I0031838

Indigenous
Mobilities

ACROSS AND BEYOND
THE ANTIPODES

Aboriginal History Incorporated

Aboriginal History Inc. is a part of the Australian Centre for Indigenous History, Research School of Social Sciences, The Australian National University, and gratefully acknowledges the support of the School of History and the National Centre for Indigenous Studies, The Australian National University. Aboriginal History Inc. is administered by an Editorial Board which is responsible for all unsigned material. Views and opinions expressed by the author are not necessarily shared by Board members.

Contacting Aboriginal History

All correspondence should be addressed to the Editors, Aboriginal History Inc., ACIH, School of History, RSSS, 9 Fellows Road (Coombs Building), Acton, ANU, 2601, or aboriginal.history@anu.edu.au.

WARNING: Readers are notified that this publication may contain names or images of deceased persons.

Indigenous
Mobilities

ACROSS AND BEYOND
THE ANTIPODES

Edited by Rachel Standfield

Australian
National
University

PRESS

ANU PRESS

Published by ANU Press and Aboriginal History Inc.
The Australian National University
Acton ACT 2601, Australia
Email: anupress@anu.edu.au
Available to download for free at press.anu.edu.au

A catalogue record for this book is available from the National Library of Australia

ISBN (print): 9781760462147
ISBN (online): 9781760462154

WorldCat (print): 1038052699
WorldCat (online): 1038052860

DOI: 10.22459/IM.06.2018

This title is published under a Creative Commons Attribution-NonCommercial-NoDerivatives 4.0 International (CC BY-NC-ND 4.0).

The full licence terms are available at creativecommons.org/licenses/by-nc-nd/4.0/legalcode

Cover design and layout by ANU Press.

Cover image: State Library of NSW, Tippahee [Te Pahi], a chief of New Zealand, 1808 / painted by James Finucane, call number SV*/Mao/Port/14, file number FL1601774.

This edition © 2018 ANU Press

Contents

Acknowledgements

This publication is the outcome of a workshop held at the Ōtākou Marae, southern New Zealand, in November 2014, which was jointly hosted by the Monash Indigenous Studies Centre, the Department of History and Art History and the Centre for Research on Colonial Culture at the University of Otago. My thanks go to Lynette Russell and Tony Ballantyne, whose commitment to comparative and connected historical scholarship, and to a management style based in collegiate relationships, facilitated both the workshop and this edited collection. Thank you to the speakers and participants at that workshop, particularly Jane Carey for her participation and enthusiastic support, and to the contributors to this volume for their patience through delays and changing circumstances.

I would particularly like to thank Mike Stevens for his role in organising the workshop, for our time studying and now researching together, but also for much more than this—for years of friendship between us (and now our families), generous hospitality and for introducing me to the taonga of coming to know Ngāi Tahu people and culture. I pay my respects to Ngāi Tahu ancestors and people discussed in this book, as well as to all the other Indigenous communities, both ancestors and their contemporary descendants, whose histories we trace.

Thank you to my colleagues in the history research group at Monash University for their feedback on the introductory chapter, especially Charlotte Greenhalgh, Kat Ellinghaus and Christina Twomey whose insightful comments helped immeasurably. To John Bradley, thank you for being such a champion of interdisciplinary and engaged research, and for the conversations, reading of each other's work and help to engage with other epistemologies.

Aboriginal History and Rani Kerin have been excellent to work with; as authors we thank them for their efforts and their persistence in supporting publications on Indigenous histories and perspectives. Thank you also to our peer reviewers whose insights improved the work. Special thanks must go to Heather Goodall for her encouragement and advice.

My thanks go to the State Library of New South Wales for the cover image and for their excellent support of researchers working with their collections. Finally, the publication of this collection would not have been possible without the generous support of the Faculty of Arts at Monash University, for which I am grateful.

Rachael Standfield
February 2018

Contributors

Tony Ballantyne is a Professor of History and Pro Vice-Chancellor, Humanities, at the University of Otago. He has published widely on New Zealand's colonial pasts, the cultural history of the modern British Empire and on the place of empires in world history.

Regina Ganter is a Professor in the School of Humanities, Languages and Social Sciences at Griffith University. She is also Director of the Harry Gentle Resource Centre at Griffith University. She specialises in interactions between Indigenous, Asian and European peoples in Australia and is the multi–award winning author of *The Pearl-Shellers of Torres Strait* (1994) and *Mixed Relations* (2006). Her most recent monograph is *The Contest for Aboriginal Souls: European Missionary Agendas in Australia* (2018), a companion to her web-directory of intercultural encounters between Indigenous people and German-speaking missionaries in Australia.

Kristyn Harman is a historian at the University of Tasmania. She specialises in cross-cultural encounters across Britain's nineteenth-century colonies and twentieth-century Australasia. Kristyn is the author of *Cleansing the Colony: Transporting Convicts from New Zealand to Van Diemen's Land* (2017) and was the winner of the 2014 Australian Historical Association Kay Daniels Award for her book *Aboriginal Convicts: Australian, Khoisan, and Māori Exiles* (2012).

Shino Konishi is a historian based at the University of Western Australia. She is the author of *The Aboriginal Male in the Enlightenment World* (2012) and co-editor, with Maria Nugent and Tiffany Shellam, of *Indigenous Intermediaries: New Perspectives on Exploration Archives* (2015) and *Brokers and Boundaries: Colonial Exploration in Indigenous Territory* (2016). She is Aboriginal and identifies with the Yawuru people of Broome.

Lachy Paterson is an Associate Professor in Te Tumu—School of Māori, Pacific and Indigenous Studies, University of Otago, where he teaches te reo Māori (Māori language) and Māori history. Lachy draws on reo-Māori texts, such as newspapers, to explore aspects of Māori social, cultural and political history. He is the author of *Colonial Discourses: Niupepa Māori, 1855–1863* (2006) and co-author, with Angela Wanhalla, of *He Reo Wāhine: Māori Women's Voices from the Nineteenth Century* (2017).

Lynette Russell is Professor and Director of the Monash Indigenous Studies Centre. She has published widely in the areas of theory, Indigenous histories, post-colonialism and representations of race, museum studies and popular culture. Her 2012 book, *Roving Mariners: Aboriginal Whalers and Sealers in the Southern Oceans 1790–1870*, explores Aboriginal mobility, entrepreneurship and enterprise in maritime industries.

Tiffany Shellam is a Lecturer in History at Deakin University. Her research focuses on the encounters between explorers and Indigenous people in the early nineteenth century, and later relationships between Indigenous people, settlers and missionaries. She is the author of *Shaking Hands on the Fringe: Negotiating the Aboriginal World at King George's Sound* (2009) and co-editor, with Shino Konishi and Maria Nugent, of *Indigenous Intermediaries: New Perspectives on Exploration Archives* (2015) and *Brokers and Boundaries: Colonial Exploration in Indigenous Territory* (2016).

Rachel Standfield is a Lecturer in Indigenous Studies at the Monash Indigenous Studies Centre. Her work explores histories of cross-cultural encounters and the agency of Indigenous peoples in Australia and New Zealand as they encountered Europeans on their country. She is the author of *Race and Identity in the Tasman World* (2012).

Michael J. Stevens (nō Kāi Tahu ki Awarua) is a freelance historian and former Senior Lecturer in History at the University of Otago. His research focuses on knowledge born out of cross-cultural entanglement and colonisation in the long nineteenth century. He focuses primarily on southern New Zealand's colonial and maritime histories, especially as they relate to Kāi Tahu families and communities.

Angela Wanhalla is an Associate Professor in the Department of History and Art History, University of Otago. She has published widely on the relationship between race, intimacy and colonialism, including *Matters of the Heart: A History of Interracial Marriage in New Zealand* (2013).

1

Moving Across, Looking Beyond

Rachel Standfield

Mobility has become one of the key themes of new imperial history writing as scholars trace the movement of people, things and ideas across imperial spaces and national boundaries, exploring the networks that lay at the heart of imperial endeavour. Developing out of attempts to unsettle and destabilise the connection between the nation and historical scholarship from the mid-twentieth century, histories of mobility have brought a focus on the 'transnational realities' that 'threaten to weaken the hegemonic claim of the nation'.[1] Recognising that histories of the nation tend to focus on what is distinctive rather than what is shared,[2] historians of British imperialism have turned the gaze back upon what is held in common in imperial spaces. Building on metaphors of British imperialism as networked—such as the webs of empire theorised by Tony Ballantyne or the view of imperial networks espoused by Alan Lester—imperial histories of mobility have given scholars the freedom to trace the paths by which people, goods and ideas have been disseminated throughout the British imperial world.[3] Following the tracks of mobile lives provides a means of tracing connections between disparate imperial sites and understanding the particular local circumstances of varied

---

1 Byrnes 2009: 126.
2 Curthoys 2003: 84.
3 Ballantyne 2002; Lester 2001.

colonial locations, while managing the complex scholarship of multiple historiographies and dispersed archives that can make transnational histories so challenging.[4]

There have been significant developments in scholarship in the area of histories of mobilities. Numerous scholars have examined the travels of Europeans and the meanings of mobility for European people and settler colonists, but the mobility of Indigenous peoples has received less attention.[5] Historians of Indigenous life and colonisation have begun to rectify this gap in scholarship by exploring the patterns of Indigenous mobility. There is a small but growing body of work that engages with the mobile Indigenous subject in imperial and colonial historical contexts. This scholarship responds to Tony Ballantyne and Antoinette Burton's claim, in *Moving Subjects*, that work on mobility in general, and intimate cross-cultural encounters in particular, by depicting Europeans as global subjects, has rendered Indigenous people as purely 'local' in contrast to the figure of the mobile European. In much historical scholarship, 'mobility becomes the property of colonizers, and stasis the preternatural condition of the indigene', yet, as discussed below, in Australia, Indigenous movement was central to colonial discourses that denied land rights and led to colonial policies to 'settle' populations.[6] Alan Lester and Zoe Laidlaw contend that 'Western agents and networks are often seen as global and mobile', whereas 'indigeneity is too frequently defined as local and static, leaving the problem of where and how Indigenous people connect with trans-global networks ill-defined'.[7] Jane Carey and Jane Lydon, in *Indigenous Networks: Mobility, Connections and Exchange*, posited that 'stereotypically, Indigenous people are seen as either autochthonous and fixed, or as displaced and inauthentic'.[8] Ballantyne and Burton contended that one effect of the binary between the mobile European subject and the fixed Indigenous subject is that 'the agency of the Indigenous subject … is rarely apprehended, let along recognized, as a subject of historical inquiry in its own right'.[9]

---

4   Lambert and Lester 2006.
5   See, for example, Russell, Deacon and Woollacott 2008; Deacon, Russell and Woollacott 2010; Curthoys and Lake 2005.
6   Ballantyne and Burton 2009: 5.
7   Lester and Laidlaw 2015: 6.
8   Carey and Lydon 2014: 1.
9   Ballantyne and Burton 2009: 6.

This collection aims to contribute to this emerging body of work, recognising Indigenous people as subjects in their own right by exploring Aboriginal and Māori movement in the nineteenth century. Authors in this collection examine the ways that Indigenous people moved, their motivations for doing so, and the ways that travel affected the travellers, other members of their communities and the non-Indigenous people they encountered. Chapters consider the cultural aspects of travel for Indigenous communities on both sides of the Tasman, exploring motivations for both individuals and communities to travel, and looking at the effect that Indigenous travel had on Indigenous individuals, Indigenous communities and non-Indigenous people. Authors here insist that Indigenous mobility in imperial and colonial contexts must be considered an extension of pre-colonial travel, embodying Indigenous values and community-specific motivations for travel. Setting out this context helps to draw out the Indigenous-specific experience of travel when looking at imperial and colonial contexts, which helps to challenge the assumption that Indigenous people were merely engaged in travel for European purposes or along European lines. By understanding the context of pre-colonial Indigenous mobility, we can focus on Indigenous mobility in imperial and colonial contexts, seeing it as more than simply travelling or working with Europeans.

In keeping with the geographical locations of the authors, the work follows an antipodean theme, considering Māori and Aboriginal mobility in imperial and colonial contexts. This introduction sets out the broad contours of Indigenous Australian and Māori travel, engaging with mobility in both pre-colonial and colonial contexts, and considering the meanings accorded mobility in colonial contexts on opposite sides of the Tasman. As well as investigating the movement of Indigenous people across national borders, the chapters investigate Indigenous mobility within settler colonies and nations, recognising the importance of Indigenous people travelling to other Indigenous communities, across iwi, nation or language group borders, as a cross-cultural encounter. The contributors—scholars in Indigenous studies, historians of Indigenous societies and Indigenous academics—share interests in the intersections of Indigenous cultures and history, and ongoing implications of colonisation for Indigenous communities in Australia and New Zealand, and they bring these interests to bear on the history of mobility.

Although the field of research is small, several pivotal studies of mobile Indigenous subjects in imperial and colonial historical contexts have laid the groundwork for this collection. In a study of nineteenth-century humanitarian networks, Elizabeth Elbourne recognised the omission of Indigenous people from the significant body of work on the movement of humanitarian discourses, and humanitarians themselves. Existing work gave 'relatively little attention' to the interactions of Indigenous people with the British or with other Indigenous groups, Elbourne argued. Her analysis showed a range of connections between Indigenous groups and people who travelled to England via British humanitarian networks. Significantly, she noted that British imperial networks 'not only contributed to the creation of British policy towards Indigenous people, but also involved Indigenous people directly'.[10] Further, Elbourne argued that 'imperial networks … *affected* Indigenous interlocutors themselves'.[11] Building on this argument, we maintain that Indigenous people were not only *affected* themselves, they also affected the Europeans they encountered through humanitarian networks or other types of connections. Authors in this volume seek to recover the ways in which Indigenous people affected mobility, such as through being involved in its creation, shaping its operations, making use of networks for their own ends and travelling for the sake of travel. Special attention is paid to cases that demonstrate Indigenous agency—that is, cases in which Indigenous people chose to engage with or to ignore (or even to shun) connections with Europeans.

Lynette Russell's recent monograph, *Roving Mariners: Australian Aboriginal Whalers and Sealers in the Southern Oceans, 1790–1870*, detailed the mobile lives of Tasmanian Aboriginal men and women in the whaling and sealing industries.[12] This followed earlier research into the trans-Tasman career of Tommy Chasland or Chasling, an Aboriginal man who made his home in the mixed Māori and Pākehā sealing and whaling communities of southern New Zealand.[13] Russell argued that mobility allowed Aboriginal people to 'create a space' for themselves, despite dispossession and colonial intervention.[14] She documented the 'attenuated agency' that Aboriginal people could (and did) exert through

---

10 Elbourne 2005: 62.
11 Elbourne 2005: 59.
12 Russell 2012.
13 Russell 2008.
14 Russell 2012: 4.

their mobility; she neither assumed that Indigenous people were unfettered agents, nor that their interactions with colonial systems rendered them powerless.[15]

Māori mobility in the early decades of the nineteenth century is well documented in the New Zealand historiography, and is thus well known. The work of Anne Salmond, Judith Binney, Alison Jones and Kuni Jenkins, and Ballantyne has illuminated the international journeys of a cohort of Māori, predominantly chiefs and young men, and one young woman, Atahoe.[16] The journeys to Australia and beyond by Tuki, Huru, Te Pahi, Ruatara and Hongi Hika are familiar to readers, so much so that the journeys made by this group of men from the north of the North Island have, in many respects, come to overshadow other journeys, such as those made by Māori within the New Zealand archipelago; the overseas journeys of Māori from other parts of the country; and the less frequent, but no less remarkable, journeys of Māori women. Moreover, as several of the chapters in this collection argue, there is relatively little attention paid to how these journeys affected the nature of relationships forged with Europeans or communities at home.

The mobility of people and ideas in Indigenous protest movements has captured the attention of historians. In the Australian context, John Maynard has investigated the impact of mobile black maritime workers on the development of Aboriginal political activism in the early twentieth century.[17] Ravi de Costa, in his work on international Indigenous politics, represented Indigenous transnationalism as an extension of pre-existing Indigenous 'norms about access to resources, diplomacy and mobility across others' territories, in trade and the sharing of culture'.[18] Such insights are carried through into chapters in this volume that consider the crossing of borders of Indigenous nations (i.e. movement across Indigenous lands within individual countries) to be as central to Indigenous mobility as travel overseas. Chapters here also take seriously de Costa's emphasis on mobility as a 'norm'. Insights offered by Pacific Studies scholarship, especially the work of Epeli Hau'ofa, likewise play a major role. Hau'ofa's seminal research on the importance of movement

15   Russell 2012: 12–13.
16   Salmond 1997; Binney 2004; Jones and Jenkins 2011; Ballantyne 2014.
17   Maynard 2005.
18   de Costa 2006: 5.

to Pacific Island cultures and lives shapes our approach to mobility, not as an exceptional occurrence, but as an outcome of culture, economics and social organisation.[19]

Fiona Paisley's work on Māori and Pākehā women's international travel associated with political activism in the twentieth century has made a significant contribution to our understanding of the role of gender in shaping Indigenous mobility.[20] While considerable attention has been paid to the movement of white women in histories of mobility,[21] building on Paisley's work, authors in this volume attempt to account for the gendered nature of Indigenous movement and the complexities of uncovering the travel of Indigenous women who are often rendered anonymous in the colonial archive. Paisley's recent monograph, *The Lone Protestor*, explored the travel of Aboriginal activist A.M. Fernando, a largely unknown campaigner working in the UK and Europe during the inter-war years. As well as bringing Fernando's work into the historical record, Paisley's arguments about his mobility—that it placed him outside national history writing and affected his politics and activism—have changed the way we think about mobility. According to Paisley, Fernando's activism was overlooked by Australian historians because his mobility made him appear peripheral to a nationally focused story.[22] Fernando linked racism in Australia to the prejudice he witnessed and was subject to in England; thus, he came to understand racism as 'transnational in context, inflamed by the colonial world order and by poverty and ignorance'.[23]

In *Indians in Unexpected Places*, Philip J. Deloria undermined dominant depictions of American Indian people as outside of modernity. His work, which examined the transformed mobility of Indian people through their early embrace of travel via the automobile, played an important role in this developing field. Departing from the more usual focus on international travel within studies of twentieth-century Indigenous mobility, Deloria examined the 'local embrace of the automobile', exploring how this allowed Indian communities to travel within 'Indian country itself'.[24] In a similar

---

19   Hau'ofa 1993.
20   Paisley 2006; Paisley 2004.
21   See, for example, chapters in Russell, Deacon and Woollacott 2010; Georgine Clarsen's work has been instrumental in Australian histories of mobility in general and gender in particular. See Clarsen 2008 and 2011.
22   Paisley 2012: xiii, xv.
23   Paisley 2012: xiv–xv.
24   Deloria 2004.

fashion, Heather Goodall and Alison Cadzow traced Aboriginal mobility on, and relationships to, the Georges River in Sydney. In tracing mobility from pre-European contact to contemporary communities, Goodall and Cadzow showed the connectedness, as well as the 'resilience', of Aboriginal people who were 'sometimes moving … and sometimes staying tenaciously in one space'.[25] Taking inspiration from this work, chapters in this volume explore the ways that Indigenous people forged new— and continued old—tracks of mobility that maintained connection to traditional country and opened up new places of connection. Goodall and Cadzow's work speaks to the strength and length of connections forged through mobile Indigenous people, and how movement over country continues despite colonisation for Aboriginal people in Sydney (even though it is mostly unknown and unrecognised by the non-Indigenous community, which has built cities over the top of country in its attempt to displace Indigenous people).

Attempting to move away from the more usual focus on Indigenous–European connection, other developments in scholarship have looked at the connections formed between different communities of Indigenous peoples via travel. Lachy Paterson examined the participation of Māori in Australian federation in 1901, focusing on meetings between Aboriginal warriors, Māori chiefs and Indian troops jointly assembled for events celebrating the establishment of the Australian nation.[26] Tracey Banivanua Mar's exploratory study of the 'parallel Indigenous discourses' of anti-colonial protest operating in Port Phillip, New Zealand and Tahiti in the 1830s and 1840s emphasised the 'fleeting and ephemeral circuitry' of connection between Indigenous peoples.[27] Seeking to restore Indigenous peoples in Papua New Guinea and the Torres Strait from the 'margins of international affairs to the centre', Frank David, Leah Lui-Chivize and Jude Philip followed the interconnected lives of three Indigenous men as they travelled through the Torres Strait seascape yabugud (road). Their apparent 'constancy and consistency … across the fields of commerce, science and religion' allowed 'for consideration of the politics of how these people manipulated events towards their own goals'.[28] Other work decentres European understandings of mobility by placing it alongside Indigenous and immigrant conceptions, analysing it as simply another

---

25   Goodall and Cadzow 2009: 25.
26   Paterson 2013.
27   Banivanua Mar 2013: 3–4.
28   David, Lui-Chivizhe and Philip 2015: 290–91.

in a constellation of meanings associated with travel. Samia Khatun, for example, focused on the various 'tracks' that 'structured mobility through Beltana' on the country of Kuyani people in northern South Australia, where tracks of story from different epistemological traditions created geographies and mobilities across the Australian landscape.[29]

Among recent work, Jane Lydon and Jane Carey's edited collection stands out. It brings together some of the most innovative and thoughtful scholars of new imperial history to recognise Indigenous participation in 'global networks of power and mobility'.[30] In his review of the collection, Michael McDonnell argued that it 'issued a challenge to imperial and transnational historians to start taking seriously Indigenous peoples as dynamic and mobile historical actors'.[31] This challenge motivates the authors in this volume. Carey and Lydon noted, insightfully, that while anthropologists and archaeologists have documented particular forms and meanings associated with Indigenous mobility, historians have not generally incorporated this into their work.[32] However, even with this recognition, most of the essays in *Indigenous Networks* focused on Indigenous people tapping into European networks and working with Europeans, which, given the collection's emphasis on Indigenous participation in 'global networks of power', is understandable. By contrast, the contributors to this collection emphasise that, while Indigenous movement could be about global imperial and colonial networks, it could also be for purely Indigenous purposes: for community and individual economic wellbeing, to meet other Indigenous or non-Indigenous peoples and experience different cultures, to gather knowledge or experience desired within an Indigenous worldview and to escape from colonial intrusion. The essays presented here attempt to decentre, where possible, the role of Europeans within Indigenous travel; they emphasise Indigenous perspectives on, reasons for and agency in their own mobility. This involves looking at Indigenous communities—their arrangement of culture and economic and social contexts—as the primary locus of life.

---

29 Khatun 2015.
30 Carey and Lydon 2014: 1.
31 McDonnell 2015.
32 Carey and Lydon 2014: 1.

Analytic Possibilities of Scholarship on Indigenous Mobilities

A focus on specific Indigenous communities as the locus of life assists authors to further question and unsettle the role of the nation within historical scholarship. Karen Fox, reflecting on trends in the writing of Indigenous histories in Australia and New Zealand, observed that 'transnational history seeks to move beyond the nation, looking across national borders, considering the importance of factors outside the nation and critiquing nationalist approaches to the past'.[33] This issue of 'moving beyond' and 'looking across' nations has constituted both a promise and a problem in studies of historical mobility. Such studies have focused on the movement of Europeans and have assumed that a colonial or a 'national' border is defined by the non-Indigenous state. Consequently, the nation has both been problematised and, potentially, reinforced as the primary analytic category. Histories that trace and respect the continued production of Aboriginal geographies can help rally against scholarship that, even as it seeks to explain the processes of dispossession, can, as Khatun observed, 'replicate precisely the phenomenon they seek to critique: the erasure of Aboriginal geographies'.[34]

Indigenous geographies persist within settler colonial spaces in the form of Indigenous nations, language groups, tribal groups and iwi. These, of course, existed prior to the settler colonial state and they continue throughout colonial history into the present. Importantly, they continue to exist even when Indigenous people have been dispossessed from their territory. As Penny van Toorn asserted: 'New borders and boundaries don't necessarily supplant old ones. Australia is a palimpsest in which new and old borders and boundaries intersect and shift underfoot over time'.[35] For Indigenous people, this provides a completely different meaning to the concept of border crossing in travel; to consider this is to bring a different dimension to the analysis of mobilities in settler colonial spaces—one that speaks to the importance of seeing Indigenous people travelling to other communities and across iwi, nation or language group borders as participating in cross-cultural encounters. As John Taylor and Martin Bell observed, 'migration' and 'diaspora' in the Indigenous sense generally

---

33   Fox 2012: 425.
34   Khatun 2015.
35   van Toorn 2010: 41.

applies to movement within, rather than between, nation states.[36] As such, mobility between Indigenous nations, language groups or other tribal formations should be seen as a form of migration that deserves the same recognition as international mobility. Analysing Indigenous mobility in Indigenous-centric ways has the potential to shed new light on well-worn historical explanations, and thus operates as an implicit challenge to history as a discipline.

Recognition of different boundaries to be crossed brings with it recognition of the political forms that underpin border crossings. Indigenous nations have their own polity, territory, unique social organisation and culture. To recognise these as the basis for different forms of movement is to recognise the different territories and polities that have created the borders. It is also to recognise that the category of the 'nation', so important to historical writing in the twentieth and twenty-first centuries, is imposed over the top of Indigenous political structures and territoriality. Further, it is to recognise that, while Indigenous forms are older, they are continuing, and that this continued presence tends to be ignored within the trajectories of histories of the nation. As Giselle Byrnes noted, the nation is not simply a remnant of 'nineteenth-century colonial ambition', it is 'a colonizing tool'; historiography that ignores Indigenous nations in their myriad and diverse forms effectively replicates the silencing and repression of Indigenous political systems.[37] Paying attention to the different meanings, rituals and cultures of movement within Indigenous societies may provide a way to foreground Indigenous peoples and nations within history writing.

Focusing on Indigenous mobility forces us to interrogate colonial sources, asking questions about how they represent Indigenous people who travel. Indigenous people often come into historical sources when—and precisely because—they are mobile. Indigenous movement is captured in documents generated by those who utilised Aboriginal or Māori mobility, such as explorers or ship's captains, or by those who displayed concern about their mobility, such as colonial officials, missionaries or protectors. Yet, within these sources, the motivations for, and meanings of, Indigenous mobilities are rarely fully understood or discussed—or, indeed, even considered. Thus, the way we read these accounts is vital, for it determines how we understand Indigenous mobilities.

36   Bell and Taylor 2004: 263.
37   Byrnes 2009: 125.

Rather than accepting the perspectives provided by European authors, determining Indigenous motivation and meaning involves searching for an Indigenous-centric interpretation. New work is helping to provide a model here. Through her careful reading of sources, Banivanua Mar's work on anti-colonial protest in Port Phillip, New Zealand and Tahiti exposed a 'counter-imperial and Indigenous circuitry' that developed out of fleeting physical contact between Indigenous peoples.[38] Likewise, Lachy Paterson's close reading of Māori- and English-language sources provided new insights into the development of an 'imperial discourse of racial fraternity' between Māori and Indian troops who visited Australia and New Zealand.[39] Ian Clarke and Fred Cahir's work on Māori visits to, and life in, Victoria also demonstrated the benefits of careful examination of extensive archival material.[40]

Closely examining issues of continuity and change between pre-colonial and colonial Indigenous mobility has the potential to problematise and complicate notions of European travel as well. Imperial and colonial agents often travelled along Indigenous routes, particularly (but not exclusively) in the early stages of settlement, guided by the knowledge of Indigenous peoples.[41] In addition, Europeans often travelled according to Indigenous protocols, although they were not always aware of doing so. Paying close attention to routes, protocols and other forms of Indigenous knowledge complicates power relations that might otherwise be taken for granted, especially in cases where Indigenous people are said to be 'accompanying' Europeans. Indigenous mobility or travel was far more likely to be documented in the colonial archive when it involved Europeans. In reviewing such sources, it is important to consider whether the Europeans involved were being used by the Indigenous travellers as a means to an end—that is, as a way to facilitate travel. Mobility could take place for new or old reasons and could occur along new or old routes, and could be prompted by Indigenous-specific motivations, including cultural reasons or other reasons.

Consideration of the various motivations underlying Indigenous mobilities allows scholars to focus on Indigenous agency in multiple contexts, exploring how agency functions in racialised and highly

---

38   Banivanua Mar 2013.
39   Paterson 2013.
40   Cahir and Clark 2014.
41   Pratt 2007; Shellam, Nugent, Konishi and Cadzow 2016; Byrnes 2001.

regulated environments. Scholarship in this volume considers the lure of the sea for Aboriginal people and Māori. Gopal Balachandran has shown how Indian seafarers, although they 'manned the world's ship', have 'languished as a historically invisible underclass'.[42] Indian seafarers' lives were circumscribed and controlled by racialised policies and practices at every level, regulated in minute detail through 'routine bureaucratic agency' designed to render their presence invisible, even as their labour was central to world shipping.[43] Janet Ewald's work has detailed racialised policies, such as the Asiatic Articles, that were applied to shipping labour and, importantly, the transformative possibilities of labouring on ships in the early nineteenth century. She observed:

> Atlantic and Indian Ocean ports were sites for social transformations. Landsmen became seaman ... [b]ut seamen also became landsmen when sailors turned to port work between voyages.[44]

Slaves 'loosened or broke ties with their masters', making ships and port environments important places for possibility as well as restriction.[45] Ewald's insights have been extended by Alison Bashford in her recent call for 'terraqueous' histories that attend to the connections and multiple meanings that diverse communities attribute to crossings between land and sea.[46]

In contrast to these restrictive and controlling regulations, Māori and Pacific Islander sailors, at least in the early years of Australian colonisation, were protected by a governor's order that stipulated they could only be removed from New Zealand with the consent of chiefs, and that masters of ships could not 'discharge any sailor or sailors, or other persons' in New Zealand without the 'permission of the chief or chiefs of the place'.[47] The order was designed to protect trade interests and avoid the possibility of retaliation against shipping during a period in which Indigenous communities retained significant power, controlling access to resources and labour. Of course, racialised structures, policies and practices were still a factor for Aboriginal people and Māori when travelling on board ships; however, this example shows that the application of racialised forms of regulation was uneven, specific and not always designed to exploit

---

42   Balachandran 2012: 4, 10.
43   Balachandran 2012: 10.
44   Ewald 2000: 73.
45   Ewald 2000: 73.
46   Bashford 2017: 261–62.
47   McNab 1908: 328–29.

labour. Indeed, as Heather Goodall, Devleena Ghosh and Lindi Todd have shown, even with highly restrictive policies in place, individuals could slip between the cracks and subvert systems. They maintain that the presence of regulation in archival records is not evidence of the success of that regulation:

> The official records, the catalogues and the schedules [that] European imperial powers were so well able to produce are actually the archives of mechanisms for control rather than proof that the controls worked … we are looking at claims of achievement of the 'settler' goal, in which such documents are reflective of hopes, desires or fantasies rather than accomplished facts.[48]

As Russell argues in this volume, the sea offered a means of escape from land-based systems of surveillance and severe restrictions of movement for some Indigenous peoples. Attention to Indigenous mobilities offers the possibility of understanding agency in different land- and sea-based contexts, as well as the promise of a more nuanced understanding of how racial thought shaped policies of 'protection' and restriction.

Aboriginal and Māori Cultures of Mobility

We contend that Māori and Aboriginal peoples undertook distinct forms of mobility in colonial history; each of the chapters in this volume attempts to elucidate these forms of travel. To delineate what is unique about Indigenous mobilities in imperial and colonial situations in the region, it is necessary to have a general understanding of the features of Aboriginal and Māori mobility. Taylor and Bell have called for 'sustained attention in ongoing research' to Indigenous mobilities. They maintain that:

> A primary focus should be given to further elaborating the way in which mobility dynamics and settlement outcomes are shaped by the changing interface between Indigenous culture and the encapsulating state. An enhanced understanding of these interactions, in diverse settings and at varying temporal and spatial scales, is fundamental to articulation of a robust and comprehensive theory of mobility among Indigenous peoples.[49]

---

48 Goodall, Ghosh and Todd 2008: 47.
49 Bell and Taylor 2004: 263.

Authors in this volume similarly argue that care must be taken to understand and account for Indigenous cultural forms and the effect they have on mobility.

Mobility is a vital feature of Indigenous Australian life. As Goodall and Cadzow have explained, 'mobility was and is as much a defining characteristic of Aboriginal cultures as affiliations with meaningful bounded places'.[50] De Costa has argued that a 'mobility ethos' underpinned 'classical' Aboriginal society. Writing about Indigenous communities in terms of philosophies of diplomacy, de Costa asserted that cosmological ideas of 'interrelatedness and the connection of all things' shaped Indigenous communities, informing their embrace of 'mobility and its corollary of openness'.[51] Songlines and Dreaming narratives travel across regions; this means that neighbouring communities shared connections to particular stories. One group's 'authoritative reading' of a narrative does not preclude others having relationships to country or songlines. As de Costa explained, 'such connections give Indigenous peoples a context for engagement as well as reason to be mobile, to maintain their connections across different countries'.[52] In practical terms, mobility was, and is, required for ceremonial responsibilities tied to these cosmological narratives. Connections to common Dreaming narratives brought people together, often across large areas, to join for ceremonial purposes. An iconic and continuing ceremonial journey is that undertaken as part of Central Australian initiation practices:

> According to customary practice, just prior to circumcision, boys were taken by their guardians on a journey to visit people in the region to gather them together for the actual ceremony. In the past this was done on foot over several months; today some initiation candidates, but not all, go off on a tour with their guardian using various forms of transport.[53]

As Peterson noted, in 1994, a journey undertaken prior to initiation of a young Western Desert man extended over 2,500 kilometres on the outward journey and gathered over 600 people for the ceremony.[54]

---

50   Goodall and Cadzow 2009: 21.
51   de Costa 2007: 16.
52   de Costa 2007: 15.
53   Peterson 2004: 230.
54   Peterson 2004: 230.

As well as movement for ceremony, Indigenous Australians engaged in circular mobility in which people moved within their own country and wider region for economic, social and cultural reasons. Before colonisation, 'varying degrees of movement were required in pursuit of survival', and the extent of this movement was dependent on the nature of an Aboriginal nation's country. People living on resource-dense country engaged in 'highly localized movement', whereas desert people travelled over long distances.[55] This regular and structured mobility in circular patterns formed 'functional regions' for Aboriginal people, which, in contemporary Australia, 'reflect persistence of the customary alongside change'.[56] The movement around country for the purposes of food hunting and gathering followed seasonal patterns to exploit resource availability throughout the year. Jon Altman, in his fieldwork among eastern Kuninjku people in north-central Arnhem Land in 1979–80, followed the community's travel throughout their land over six distinct seasons— three dry, three wet—as they harvested food and managed the land.[57] Later work by Altman and Melinda Hinkson showed how Kuninjku's adoption of trucks facilitated movement back to country in the 1970s. The Kuninjku community saved considerable money to purchase vehicles to move back to country. The timing of these purchases allowed Kuninjku to reverse processes of centralisation of Aboriginal language groups in Maningrida in Arnhem Land, as it coincided with legislation for land rights, self-determination and financial assistance for the outstation movement. Kuninjku became highly engaged with the commercial arts market, developing an 'eclectic hybrid economy' that combined 'income from the state and earnings from arts production with a robust harvesting economy'.[58] Kuninjku vehicles were used in accordance with Kuninjku values; the incorporation of trucks into the Kuninjku world reflected kinship structures, respect for seniority, gendered structures and avoidance relationships.[59]

Connection to sea country and waterways have also shaped mobility. Amanda Kearney and John Bradley investigated the relationship between modes of sea travel and Yanyuwa peoples' interactions with sea country. Hailing from the south-west Gulf of Carpentaria, Yanyuwa peoples

---

55   Peterson 2004: 223.
56   Taylor and Bell 2004b: 17.
57   Taylor and Bell 2004b: 18; Altman 1987.
58   Altman and Hinkson 2007: 188.
59   Altman and Hinkson 2007.

derive their identity from being 'saltwater people'.[60] Kearney and Bradley charted the changing technology that Yanyuwa used for journeys by sea and their shifting ideologies of movement as technology changed. They found that Yanyuwa embraced changing boat technology as Indigenous communities elsewhere embraced the car. They concluded that, unlike in non-Indigenous communities where cars are seen as 'instruments of autonomy', in Indigenous communities, boats and cars are tools 'for connecting, rather than disconnecting'; they are also ways to 'resist alienation'.[61]

According to Kearney and Bradley, elders who had witnessed the rise in the use of mechanised transport during their lifetime felt that 'really travelling' required walking, partly because the speed of mechanised transport jeopardised the unpredictable encounters between people and country that occurred during walking.[62] Yet, conversely, the same technology applied to the sea resulted in new parts of sea country being opened up to Yanyuwa, and better and more regular access to the sea, including parts that colonial processes had severely curtailed. Noticing similar processes on rivers, Goodall and Cadzow observed that technologies for travel on rivers 'have changed and will continue to change'; however, this simply shows that 'mobility was and still is crucial in people's lives'. They argue that 'even land vehicles are still moving on routes shaped by the river valleys'.[63] Goodall and Cadzow demonstrated that the adoption of new technologies of movement to continue mobility for 'traditional' purposes is not simply a feature of remote Indigenous communities; instead, it operated and operates in Sydney too. However, it seems that these encounters were not that interesting to non-Indigenous people. As Victoria Haskins has explained with reference to Aboriginal people who embraced automobiles:

> [It did] not capture white imaginations. It could not provide the same satisfaction as imagining the more mysterious people of the central and northern regions of Australia confronting the gleaming symbol of white man's modernity and technological prowess.[64]

60   Kearney and Bradley 2015.
61   Kearney and Bradley 2015: 174.
62   Kearney and Bradley 2015: 174.
63   Goodall and Cadzow 2009: 21.
64   Haskins 2008: 72.

Mobility is a feature of Aboriginal social life. Aboriginal people travel to maintain connections with kin. Such movement is not confined to rural and remote Australia. It is a feature of the lives of urban Aboriginal people in both contemporary and historical settings. Aboriginal people from early in colonial history have travelled between new residences and their home country. As Taylor and Bell have observed:

> From the early stages of urbanization, Indigenous people sought to maintain links between their new residential bases and family in the hinterland from which they were drawn. This was accomplished by engaging in frequent mobility between the two.[65]

It should be emphasised that urban sites are also Indigenous country; it is not only the 'hinterland' that is Indigenous.

In Aboriginal life, both mobility and fixedness play important roles in a person's identity. Peterson explained how 'mobility is fundamental to an Aboriginal individual's social identity', as networks and relationships—hence shared identity—are renewed through travel. Travel also offers personal autonomy, as people move to escape the control or direction of others. Yet fixedness was also crucial: 'relationships to place and country were central to Aboriginal political identity', as community and personal identity is drawn from relationships to specific areas of land.[66] Hence, coming back to one's own country and returning to place were vital parts of travel. These two aspects of Aboriginal cultural life are encapsulated in the importance accorded to boundary-crossing protocols. As Turnbull observed:

> Australian Aboriginal groups had a highly articulated understanding of their own territory and kinship and had a well developed form of social organisation reflected in boundary practices and protocols governing the ways authority and ownership should be acknowledged and how permission should be sought and granted. This systems of norms and signs that made negotiated boundary-crossing permissions possible reveals a politics and territorial distribution and also provides the conditions for the possibility of trust and the movement of knowledge along networks or 'strings' of connectedness.[67]

---

65   Taylor and Bell 2004b: 20.
66   Peterson 2004: 224.
67   Turnbull 2004: 175.

Mobility was, and is, of fundamental importance to Māori culture and life as well. It was, and is, central to the identity of individuals and communities; the arrival of waka (traditional Māori canoes) after long sea-journeys from Hawaiiki features in the foundation stories of iwi (Māori tribes) across the country. Oral histories of ancestral journeys of exploration by land and sea explain a community's journey of arrival as well as their claims to tribal lands.[68]

Mobility remained important in everyday life in the pre-colonial period. People travelled for a range of purposes: to visit family, to harvest food, to trade for both food and objects of material culture and to engage in war.[69] Māori society has been described as 'highly mobile' during the 'early pre-contact period'. According to Manahuia Barcham, mobility increased during the 'classical' period of Māori history, 'as endemic warfare, due in large part to a shrinking resource base especially in terms of food (particularly meat), led these groups to engage in increased levels of warfare and conquest'.[70] The Kāi Tahu groups that moved from the east coast of the North Island in the eighteenth century, marrying into and also defeating other communities as they moved south, eventually coming to establish their territory throughout most of the South Island, show how mobility shaped the histories of communities.[71] Mobility was vital to Kāi Tahu's pre-colonial life, as Michael Stevens' chapter in this collection describes, with people moving into the south and then continuing to travel seasonally to take advantage of food resources, including extended stays offshore to carry out the annual tītī (sooty shearwater or mutton-bird) harvest.[72] The birds, preserved and packed for long-term storage, were traded over long distances to communities in the north. This community-specific movement of both people and goods remains central to Kāi Tahu culture and identity today.

These already high levels of Māori mobility escalated after initial contact with Europeans. There was an intensification of 'warfare-induced mobility' as muskets were introduced to New Zealand by Europeans.[73] As Barcham observed:

---

68   Taonui n.d.
69   Ballantyne 2011: 63.
70   Barcham 2004: 163.
71   Anderson 1998: 57–62.
72   Stevens 2006.
73   Barcham 2004: 163.

The period of the early nineteenth century was thus characterized by extremely high levels of mobility for Māori as large numbers of people were displaced as they attempted to escape the various conflicts that raged over the country during this period.[74]

Many people moved by choice to exploit new opportunities for knowledge, goods or contacts that developed around centres where Europeans congregated; the forcible movement of slaves also occurred.[75] As chapters in this volume demonstrate, the early nineteenth century saw Māori exploit opportunities to travel overseas; Port Jackson became an important destination for Māori travel, as well as a transit point for travel further afield. This international migration has remained a feature of Māori life, placing 'Māori somewhat at odds with other Indigenous populations', as Taylor and Bell have noted (although other Pacific peoples may also have high levels of overseas migration).[76] Ian Pool concluded that:

> It is possible that the migrations of the early nineteenth century far exceeded mobility in previous periods, and may have been more important proportionally than subsequent inter regional movements until rapid urbanisation occurred after World War II.[77]

Colonisation from 1840 brought changes that significantly reduced Māori mobility as land was alienated swiftly in comparison to many areas of Australia. Moreover, there were other political implications of colonisation, as Ballantyne established:

> The consolidation of British rule not only reduced Māori mobility but also calcified takiwā and rohe [boundaries] … Under colonial rule tribal boundaries that had only taken shape in the previous couple of decades were now seen as durable and 'traditional'.[78]

Reduced mobility during the colonial period did not mean that Māori were not mobile during this period, as contributions in this volume by Lachy Paterson, Angela Wanhalla and Michael Stevens attest.

---

74 Barcham 2004: 163–64.
75 Ballantyne 2011: 64.
76 Taylor and Bell 2004a: 6.
77 Pool 2013.
78 Ballantyne 2011: 64.

The Politics of Aboriginal and Māori Mobility

Not only were Aboriginal and Māori mobilities different in form and nature, and specific to the cultural, economic and social lives of particular communities, they were read and reacted to differently within imperial and colonial situations. Māori, as outlined above, were noted for having engaged in international travel, using the arrival of European ships in their waters as an opportunity to travel to New South Wales and further afield from the early nineteenth century. The early journeys were often made by young men of chiefly status, although, as Wanhalla discusses here, this was not exclusively the case, as women also crossed the Tasman Sea. The social position of the travellers, combined with British interest in observing a new culture, meant that visiting Māori excited considerable interest in New South Wales. They were often met and entertained by colonial officials, including governors, leading to the view that such visits were 'diplomatic relations'.[79] According to British colonists, these international travellers showed appropriate respect, interest and capacity for improvement in making the journey to investigate British society in the region. What, to colonists in New South Wales, seemed a recognition of British superiority and a curiosity about technology and civilisation was, for Māori, a chance to gain advantages at home for the benefit of their communities. The relationships forged and knowledge developed during those visits to Australia also opened up resources in New Zealand for the British—resources that could be accessed with the permission of chiefs, with Māori labour and, it was assumed, without conflict. At this time, Māori and Pacific peoples' labour on ships was becoming an important part of the region's workforce, and this form of mobility led to efforts at 'protection' by the New South Wales colonial government, as it was keen to prevent mistreatment that could jeopardise access to resources or lead to violent conflict.[80]

Regina Ganter's contribution here documents northern Aboriginal international travel and engagement—forms of Indigenous mobility that have not informed racial discourses due to their northern focus and their connections forged to Asian, rather than European, communities. The absence of such journeys from Australian historiography has resulted in the concomitant absence of representations of Aboriginal people as

---

79   Salmond 1997.
80   Standfield 2012: Chapter 1.

curious or interested in improvement. By contrast, the international travel that Māori undertook during the contact period (and have undertaken in a sustained way ever since), produced a particular view of Māori that, as several chapters in this volume argue, influenced New Zealand's imperial history and histories of the region. Many Māori have also been involved in internal migration, moving from rural to urban environments. Melissa Matutina Williams has explored Panguru migration from Hokianga to Auckland during the mid-twentieth century, a migration that was part of her own family history. Her oral histories retain a tribal focus because, as she explained:

> The people who migrated out of Panguru did not migrate out of their whakapapa and, by extension, their connection to the whenua. Tribal connections were not cut by geographical space, state policy or academic theory. You remain part of a tribal story regardless of where you live or the degree of knowledge or interaction you may have with your whanaunga and tribal homeland.[81]

Challenging the idea that migration necessarily produces emotions of loss and isolation, Nepia Mahuika showed that such assumptions are complicated by inter-iwi connections—engagement between those migrating and the people of Auckland, Wellington or other New Zealand cities—as well as the connections that many migrants continue to foster with their whānau (family) and iwi at home. Unproblematic depictions of loss or dislocation fail to account for mātauranga Māori (Māori knowledge) and related creation narratives, rooted in land, through which iwi share connection to New Zealand geographies. As well as tribal identities, historians must be cognisant of the identification that many people have to being 'Māori'.[82] This is not to say that migrants did not experience feelings of isolation or loss, but that these were caused by more complex processes than moving to an urban location.[83]

Significant meaning has been accorded to Aboriginal mobility in the Australian colonial context. Aboriginal movement has been highly politicised, racialised and used as a justification for colonisation. From the outset of colonisation, Aboriginal movement was viewed as 'wandering'— that is, as taking a form that precluded land ownership. David Turnbull characterised wandering as 'the first-order descriptor invoked whenever

---

81   Williams 2015: 28.
82   Mahuika 2009.
83   Mahuika 2009: 140.

indigenes are described ... implying a timeless, placeless, and directionless existence'.[84] He argued that land, to be seen as 'empty', did not have to be free of inhabitants; it was sufficient to have inhabitants who were seen as 'wanderers with no complex organisation or laws'.[85] To be deemed as wanderers rendered an Indigenous population as placeless in the eyes of European colonisers:

> Having no place meant no organization, no law, no labor, no cultivation, no property, no boundaries. All of which were essential components of enlightenment rationality and the complete antithesis of wandering, revealing both the profoundly place-based, static and boundaried spatial ontology underpinning modern rationality and epistemology and the profound tension in which it was constituted.[86]

Aboriginal movement through country—the ordered, regular, seasonal circular mobility that was highly attuned to the landscape—was characterised as irrational and read as being antithetical to Indigenous rights in land. These views had powerful effects on Aboriginal people, underpinning government and legal discussions that ignored Aboriginal sovereignty and land ownership and justified the appropriation of land for European uses. These ideas continue to hold great power, for while the legal basis of the concept of terra nullius has been overturned, Indigenous authors have stressed that a psychological terra nullius continues unabated within Australian society.[87]

The serious negative connotations associated with Aboriginal movement created a focus in colonial policies on restricting movement. The 'problem' of Indigenous mobility, as Australian colonial authorities envisioned it, meant that policies and practices focused on regulating Indigenous movement loomed large in the tactics undertaken by government. These involved restrictions on movement over country, policies of forced movement in which populations were shifted off country and on to reserves, and ongoing policies of removing Indigenous children from families—all carried out in the name of civilisation: to 'settle' Aboriginal people. Such policies had practical benefits for colonial

---

84   Turnbull 2004: 175.
85   Turnbull 2004: 175.
86   Turnbull 2004: 175.
87   Behrendt 2003: 3. Senator Aiden Ridgeway described this in 2001 as a 'terra nullius of the mind'. See Standfield 2004.

society; they helped curtail Aboriginal physical resistance and removed Aboriginal people from country, making additional areas of land available for colonial occupation.

These readings of Australian Aboriginal mobility are not confined to the early period of colonial history; they continued to shape views of Aboriginal people throughout the twentieth century and they persist into the present. As Peterson has observed, the idea of Aboriginal people going 'walkabout' is 'one of the most mythological aspects of Australian Aboriginal behaviour'.[88] Walkabout is 'usually understood in terms of some urge that results in Aboriginal people leaving a locality without notice to travel for travel's sake'.[89] This idea has such power that Aboriginal people are seen as a 'walkabout race'. According to Sarah Prout, notions of unpredictable Aboriginal movement shape non-Indigenous interactions with Aboriginal people in the context of service provision in Western Australia.[90] The trope of Aboriginal people as wandering has been powerful, and consistent, throughout Australian colonial history.[91] In fact, Ann Curthoys has argued that the idea of Indigenous people as fixed and local does not apply to Aboriginal people, as 'the idea of Aboriginal people as nomads with no attachment or claim to the land was far more prominent in settler discourse'.[92]

Movement is not only an important factor in Aboriginal culture and identity; it has proved to be vitally important in resisting colonial incursions and restrictions on movement. Peterson has described 'walkabout' as:

> An everyday form of resistance: Aboriginal people avoided letting employers know they intended leaving because they denied their employers' right to control their lives. Further, the employers' assumption that the urge to leave was biologically based helped reproduce unheralded departures because such an assumption meant that people were rarely called on to account for their movements.[93]

---

88   Peterson 2004: 223.
89   Peterson 2004: 223.
90   Prout 2009.
91   See, for example, Karen Fox's discussion of the concept of walkabout being applied to Yvonne Gollagong's tennis performances to explain occasional lapses of concentration. Fox 2011: 57–59.
92   Carey and Lydon 2014: 9.
93   Peterson 2004: 223.

Denis Byrne analysed the way that Aboriginal people subverted the cadastral grid laid by colonisers as they took over new areas of land in Australia from 1788. Mobility was key to Aboriginal people maintaining relationships to country, even when land was no longer easily available to them, as it was 'owned' by others. As Byrne explained, Aboriginal people negotiated 'moving through the "openings" between the private properties of the cadastral grid', developing 'a web of tactical relationships with those white landowners prepared to be friendly or, at least, not to be hostile'.[94] Similar processes occurred in New Zealand; where access to mahinga kai (food gathering places) was closed off to Māori, negotiation of the cadastral grid became necessary.

***

The antipodean theme and the comparisons drawn in our volume grow out of relationships between the contributing authors, and between the authors and their own mobility. The volume reflects the commitment of those authors to take their scholarship beyond national borders, strengthening their work by understanding what is common and what is unique in comparison to other histories in the region. The contributors demonstrate that engagement with Indigenous social, cultural and political organisation can enable understanding of the specific and ontologically and epistemologically driven mobilities of Indigenous communities. Chapters by Konishi, Shellam, Wanhalla, Standfield, Ganter and Stevens focus on the specific culturally imbued meanings of movement. Chapters by Konishi, Shellam and Wanhalla are sensitive to travel between distinct Indigenous nations or tribal areas. Konishi explores evidence for Aboriginal boundary-crossing rituals in early European exploration journals, demonstrating how European exploration accounts can help us to understand pre-colonial Aboriginal mobility, rituals of negotiated boundary crossing and the vital role played by Aboriginal intermediaries in European exploration. Shellam investigates the travels of Miago, a Nyungar man from south-west Western Australia, and considers the cultural knowledge of the new Aboriginal communities he developed on his journeys. Wanhalla explores the international and local mobility of two Indigenous women—a Canadian Aboriginal woman and a Kāi Tahu woman—and considers their parallel lives spent living on, and adjacent

94   Byrne 2010: 113–14.

to, the Taieri Native Reserve in New Zealand's South Island. Russell reads Aboriginal travel in the colonial period as an extension of pre-colonial mobility, as does Stevens in regard to his own Kāi Tahu people.

The volume demonstrates the limitations of language to explain the complexity of histories of Indigenous mobilities. Chapters expressly interrogate the often implicit assumptions of scholars that Indigenous peoples are wholly 'grounded' in their land, fixed either through attachment to country or through colonial control in which policies of colonial containment are assumed to be wholly successful in stopping Indigenous movement. The weight of these assumptions, combined with the drive to homogeneity that blanket categories of 'Indigenous' tend to encourage, can make even recognising Indigenous movement a difficult undertaking. Through careful empirical work, chapters here interrogate these tropes of indigeneity and bring to light the complex experiences and histories of Indigenous individuals and groups. Cognisant of Indigenous agency and its limitations, authors display awareness of culturally driven travel; Indigenous people who grasped opportunities for travel opened up by imperial and colonial associations; and, conversely, of the colonial situations that restricted Indigenous movement or forced (or coerced) travel. Both Russell and Harman focus on the mobility of Tasmanian Aboriginal people in the nineteenth century, investigating how Aboriginal people reacted to restraints placed on their movement and their creative exploitation of opportunities for movement. Harman explores the constrained mobility of Aboriginal people living at the Oyster Cove settlement, highlighting their agency in grasping opportunities— sanctioned by colonial officials or not—to maintain mobile lifestyles. Russell documents the mobility of Tasmanian Aboriginal people within colonial coastal industries, considering these new opportunities as extensions of 'traditional' Aboriginal mobilities. Her chapter shows how opportunities to work on ships, even within racially structured shipping environments, offered an escape from the containment and surveillance of land-based colonial regimes.

The collection aims to decentre the role of Europeans by undermining assumptions that Europeans were always central to Indigenous travel. Chapters by Paterson and Ganter explore Indigenous and non-European encounters through travel. While Paterson explores Māori–Rarotongan contact, Ganter probes the effects of Aboriginal encounters with Asian communities on Aboriginal identities and cultural values. Several chapters examine early Aboriginal and Māori travel. Taking a long-run view, chapters by Paterson and Stevens examine the ongoing movement of Kāi Tahu and Ngāti Whātua people respectively, looking at their established connections with particular peoples and places, and examining how specific destinations have shaped these communities. Ganter too investigates the re-establishing of connections after sustained periods of government control that quashed long-established trade connections.

Two chapters take mobilities further than the usual focus on people, exploring the movement of objects and ideas that travelled with Indigenous people. Curthoys and Lake emphasised that transnational history 'seeks to understand ideas, things, people and practices [that] have crossed national boundaries'.[95] However, as Ballantyne has argued, by seeing the British as 'unfettered and unchanged' by Indigenous peoples, new imperial history has failed to account for Indigenous experience.[96] For Indigenous mobilities to be truly integrated into mobilities scholarship, Indigenous goods, practices and values must be understood as affective—that is, as capable of influencing encounters and relationships between Indigenous and non-Indigenous people, mirroring the way that Europeans' goods, practices and values are assumed to have affected Indigenous people. Ballantyne's offering in this volume explores how mobility shaped early printed texts in New Zealand and how these texts were, themselves, mobile, opening up new forms of knowledge and being imbued with different meanings as they travelled through Māori communities. Standfield's chapter follows the movement of both people and ideas between New Zealand and Port Jackson in the early nineteenth century, arguing that Māori values of reciprocity in relationships shaped the reception of missionaries in New Zealand, and that the mobility of Indigenous values and ideas is a vital aspect of cross-cultural contact that has the power to influence imperial activity.

Overall, this volume hopes to contribute to a developing field of scholarship on Indigenous mobilities in which Indigenous people and communities are recognised and respected as distinct; as having their own motivations for travelling, and for living their cultures while travelling; as crossing boundaries other than those imposed by Europeans; as expressing boundary-crossing protocols; and as undertaking shorter journeys that

---

95   Curthoys and Lake 2005.
96   Ballantyne 2010: 451.

might have as much significance as travelling the globe. In short, we hope that Indigenous people can emerge from the archives as active voyagers recognised in histories as expressing their own ambitions and agency.

References

Altman, Jon 1987, *Hunter-Gatherers Today: An Aboriginal Economy in North Australia*, Australian Institute of Aboriginal Studies, Canberra.

Altman, Jon and Melinda Hinkson 2007, 'Mobility and modernity in Arnhem Land: The social universe of Kuninjku trucks', *Journal of Material Culture* 12(2):181–203. doi.org/10.1177/1359183507078122

Anderson, Atholl 1998, *The Welcome of Strangers: An Ethnohistory of Southern Maori AD 1650–1850*, University of Otago Press, Dunedin.

Balachandran, Gopal 2012, *Globalizing Labour? Indian Seafarers and World Shipping, c. 1879–1945*, Oxford University Press, New Delhi.

Ballantyne, Tony 2002, *Orientalism and Race: Aryanism in the British Empire*, Palgrave, Bassingstoke, New York. doi.org/10.1057/9780230508071

Ballantyne, Tony 2010, 'The changing shape of the modern British Empire and its historiography', *The Historical Journal* 55(2): 429–52. doi.org/10.1017/S0018246X10000117

Ballantyne, Tony 2011, 'On place, space and mobility in nineteenth century New Zealand', *New Zealand Journal of History* 45(1): 50–70.

Ballantyne, Tony 2014, *Entanglements of Empire: Missionaries, Maori and the Question of the Body*, Duke University Press, Durham. doi.org/10.1215/9780822375883

Ballantyne, Tony and Antoinette Burton 2009, 'Introduction: The politics of intimacy in an age of empire', in *Moving Subjects: Gender, Mobility, and Intimacy in an Age of Global Empire*, Tony Ballantyne and Antoinette Burton (eds), University of Illinois Press, Urbana: 1–28.

Banivanua Mar, Tracey 2013, 'Imperial literacy and Indigenous rights: Tracing transoceanic circuits of a modern discourse', *Aboriginal History* (37): 1–28.

Barcham, Manahuia 2004, 'The politics of Maori mobility', in *Population Mobility and Indigenous Peoples in Australasia and North America*, John Taylor and Martin Bell (eds), Routledge, London and New York: 163–83.

Bashford, Alison 2017, 'Terraqueous histories', *The Historical Journal* 60(2): 253–72. doi.org/10.1017/S0018246X16000431

Behrendt, Larissa 2003, *Achieving Social Justice: Indigenous Rights and Australia's Future*, The Federation Press, Sydney.

Bell, Martin and John Taylor 2004, 'Conclusion: Emerging research themes' in *Population Mobility and Indigenous Peoples in Australasia and North America*, John Taylor and Martin Bell (eds), Routledge, London and New York: 262–67.

Binney, Judith 2004, 'Tuki's universe', *New Zealand Journal of History* 38(2): 215–32.

Byrne, Denis 2010, 'Nervous landscapes: Race and space in Australia', in *Making Settler Colonial Space: Perspectives on Race, Place and Identity*, Tracey Banivanua Mar and Penelope Edmonds (eds), Palgrave Macmillan, Houndsmill and New York: 103–28. doi.org/10.1057/9780230277946_8

Byrnes, Giselle 2001, *Boundary Markers: Land Surveying and the Colonisation of New Zealand*, Bridget Williams Books, Wellington. doi.org/10.7810/9781877242908

Byrnes, Giselle 2009, 'Nation and migration', *New Zealand Journal of History* 43(2): 123–32.

Cahir, Fred and Ian D. Clark 2014, 'The Maori presence in Victoria, Australia, 1830–1900: A preliminary analysis of Australian sources', *New Zealand Journal of History* 48(1): 109–26.

Carey, Jane and Jane Lydon 2014, 'Introduction: Indigenous networks, historical trajectories and contemporary connections', in *Indigenous Networks: Mobility, Connections and Exchange*, Jane Lydon and Jane Carey (eds), Routledge, New York: 1–26.

Clarsen, Georgine 2008, *Eat My Dust: Early Women Motorists*, Johns Hopkins University Press, Baltimore.

Clarsen, Georgine 2011, 'The flip side: Women on the redex around Australia reliability trials of the 1950s', *Humanities Research* 17(2): 17–36.

Curthoys, Ann 2003, 'We've just started making national histories, and you want us to stop already?', in *After the Imperial Turn: Thinking With and Through the Nation*, Antoinette Burton (ed.), Duke University Press, Durham: 70–89.

Curthoys, Ann and Marilyn Lake (eds) 2005, *Connected Worlds: History in Transnational Perspective*, ANU E Press, Canberra.

David, Frank, Leah Lui-Chivizhe and Jude Philip 2015, 'Individuals in Kulkalgal history', *Journal of Australian Studies* 39(3): 290–306. doi.org/10.1080/14443058.2015.1051086

Deacon, Desley, Penny Russell and Angela Woollacott (eds) 2010, *Transnational Lives: Biographies of Global Modernity, 1700–Present*, Palgrave Macmillan, Bassingstoke, New York.

de Costa, Ravi 2006, *A Higher Authority: Indigenous Transnationalism and Australia*, UNSW Press, Sydney.

de Costa, Ravi 2007, 'Cosmology, mobility and exchange: Indigenous diplomacies before the nation-state', *Canadian Foreign Policy* 13(3): 13–28. doi.org/10.1080/11926422.2007.9673440

Deloria, Philip J. 2004, 'Technology: I want to ride in Geronimo's Cadillac', in his *Indians in Unexpected Places*, University Press of Kansas, Lawrence: 136–82.

Elbourne, Elizabeth 2005, 'Indigenous peoples and imperial networks in the early nineteenth century: The politics of knowledge', in *Rediscovering the British World*, Phillip Buckner and R. Douglas Francis (eds), University of Calgary Press, Calgary: 59–85.

Ewald, Janet J. 2000, 'Crossers of the sea: Slaves, freedmen, and other migrants in the northwestern Indian Ocean, c. 1750–1914', *The American Historical Review* 105(1): 69–91.

Fox, Karen 2011, *Maori and Aboriginal Women in the Public Eye: Representing Difference, 1950–2000*, ANU E Press, Canberra.

Fox, Karen 2012, 'Globalising indigeneity? Writing Indigenous histories in a transnational world', *History Compass* 10(6): 423–39. doi.org/10.1111/j.1478-0542.2012.00855.x

Goodall, Heather and Allison Cadzow 2009, *Rivers and Resilience: Aboriginal People on Sydney's Georges River*, UNSW Press, Sydney.

Goodall, Heather, Devleena Ghosh and Lindi R. Todd 2008, 'Jumping ship—skirting empire: Indians, Aborigines and Australians across the Indian Ocean', *Transforming Cultures eJournal* 3(1): 44–74.

Haskins, Victoria 2008, 'The smoking buggy', in *Off the Beaten Track: A Journey Across the Nation*, Alison Russell (ed.), National Motor Museum, Birdwood: 72–81.

Hau'ofa, Epeli 1993, 'Our sea of islands', in *A New Oceania: Rediscovering Our Sea of Islands*, Eric Waddell, Vijay Naidu, and Epeli Hau'ofa (eds), School of Social and Economic Development, University of the South Pacific and Bleake House, Suva: 2–16.

Jones, Alison and Kuni Jenkins 2011, *He Kōrero—Words Between Us: First Māori-Pākehā Conversations on Paper,* Huia Publications, Auckland.

Kearney, Amanda and John J. Bradley 2015, 'When a long way in a bark canoe is a quick trip in a boat', *Quaternary International* 385: 166–76. doi.org/10.1016/j.quaint.2014.07.004

Khatun, Samia 2015, 'Beyond blank spaces: Five tracks to late-nineteenth century Beltana', *Transfers* 5(3): 68–86.

Lambert, David and Alan Lester (eds) 2006, *Colonial Lives Across the British Empire*, Cambridge University Press, Cambridge.

Lester, Alan 2001, *Imperial Networks: Creating Identities in Nineteenth Century South Africa and Britain*, Routledge, London and New York.

Lester, Alan and Zoe Laidlaw 2015, 'Indigenous sites and mobilities: Connected sites in the long nineteenth century', in *Indigenous Communities and Settler Colonialism: Land Holding, Loss and Survival and an Interconnected World*, Zoe Laidlaw and Alan Lester (eds), Palgrave Macmillan, London: 1–23. doi.org/10.1057/9781137452368_1

Mahuika, Nepia 2009, 'Revitalizing Te Ika-a-Maui: Māori migration and the nation', *New Zealand Journal of History* 43(2): 133–49.

Maynard, John 2005, '"In the interests of our people": The influence of Garveyism on the rise of Australian Aboriginal political activism', *Aboriginal History* 29: 1–22.

McDonnell, Michael A. 2015, 'Indigenous networks: Mobility, connections and exchange', *Australian Historical Studies* 46(2): 312–13. doi.org/10.1080/1031461X.2015.1040580

McNab, Robert (ed.) 1908, *Historical Records of New Zealand, Volume 1*, Government Printer. Wellington, www.enzb.auckland.ac.nz/document?wid=3870&page=0&action=null

Paisley, Fiona 2004, '"Performing New Zealand": Maori and Pakeha delegates at the pan-Pacific women's conference, Hawai'i, 1934', *New Zealand Journal of History* 38(1): 22–38.

Paisley, Fiona 2006, 'Glamour in the Pacific: Cultural internationalism and Maori politics at pan-Pacific women's conferences in the 1950s', *Pacific Studies* 29(1): 54–81.

Paisley, Fiona 2012, *The Lone Protestor: AM Fernando in Australia and Europe*, Aboriginal Studies Press, Canberra.

Paterson, Lachy 2013, 'The similarity of hue constituted no special bond of intimacy between them', *Journal of New Zealand Studies* 14: 19–40.

Peterson, Nicolas 2004, 'Myth of the "walkabout": Movement in the Aboriginal domain', in *Population Mobility and Indigenous Peoples in Australasia and North America*, John Taylor and Martin Bell (eds), Routledge, London and New York: 223–38.

Pool, Ian 2013, *Te Iwi Maori: Population Past, Present and Projected*, Auckland University Press, Auckland.

Pratt, Mary Louise 2007, *Imperial Eyes: Travel Writing and Transculturation*, Routledge, London, New York.

Prout, Sarah 2009, 'Security and belonging: Reconceptualising Aboriginal spatial mobilities in Yamatji country, Western Australia', *Mobilities* 4(2): 177–202. doi.org/10.1080/17450100902905105

Russell, Lynette 2008, '"A New Holland half-caste": Sealer and whaler Tommy Chaseland', *History Australia* 5(1): 08.1–08.15.

Russell, Lynette 2012, *Roving Mariners: Australian Aboriginal Whalers and Sealers in the Southern Oceans, 1790–1870*, State University of New York Press, Albany.

Russell, Penny, Desley Deacon and Angela Woollacott 2008, *Transnational Ties: Australian Lives in the World*, ANU E Press, Canberra.

Salmond, Anne 1997, *Between Worlds: Early Exchanges between Maori and Europeans, 1773–1815*, Viking Press, Auckland.

Shellam, Tiffany, Maria Nugent, Shino Konishi and Alison Cadzow 2016, *Brokers and Boundaries. Colonial Exploration in Indigenous Territory*, ANU Press, Canberra. doi.org/10.22459/BB.04.2016

Standfield, Rachel 2004, 'A remarkably tolerant nation? Constructions of benign whiteness in Australian political discourse', *Borderlands e-journal* 3(2).

Standfield, Rachel 2012, *Race and Identity in the Tasman World, 1769–1840,* Pickering and Chatto, London.

Stevens, Michael J. 2006, 'Kāi Tahu me te Hopu Tītī ki Rakiura: An exception to the "colonial rule"?', *Journal of Pacific History* 41(3): 273–91. doi.org/10.1080/00223340600984737

Taonui, Rāwiri n.d., 'Ngā Waewae tapu—Māori exploration', *Te Ara— The Encyclopaedia of New Zealand*, teara.govt.nz/en/nga-waewae-tapu-maori-exploration

Taylor, John and Martin Bell 2004a, 'Introduction: New world demography', in *Population Mobility and Indigenous Peoples in Australasia and North America*, John Taylor and Martin Bell (eds), Routledge, London and New York: 1–10.

Taylor, John and Martin Bell 2004b, 'Continuity and change in Indigenous Australian population mobility', in *Population Mobility and Indigenous Peoples in Australasia and North America*, John Taylor and Martin Bell (eds), Routledge, London and New York: 13–43.

Turnbull, David 2004, 'Narrative traditions of space, time and trust in court: *Terra nullius*, "wandering", the *Yorta Yorta* native title claim, and the Hindmarsh Island bridge controversy', in *Expertise in Regulation and Law*, Gary Edmond (ed.), Aldershot and Burlington, Ashgate: 166–83.

van Toorn, Penny 2010, 'Writing the entrapped nations of Indigenous Australia into being', in *Transnational Lives: Biographies on Global Modernity, 1700–present*, Penny Russell, Desley Deacon and Angela Woollacott (eds), Palgrave Macmillan, Houndmills, Basingstoke: 41–53. doi.org/10.1057/9780230277472_4

Williams, Melissa Matutina 2015, *Panguru and the City: Kāinga Tahi, Kāinga Rua: An Urban Migration History*, Bridget Williams Books, Wellington.

2

Crossing Boundaries: Tracing Indigenous Mobility and Territory in the Exploration of South-Eastern Australia

Shino Konishi

In 'Expulsion, Exodus and Exile in White Australian Historical Mythology', Ann Curthoys examined how Indigenous mobility was problematised in settler colonial discourses. She drew on Gamatj leader and former Australian of the Year Galarrwuy Yunupingu's observation that Aboriginal people were derisively represented as aimless wanderers and nomads, perpetually on 'walkabout', while the colonists claimed for themselves the mantle of settlers and natives, ostensibly defending their homelands from marauding Aboriginal people.[1] Curthoys highlighted the tension between movement and place, and the ways in which certain kinds of mobility or, to be more specific, the mobility of certain kinds of people—namely, nomadic Indigenous people—have been historically coded as 'dysfunctional' and 'rootless'.[2]

Colonial discourses constructed Indigenous mobility as aimless wandering—an almost animalistic roaming driven by the search for food and the need to eke out survival. According to Sarah Prout and Richard

---

1   Curthoys 1999: 14.
2   Cresswell 2010: 20.

Howitt, 'Indigenous hunter-gatherer lifestyles were interpreted by arriving British settlers as evidence of their backward and uncivilized existence'.[3] Such constructions fuelled the colonial fantasy of terra nullius—that the lands the British ostensibly discovered belonged to no one.

Alan Frost's 'New South Wales as Terra Nullius: The British Denial of Aboriginal Land Rights', published in 1981, was one of the first significant historical studies of European perceptions of Aboriginal people and the conception of terra nullius.[4] He argued that upon the *Endeavour*'s arrival in 1770, the British inevitably assumed that Aboriginal people lacked sovereignty and property rights because 'Aborigines had scarcely begun to develop social, political or religious organization's as the Europeans understood these'.[5] For Frost, a crucial factor underpinning the British belief that New South Wales was not owned by Aboriginal people was their apparent failure to 'subdue and cultivate the earth so as to obtain "dominion" over it'. He saw Indigenous mobility as a sign of their failure to progress beyond the '"first stage" … of civilization'. Frost cited Joseph Banks' observation that they 'seemed "never to make stay in their houses but wander[ed] from place to place like the Arabs"'.[6] Such Eurocentric perceptions of Aboriginal mobility were construed by Frost as an inevitable response to the seemingly abject poverty of Aboriginal material culture, as well as their local environments, which were devoid of recognisable food sources to cultivate. Hence, Frost believed that the British had little option but to see Australia as a terra nullius, as he explained:

> The Aborigines had not enclosed the country to depasture herds and flocks, nor had they wrought an agriculture upon it. And just as they did not labour in the sweat of their brow for their food, neither did they manufacture to any degree. Their few utensils, weapons and ornaments were crude in the extreme—mere pieces of wood, stone, shell, bark, bone or hair, fashioned in rudimentary ways to meet only basic needs.[7]

---

3   Prout and Howitt 2009: 398.
4   Frost 1981. This work is more widely discussed than earlier historical analyses of terra nullius in Australia, such as Scott (1940). Fitzmaurice (2007: 5–6) argued that 'between Ernest Scott and [Wiradjuri activist and lawyer] Paul Coe's use of terra nullius in 1978, discussions of res nullius, territorium nullius and terra nullius in application to Australian history were rare'.
5   Frost 1981: 520.
6   Frost 1981: 519.
7   Frost 1981: 519.

In the decades after Frost's essay was published, historians such as Henry Reynolds countered the view that eighteenth-century British colonists were oblivious to Aboriginal modes of land tenure, demonstrating that some seventeenth- and eighteenth-century jurists held that nomadic peoples maintained sovereignty over their land.[8]

Further challenging the settler discourse that Aboriginal people were aimless wanderers, Indigenous scholars such as Dale Kerwin and Bruce Pascoe demonstrated that Aboriginal people, far from eking out a meagre existence, systematically managed the environment through a range of seasonal practices, such as harvesting fish and eels, collecting seeds and preparing the soil through deliberate firing.[9] In *The Biggest Estate on Earth: How Aborigines Made Australia*, Bill Gammage contended that Western recognition of such practices is not a recent development (i.e. it did not follow anthropologist Rhys Jones' 1969 coining of the term 'fire-stick farming'), as some individuals acknowledged such practices during the colonial period. For example, citing Edward Curr's 1883 claim that no other 'section of the human race has exercised a greater influence on the physical condition of any large portion of the globe than the wandering savages of Australia', Gammage argued that Curr 'defied a European convention that the wanderers barely touched the land'.[10]

When combined with the legacy of terra nullius and, since 1993, the introduction of native title legislation, the construction of Indigenous mobility as aimless wandering has led many Aboriginal people to minimise their histories of mobility in favour of asserting their fixed connections to place and ties to particular country. In *Rivers and Resilience: Aboriginal People on Sydney's Georges River*, Heather Goodall and Allison Cadzow argued that the trope of aimless wandering made it difficult for Aboriginal people to rehabilitate and extol their cultures of mobility lest it 'obstruct the recognition of their rights to land'.[11] Indeed, such a strategy can be prudent, as evident from the difficulties the Wongatha people of the Western Desert, who regularly migrated around the area east of Mount Margaret in the Western Australian goldfields, faced in proving they 'had

8   Reynolds 2003. Note that the first edition of this book was published in 1987. In 1992, in the Mabo decision, the High Court dismissed the legal fiction that Australia was terra nullius before British occupation and recognised native title.
9   Kerwin 2010; Pascoe 2014. 'Fire-stick farming' was a term coined by archaeologist Rhys Jones in 1969.
10   Gammage 2012: 2.
11   Goodall and Cadzow 2009: 21.

a long term attachment' to their land.[12] Yet, mobility has long been a key characteristic of Aboriginal experience, ranging from the ceremonial gatherings and extensive trade journeys that marked Indigenous life before (and, to a significant and often unrecognised degree, after) colonisation, through to the forced and voluntary movements that have continued in different ways through to the present. As Goodall and Cadzow attested, 'mobility was and is as much a defining characteristic of Aboriginal cultures as affiliations with meaningful bounded places'.[13]

This chapter examines the tension between mobility and place, in particular, the notion espoused by Frost that Eurocentric perceptions of Indigenous mobility inevitably prevented colonists from recognising Aboriginal sovereignty and connections to land. Reynolds showed that a colonial blindness to Indigenous sovereignty was not universal;[14] my aim is to demonstrate that this sentiment was not just an abstract philosophy, but was acknowledged, explicitly and implicitly, in explorers' accounts of their interactions with Aboriginal people. Focusing on maritime and overland explorers' accounts of Aboriginal people in south-eastern Australia, the chapter highlights the kinds of Indigenous movement that occurred before and during the early stages of colonisation in Australia. My aim is to explore the ways in which Indigenous people in the eighteenth and nineteenth centuries expressed to European strangers that they were both mobile *and* bounded to particular places, and the extent to which European interlocutors understood these articulations.

***

New imperial histories have begun to explicitly engage with the role of mobility in the creation and maintenance of empire, as well as in the development of Western notions of modernity.[15] As Nan Seuffert observed, the 'circulation of capital and commodities, technologies of transportation and communication, traveling ideologies and systems of governance and surveillance as well as the movement' of individual agents of empire, such as settlers, colonial administrators and so on, all 'shaped the politics and the period'.[16] Explorers played a key role in the expansion of empire as their expeditions into ostensibly uncharted territories opened up new routes for

---

12 Muller 2014: 59.
13 Goodall and Cadzow 2009: 21.
14 Reynolds 2003.
15 See Ballantyne 2014; Carey and Lydon 2014.
16 Seuffert 2011: 10.

the empire as well as producing new information about local resources that justified further expansion. Significantly, in many parts of Australia, it was explorers who first encountered Aboriginal people and their lands. It was their representations of Aboriginal peoples and landscapes, widely disseminated through the publication and circulation of their journals, that shaped the expectations of later explorers and colonists. Certainly, some explorers contributed to Eurocentric constructions of Aboriginal mobility as aimless wandering.

Nicolas Peterson has observed that one of the 'most mythologised aspects of Australian Aboriginal behaviour has been the "walkabout"', which, he explained, is considered to be the seemingly 'internal urge' to suddenly 'travel for travel's sake'.[17] Peterson highlighted how colonial discourses presented Indigenous movement as essentially inexplicable and irrational, for such discourses did not accommodate the reasons Aboriginal people had for moving on. For instance, Aboriginal workers in the pastoral industry were often not permitted to leave work to 'attend a ceremony, or to visit kin'; consequently, such workers had to leave without notice.[18] However, the Western rendering of Indigenous mobility as inexplicable or, at best, predicated on momentary needs, predates the colonial coopting of Aboriginal labour. Seuffert suggested that 'distinctions between "settler" and "nomad"' were 'integral' to nineteenth-century 'concepts of civilization', for ideas of civilisation and settlement were juxtaposed by notions of savagery and wandering.[19] Such a construct was mobilised in Captain James Cook's 1770 account of the Aboriginal people of New South Wales:

> I do not look upon them to be a warlike people; on the contrary, I think them a Timerous and inoffensive race, no ways inclined to Cruelty … neither are they very numerous. They live in small parties along by the Sea Coast, the banks of Lakes, Rivers, Creeks, etc. They seem to have no fixed habitation, but move about from place to place like wild beasts in search of Food.[20]

This description is arguably one of the most influential European descriptions of Aboriginal society. It informed the eventual decision by the British to establish a penal colony in New South Wales in 1788.

---

17 Peterson 2003: 223.
18 Peterson 2003: 223.
19 Seuffert 2011: 11.
20 Cook 1955: 433.

Cook's journal, as well as those of his fellow *Endeavour* shipmates, botanist Joseph Banks and lieutenant James Matra, who separately petitioned the government to establish a colony in New South Wales, initiated the myth that Aboriginal people did not own their land. The *Endeavour* accounts suggested that Aboriginal people would simply move off the land and make way for the colonists, rather than violently oppose their settlement.[21] By contrast, Maria Nugent observed that Cook's interactions with Aboriginal people at Kamay, or Botany Bay, revealed that they did not aimlessly 'move about from place to place'; instead, each clan and people had a bounded sense of territory, and had instituted elaborate protocols for entering other's country.[22] Discussing Australia more broadly, Sylvia Hallam noted that:

> Meetings between different Australian communities were, before the coming of Europeans, (and remain for Aboriginal Australians) highly structured affairs, with elements of ceremonial preparedness for conflict, formal peacemaking, reciprocal exchange of gifts, and sometimes actual conflict and resolution of conflict.[23]

Tracing a wide range of anthropological studies and early settler accounts, Hallam argued that there was a pan-continental protocol for when Aboriginal groups encountered one another, with each side having set expectations of reciprocal obligations.[24] Yandruwandha man Aaron Paterson has recently reiterated this point, explaining that the 'customary protocols' for strangers entering Yandruwandha traditional lands include 'announcing their arrival at a distance, waiting for an invitation to enter camp, and waiting for a spot to be picked out where they could camp'. He added that, from an Indigenous perspective, such protocols seem 'so basic, so simple to understand', for they have 'been honed over millennia [and] reinforced by dire physical consequences' for any breaches.[25] However, as we shall see, Cook and later European explorers did not easily recognise or understand such protocols when they entered Aboriginal territory.

---

21 For a discussion of how Maori were perceived as protective of their territory, see Standfield 2012.
22 Nugent 2005: 13–14.
23 Hallam 1983: 134–36.
24 Hallam 1983: 134–36.
25 Paterson 2013: xv.

On 28 April 1770, Cook's *Endeavour* arrived at Kamay, a location he later named Botany Bay.[26] The surrounding land 'appeard [sic] Cliffy and barren without wood', making the smoke rising from a fire tended by a group of 10 Aboriginal people even more conspicuous. The ship immediately tacked towards the party, who then 'retird [sic] to a little eminence where they could conveniently see the ship'.[27] In the meantime, another group of Aboriginal men, perched on the shore's rocks, called out to the *Endeavour*. These men, whose black bodies were 'painted with white', were clearly perturbed by the arrival of the ship; they spoke animatedly and frequently brandished their weapons at their seemingly unwelcome visitors.[28] Concerned with seeking anchorage, Cook navigated further into the bay towards the mouth of an inlet on the southern shore of the harbour. Unlike the north side of the harbour, the south was marked by an unusual calm. Within the harbour were a number of canoes, their owners fishing, utterly unmoved by the presence of the ship; on the shore were 'a few hutts [sic]' and equally indifferent women and children emerged from the nearby wood carrying bundles of sticks.[29] With the people appearing to act as though the ship was not there, the English retired for dinner and planned their first landing.

Emboldened by the Aboriginal people's apparent indifference towards them, the British assumed that they could quietly land; however, as they approached, almost all of the people suddenly fled to the woods, leaving two lone men to oppose their landing. Rushing down to the rocks, shouting 'warra warra wai',[30] the two men threatened the boats with their spears and woomeras.[31] Cook tried to appease them by offering nails and beads, and tried in vain to gesture that they 'meant them no harm'.[32] Tiring of this mime, and hoping to scare them off, Cook had a musket fired over their heads.[33] Though one man dropped his bundle of spears in shock, he quickly collected himself and 'renewed [his] threats and

---

26   Cook 1955: 304; Banks 1998: 21.
27   Banks 1998: 21.
28   Banks 1998: 22.
29   Banks found the Aboriginal peoples' indifference to the Europeans curious, and he was 'almost inclind [sic] to think that attentive to their business and deafned [sic] by the noise of the surf they neither saw nor heard her [the *Endeavour*] go past'. Banks 1998: 22.
30   This term was later interpreted as 'be gone'. Parkinson 1972: 134.
31   Banks 1998: 23.
32   Banks 1998: 23; Cook 1955: 305.
33   Banks 1998: 23. However, Cook stated that he fired the shot between the two men. Cook 1955: 305. Parkinson clarified that the purpose was to frighten them. Parkinson 1972: 134.

opposition'.[34] Cook then had another shot fired, striking one man's leg. Instead of surrendering or retreating as Cook expected, the man ran back to one of the huts to collect a wooden club and an oval shield. During this time, the British landed and both Aboriginal men hurled their spears at them. Once again, Cook had the men fired upon, finally causing them to retreat.[35]

Nugent contended that the Aboriginal response to the arrival of Cook and his men reflected Indigenous protocols for receiving strangers. Drawing on Baldwin Spencer and Frank Gillen's anthropological studies of the Arunta people of Central Australia, she observed that within Aboriginal societies, uninvited guests were ignored until they conducted the necessary requests for admission to their potential hosts' country. Nugent suggested that the two Aboriginal men's 'display of force and the [previous] cold shoulder treatment were a type of protocol to be followed when in the presence of strangers. They were perhaps designed to pave the way for some form of exchange to occur'.[36] Oblivious to these protocols, Cook failed to play the passive role designated to strangers. Had he been aware of what was expected, he may not (later) have conceived of Aboriginal people as aimless wanderers, nor seen their mobility as incommensurable with Indigenous notions of territory. Not all explorers were as unaware as Cook that Indigenous people might have conventions for greeting strangers. Some tried to anticipate Indigenous reactions to the arrival of ships and improvise formal ceremonies of encounter.

In March 1772, just two years after Cook sailed along the east coast, Marc-Joseph Marion-Dufresne's *Mascarin* and *Marquis de Castries* landed at Marion Bay in Van Diemen's Land. The French spent four days there, and were the first Europeans to come face to face with Palawa people. After anchoring at Marion Bay, the French approached the shore in three longboats. Upon seeing them, Aboriginal people, most likely from the Oyster Bay nation, lit a fire and watched their progress, shouting and gesturing at them as they neared. Marion-Dufresne evaluated the scene and, concluding that the Aboriginal people seemed friendly, made two sailors swim ashore naked and bearing gifts. According to John Mulvaney, the idea of sending the men ashore naked was so that they would emerge from the sea like 'natural man', and not frighten the Aboriginal people

34 Banks 1998: 23.
35 Matra 1771: 58; Parkinson 1972: 134; Banks 1998: 23; Cook 1955: 305.
36 Nugent 2005: 13.

with their starkly different appearance.[37] At first, the Palawa men greeted the sailors with enthusiasm and seemed to delight in their gifts of mirrors and necklaces. When Marion-Dufresne's boat landed, the captain, although clothed, was similarly welcomed. He was given a lit torch and, in turn, offered the Aboriginal people 'several pieces of cloth and some knives' and bread. The Aboriginal people mainly seemed interested in the French weapons and clothes, 'especially the scarlet ones'.[38]

Unlike Cook, the French explorers not only recognised that Aboriginal people had protocols for receiving visitors, they also imagined that they understood them. One of the officers recorded that Marion-Dufresne believed that to show he 'had come with pacific intentions' he should light a nearby pile of wood with the firebrand he had been given. This seemed to be a mistake, as one French witness believed that lighting the fire was tantamount to an Indigenous 'declaration of war', for the Aboriginal people immediately responded by hurling stones at the explorers. However, another officer offered a more prosaic explanation for the attack, suggesting that the Aboriginal people were alarmed by the sight of a third longboat approaching the shore. Irrespective of the cause, the French responded by firing, killing at least one man.[39] Despite the tragic outcome, this attempt by Marion-Dufresne to anticipate and interpret an Indigenous protocol for greeting strangers suggests that he expected that the natives would be sovereigns of their land and have a process of welcoming strangers to their country. Yet, the Oyster Bay people failed to proceed as he expected, and misread his symbolic display of 'pacific intentions'. Unlike Cook, Marion-Dufresne recognised that Aboriginal people might have a formalised system of welcome, but he misunderstood how that welcome might be performed. In consequence, he precipitously retreated to the myth of the pernicious 'savage' and concluded that the Palawa people of Van Diemen's Land were 'the most miserable people in the world, and the human beings who approach closest to brute beasts' for they seemed to 'have no fixed abode in any one place'.[40]

Yet, the European misapprehension of Indigenous mobility was not only a result of cross-cultural miscommunication and violence. Some European explorers readily fell back on pejorative assumptions about

37 Mulvaney 1989: 29.
38 Duyker 1992: 22, 31.
39 Duyker 1992: 22, 31.
40 Duyker 1992: 22.

aimless wandering even when they failed to actually meet any Indigenous people. On Cook's second voyage around the world, Tobias Furneaux, Captain of HMS *Adventure*, consort to Cook's HMS *Resolution*, landed in south-eastern Van Diemen's Land, at what became known as Adventure Bay, in 1773. While his men did not actually meet any Aboriginal people during their brief stay, they encountered signs of the Indigenous presence. Examining their empty 'Huts', Furneaux claimed that 'they will hardly keep out a show[e]r of rain'. This led him to posit that 'they have no settled place of habitation, as their houses seem'd to be built but for a few days'. He assumed that they 'wander about in small parties from place to place in search of Food', and emphasised that he believed the unseen natives' mobility was 'actuated by no other motive'.[41] He found their mobility inexplicable, adding that it was 'remarkable' that they 'never saw the least signs of either Canoe or boat'. Furneaux concluded that the locals were 'a very Ignorant and wretched set of people, tho' natives of a country producing every necessary of life, and a climate fairest in the world'.[42] His account typifies colonial discourses on what Seuffert labelled the 'savage wanderer'. Drawing on John Stuart Mill, Seuffert suggested that the savage wanderer was constructed in opposition to the civilised settler, for their movement was not 'upward and forward', but instead was characterised as 'rootless and directionless, moving over the land without advancing or progressing'.[43] For Furneaux, such mobility rendered the natives as undeserving of the bounteous land (which they wasted), and, like Cook's 1770 accounts that informed Frost, contributed to the notion of terra nullius.

Cook, Marion-Dufresne and Furneaux's obliviousness to, or misrecognition of, local Indigenous protocols were, in some respects, a consequence of their not having Aboriginal intermediaries who could mediate between the locals and strangers and explain Indigenous protocols to them. This is highlighted when we compare their accounts with those of overland explorer Paul Edmund de Strzelecki, who, through the benefit of his Aboriginal guides Charlie Tarra and Jackey, observed that there were many Aboriginal 'superstitious practices connected with the rights of hospitality'.[44]

---

41 Furneaux 1961: 735.
42 Furneaux 1961: 735.
43 Seuffert 2011: 23.
44 Strzelecki 1845: 340.

Strzelecki provided a vivid account of one such 'traditionary' practice, recalling an encounter with an unknown Aboriginal group after a few days struggling through the Snowy mountain range with little water. As they crested the unnamed mountain, Strzelecki and his guides 'beheld at [their] feet, in the shade of a thicket, the long-looked-for pond of water', surrounded by the dwellings of the 'encamped tribe'. Desperate to quench his thirst, he began to rush towards the pond when his guide[45] seized him, warning him to 'stop, or we are lost'. Instead of directly approaching the 'circle of wigwams', led by the guide, they sat down 'about sixty yards from them'.[46] After a short while, at which point Strzelecki's impatience for food and water was 'about to burst', a 'piece of burning wood was thrown towards [them] from the nearest wigwam'. His guide nonchalantly retrieved the torch and lit a fire, and began to cook a possum that they 'had in store'. All the while he seemingly ignored the local Aboriginal group, yet occasionally cast a 'sideways' look towards them. After 10 minutes, an 'elderly woman' brought water, leaving it 'midway between' the two groups' fires; a while later, fish was provided. Strzelecki was surprised to find that it was after his group's hunger and thirst had been 'appeased' that 'an old man in the camp [finally] rose and advanced towards' the expedition. Strzlelecki's guide met him halfway, and the two men discussed 'the object of [Strzelecki's] wanderings' through their country. Following their 'parley', the old man returned to his group to report back; after a 'few moments' silence, Strzelecki and his men were 'ordered to return from whence [they] came'. Strzelecki was surprised not to receive an 'invitation to join the camp'; however, since his guide informed him that there 'was no appeal against this decision', he had no option but to retreat.[47] Reflecting on this interaction, Strzelecki declared:

> Simple child of nature! Faithful to her inspirations, the native of Australia proceeds in the discharge of hospitality by a way exactly the reverse of our own: he first satisfied the wants of the traveler, and afterwards asks him those questions which in our civilization precede and regulate the kind and quantity of the hospitality to be accorded, and sometimes prompt its refusal altogether.[48]

---

45   Strzelecki does not name his guide in this account so it is not clear whether it was Charlie Tarra or Jackey.
46   Strzelecki 1845: 340.
47   Strzelecki 1845: 341.
48   Strzelecki 1845: 341.

Yet, it was not only through their protocols for welcoming strangers that Aboriginal people conveyed implicitly to Europeans that mobility could coexist with notions of territory and sovereignty. It was also made apparent to the Europeans when they observed large ceremonial gatherings of clans from different language groups.

***

Large ceremonial gatherings were most frequently observed in New South Wales around the Port Jackson colony, initially by the First Fleet chroniclers, and later by explorers who conducted excursions out of Sydney into the hinterland. With the benefit of either Aboriginal or European intermediaries, Europeans learned that clans affiliated with different places came together for social and political purposes. Peterson explained that 'prior to sedentarization' most Aboriginal societies comprised groups of households that, together, made a band; each 'band was integrated into a regional network through the personal, social, political and ceremonial ties of individuals to other individuals in nearby bands'.[49] The political ties between bands were dependent on regular travels to visit one another to trade, fight and marry, as well as to conduct a wide range of ceremonies. Even the early explorers, who did not fully grasp the meaning of these large-scale meetings, recognised that they were significant occasions. Moreover, in the Europeans' eyes, the ceremonies delineated a native space from which the Europeans were either prohibited, or allowed to enter, at the will of the Indigenous hosts.

In 1795, David Collins, judge advocate of the Port Jackson colony, had the privilege of witnessing the yoo-lahng erah-ba-diahng ceremony, whereby boys had their front tooth removed to catalyse and signify their transition to manhood.[50] Even though he did not fully grasp the significance of each part of the ceremony, Collins wrote a detailed account of the ritual. Significantly, he recognised that it was a regular event, having previously taken place in February 1791 (he had not been permitted to observe the previous ceremony). He also observed that before the ceremony took place, a large number of Aboriginal people from all over the Sydney region assembled at Farm Cove, clearing the yoo-lahng, or ceremonial space, during the day and dancing through the night. Collins recorded

---

49   Peterson 2003: 225.
50   Collins 1975: 485.

the names of some of the clans who visited and where they had come from, most notably the Cameragal people from north of the harbour who played a significant role in the ceremony.[51]

Similarly, Strzelecki learned, presumably through his Aboriginal guides Charlie Tarra and Jackey, that while the 'nature of the religion and government of the Australian natives [was] … mysterious', their society was comprised of 'three distinct classes', which were 'attained through age and fidelity to the tribe'.[52] Ceremonies, such as the Eora's yoo-lahng erah-ba-diahng, marked what Strzelecki described as the 'ceremony of admitting the youth to the first class'; this was attended by much secrecy. He explained that 'one or two tribes usually attend the meetings' of these first or second classes. By contrast, ceremonies that marked the entrance to the 'third class'—initiating 'the aged few' into the 'details of the religious mysteries'—would result in the assembly of most 'tribes within seventy miles'. These less common ceremonies were occasioned by great secrecy; as an outsider, Strzelecki was warned by his guides that he could not 'approach nearer than ten miles to the spot'.[53] While Collins and Strzelecki explicitly saw these ceremonies as religious or cultural, their recognition that as outsiders they could not attend suggests that the explorers at least implicitly recognised Indigenous dominion over certain native spaces within and beyond the colony.

In addition to the maintenance of Indigenous ceremonial spaces, Lisa Ford has shown that in the early years of the New South Wales colony, Indigenous legal spaces were also recognised, as both Aboriginal and colonial jurisdictions coexisted, despite notional claims that Aboriginal people were subject to British law.[54] She revealed various cases in which Aboriginal 'retaliatory violence' was tolerated because such cases involved the prosecution of *inter se* crimes; the British only sought to impose British jurisdiction on Aboriginal people for alleged crimes against British victims. Ford explained that 'these acts of Indigenous jurisdiction suggested an alternative spatial order' in which Aboriginal people carried out their trials in colonised places—in the streets, outside the barracks or near British landmarks—either out of convenience or as 'a defiant reminder of the legal plurality of settler space'.[55] Here, I add to Ford's

---

51   Collins 1975: 467.
52   Strzelecki 1845: 339.
53   Strzelecki 1845: 339.
54   Ford 2010: 75–78; see also Buchan 2008: 88–91.
55   Ford 2010: 75–78.

spatial argument by highlighting that Indigenous law was not only maintained through the assertion of sovereign Aboriginal spaces, but also through Indigenous cultures of mobility. This is because neighbouring Aboriginal clans and language groups travelled together to resolve legal disputes through ritualised corporal punishment, also known as 'payback'. According to Mark Finnane, 'the practice of payback' provided a means of 'exacting a satisfaction, remedying a wrong done by the other, in ways that imply a law-like exercise of a sanction, with the objective of resolving the harm done by a previous action'. As he pointed out, while the 'physical violence of such sanctions, is undeniable', it was 'also intended to be final'.[56] Therefore, as we will see, for crimes between members of different clans and language groups, the ritualised physical punishment such as 'the ordeal of spearing'[57] allowed conflicts to be resolved before they could escalate, and thus contributed to maintaining social order and peaceable relations between Indigenous groups.

In February 1824, the *Astrolabe*, captained by French explorer Jules Sébastien César Dumont d'Urville, visited Sydney. During his stay, Dumont d'Urville was taken by British officers, themselves acting as intermediaries between French visitors and local Aboriginal people, to visit the camp of Bungaree, a Garigal man from Broken Bay who had moved south to Port Jackson in 1802. Bungaree was a well-known figure in the colony, having served as an intermediary on both Mathew Flinders and Phillip Parker King's expeditions around Australia.[58] Bungaree advised Dumont d'Urville that 'a great gathering would take place near Sydney' the following day, and that it would be attended by 'several other tribes' from 'Parramatta, Kissing Point, Sydney, Liverpool, Windsor, Emu Plains, Broken Bay, Five islands, Botany Bay, and even from Hunter River etc. etc.'.[59] The purpose of the gathering was to 'punish several natives accused of various crimes'. In exchange for some rum, Bungaree agreed to take the French along with him to the meeting.

The next day, Dumont d'Urville followed behind the great procession of Bungaree and his people, with the 'chief' at the 'head of all of the warriors of his tribe … leaping and prancing through the bushes in all directions'. The excited group eventually arrived at the meeting place, 'high ground

56 Finnane 2001: 297.
57 Finnane 2001: 297.
58 For more on the role of Indigenous guides and imperial exploration, see Konishi, Nugent and Shellam 2015; Shellam, Nugent, Konishi and Cadzow 2016; Shellam in this collection.
59 Dumont d'Urville 1987: 85.

about two miles from the sea, from where the views take in both the vast harbours of Port Jackson and Botany Bay'. Dumont d'Urville assumed that the site was chosen for practical reasons, as it 'offered an immense area of flat land free of scrub'; however, it is likely that the space was deliberately chosen because it overlooked the lands of many of the greater Sydney clans, so was maintained as a significant Eora meeting place. Upon their arrival, the explorers saw that 'several tribes were already camped around the bush'. Dumont d'Urville wrote that each of the clans were 'distinguished by the designs of their body paintings, black, red, or white'. He also observed that there were only 'five or six complete tribes' present, although others had 'sent representatives who had gathered under allied chiefs'.[60]

The formal proceedings began when 'at a general signal, all the tribes got up and went to the arena in groups of fifteen to twenty men, all armed with spears, shields, clubs and boomerangs'. Six women were lined up in a semi-circle, armed with long sticks; two men 'stood up a short distance away' and only held 'long narrow wooden shields they call a *heloman*'.[61] Bungaree explained to Dumont d'Urville that the eight individuals (six women and two men) were accused of 'having caused the death of a man from the Windsor tribe, which was allied with the Liverpool tribe commanded by Coagai, and all were to receive punishment from their tribe'. After some formal speeches, 'the executions began'. One man approached the women, 'merely' hitting each of their sticks, until he came to the fifth woman, who he 'bashed … in the throat' causing her to fall to the ground. She 'lost no time in getting up again to endure the rest of her punishment'. Other men and women followed suit, and again they only 'set upon' the fifth woman. The two men were punished by ordeal, whereby 15 men in turn hurled spears at them, the accused parrying the spears 'with amazing dexterity'. Another man collected the spears to 'send them back to their owners', and Dumont d'Urville was surprised that 'often the natives being punished threw them back themselves, challenging their enemies and mocking them for their lack of skill'. Meanwhile, others from the aggrieved clans hurled boomerangs at the women, 'making them curl and whine all around them'. After the two men had 'endured a barrage of about sixty spears each', all eight accused were set free and 'no further notice was taken of them'. The 'unfortunate woman' who had

---

60   Dumont d'Urville 1987: 85.
61   Dumont d'Urville 1987: 85.

received all the blows was 'dragged off into the bush by the women of her tribe'. Dumont d'Urville reported that the reason her punishment was so 'excessive' was that she had been accused of 'another crime, separate from the one that was shared in common with her accomplices'. For the rest, they had 'merely [been] terrorized and publicly humiliated'.[62]

Importantly, it was not only crimes against individuals that were prosecuted at such gatherings; crimes against property also meted punishment. Strzelecki claimed that 'the foundation of their social edifice may, like that of civilised nations, be said to rest on an inherent sense of the rights of property'.[63] He asserted that Aboriginal people were just like 'any European political body' and were 'strongly attached to … property, and to the rights which it involves'. Thus, if one's 'territory has been trespassed upon, in hunting, by a neighbouring tribe, compensation of a reparation of the insult is asked for'.[64] Thus, in contrast to Frost's aforementioned argument that ethnocentric Europeans were blind to Indigenous territorial sovereignty and jurisdiction, some early explorers did explicitly recognise the existence of Indigenous property rights and had in place systems for asserting and protecting their rights.

***

The eyewitness accounts discussed in this chapter illustrate that some European explorers realised that Aboriginal people in New South Wales were mobile, with clans, or their representatives, visiting one another for ceremonial, judicial and political purposes. Consequently, Aboriginal people had developed protocols for crossing boundaries and entering the territory of other clans—protocols that could also accommodate meeting strangers such as the Europeans who explored Aboriginal country. As Penny Russell observed, 'respectful negotiation of territorial boundaries was vital in the mobile world of traditional Aboriginal society'.[65] Europeans in Sydney observed various clans visiting Port Jackson, home of the local Cadigal clan, from around the greater Sydney area. By distinguishing the different clans, and noting their homelands, early European accounts reveal that Indigenous mobility did not negate connections to place.

62 Dumont d'Urville 1987: 86.
63 Strzelecki 1845: 339.
64 Strzelecki 1845: 339.
65 Russell 2010: 26.

Further, all explorers recognised, to differing degrees, the formal and ceremonial aspects of the gatherings, highlighting the social, judicial and political purposes of such meetings: to mark the coming of age of young men and the attainment of 'religious mysteries' by respected elders; to punish individuals for crimes; and to either ameliorate the consequent tensions between clans, or represent closer affiliations between other clans. As Kerwin explained, journeying to attend ceremonies performed important political functions within Aboriginal societies, allowing, among other things, the opportunity to 'settle criminal matters' or to 'settle disputes of a political nature, such as land boundaries'.[66] This is evident in both Dumont d'Urville's and Strzelecki's accounts.

Attending such ceremonies also allowed Aboriginal clans to come together and 'renew their networks', which was crucial in many Aboriginal societies, as Fred Myers has shown, for it allowed Aboriginal clans to produce and maintain 'relatedness and shared identity'.[67] Thus, while not all European explorers and observers fully grasped the significance of the hospitality protocols and cultural ceremonies they witnessed, they nevertheless identified the interplay between mobility and place. Numerous influential early explorers and colonists did not, as is often claimed, equate Indigenous mobility with 'placelessness'.[68] Recognition that the trope of Aboriginal people as aimless wanderers was not as ubiquitous and as firmly held by early explorers and colonists, as has often been claimed, may have significant implications for contemporary Aboriginal communities undergoing the native title claims process. In the wake of native title legislation, Aboriginal groups have tended to downplay their cultures of mobility, highlighting instead their fixed connections to place to try and secure rights to their lands, as Goodall and Cadzow identified. Yet such approaches elide and downplay the rich cultures of mobility that have long characterised Aboriginal culture, life and custom, both before and since colonisation.

---

66 Kerwin 2010: 12.
67 Peterson 2003: 224.
68 Havemann 2005: 59.

References

Ballantyne, Tony 2014, 'Mobility, empire, colonisation', *History Australia* 11(2): 7–37.

Banks, Joseph 1998, *The Endeavour Journal of Joseph Banks: The Australian Journey*, Paul Brunton (ed.), Angus & Robertson in association with State Library of New South Wales, Sydney.

Buchan, Bruce 2008, *Empire of Political Thought,* Pickering and Chatto, London.

Carey, Jane, and Jane Lydon (eds) 2014, *Indigenous Networks: Mobility, Connections and Exchange*, Routledge, New York.

Collins, David 1975, *An Account of the English Colony in New South Wales*, Brian Fletcher (ed.), 2 volumes, A.H. & A.W. Reed in association with the Royal Australian Historical Society, Sydney.

Cook, James 1955, *The Journals of Captain James Cook on his Voyage of Discovery: Volume 1: Endeavour*, Hakluyt Society, London.

Cresswell, Tim 2010, 'Towards a politics of mobility', *Environment and Planning* 28: 17–31. doi.org/10.1068/d11407

Curthoys, Ann 1999, 'Expulsion, exodus and exile in white Australian historical mythology', *Journal of Australian Studies* 23(61): 1–19. doi.org/10.1080/14443059909387469

Dumont d'Urville, Jules S.-C. 1987, *An Account in Two Volumes of Two Voyages to the South Seas by Captain Jules S-C Dumont D'Urville of the French Navy to Australia, New Zealand, Oceania 1826–1829 in the Corvette Astrolabe and to the Straits of Magellan, Chile, Oceania, South East Asia, Australia, Antarctica, New Zealand and Torres Strait 1837-1840 in the Corvettes Astrolabe and Zélée, Vol. 1: Astrolabe 1826–1829,* Helen Rosenman (trans. and ed.), Melbourne University Press, Carlton.

Duyker, Edward (ed.) 1992, *The Discovery of Tasmania: Journal Extracts from the Expeditions of Abel Janszoon Tasman and Marc-Joseph Marion-Dufresne 1642 & 1772*, St David's Park Publishing, Hobart.

Finnane, Mark 2001, '"Payback", Customary Law and Criminal Law in Colonised Australia', *International Journal of the Sociology of Law* 29: 293–301. doi.org/10.1006/ijsl.2001.0153

Fitzmaurice, Andrew 2007, 'The genealogy of terra nullius', *Australian Historical Studies* 129: 1–15. doi.org/10.1080/10314610708601228

Ford, Lisa 2010, *Settler Sovereignty: Jurisdiction and Indigenous People in America and Australia, 1788–1836*, Harvard University Press, Cambridge, MA.

Frost, Alan 1981, 'New South Wales as terra nullius: The British denial of Aboriginal land rights', *Australian Historical Studies* 19(77): 513–23.

Furneaux, Tobias 1961, 'Furneaux's narrative', in James Cook, *The Journals of Captain James Cooks on his Voyage of Discovery, Volume 2: Resolution, Adventure*, J.C. Beaglehole (ed.), Hakluyt Society, London: 729–45.

Gammage, Bill 2012, *The Biggest Estate on Earth: How Aborigines Made Australia*, Allen & Unwin, Sydney.

Goodall, Heather, and Allison Cadzow 2009, *Rivers and Resilience: Aboriginal People on Sydney's Georges River*, UNSW Press, Sydney.

Hallam, Sylvia 1983, 'A view from the other side of the western frontier: Or, "I met a man who wasn't there …"', *Aboriginal History* 7(2): 134–56.

Havemann, Paul 2005, 'Denial, modernity and exclusion: Indigenous placelessness in Australia', *Macquarie Law Journal* 5: 57–80.

Kerwin, Dale 2010, *Aboriginal Dreaming Paths and Trading Routes: The Colonisation of the Australian Economic Landscape*, Sussex Academic Press, Brighton.

Konishi, Shino, Maria Nugent and Tiffany Shellam (eds) 2015, *Indigenous Intermediaries: New Perspectives in Exploration Archives*, ANU Press, Canberra. doi.org/10.22459/II.09.2015

Matra, James 1771, *A Journal of a Voyage Round the World, In His Majesty's Ship Endeavour, In the Years 1768, 1769, 1770, and 1771; Undertaken in Pursuit of Natural Knowledge, at the Desire of the ROYAL SOCIETY*, T. Becket and P.A. De Hondt, London, reproduced in Alan Frost 1995, *The Precarious Life of James Mario Matra: Voyager with Cook, American Loyalist, Servant of Empire*, Miegunyah Press, Carlton.

Muller, Craig 2014, 'The 'allurements of the European presence': Examining explanations of Wongatha behaviour in the northern Goldfields of Western Australia', *Aboriginal History* 38: 59–87.

Mulvaney, Derek John 1989, *Encounters in Place: Outsiders and Aboriginal Australians, 1606–1985*, University of Queensland Press, St Lucia.

Nugent, Maria 2005, *Botany Bay: Where Histories Meet*, Allen & Unwin, Crows Nest.

Parkinson, Sydney 1972 [1773], *A Journal of a Voyage to the South Seas, in his Majesty's Ship The Endeavour*, Australiana Facsimile Editions A34, Libraries Board of South Australia, Adelaide.

Pascoe, Bruce 2014, *Dark Emu: Black Seeds: Agriculture or Accident?*, Magabala Books, Broome.

Paterson, Aaron 2013, 'Introduction: A Yandruwandha perspective', in *The Aboriginal Story of Burke and Wills: Forgotten Narratives*, Ian D. Clark and Fred Cahir (eds), CSIRO Publishing, Collingwood: xiii-xvi.

Peterson, Nicolas 2003, 'Myth of "walkabout": Movement in the Aboriginal domain', in *Population Mobility and Indigenous Peoples in Australasia and North America*, Martin Bell and John Taylor (eds), Taylor and Francis, Hoboken: 223–38.

Prout, Sarah, and Richard Howitt 2009, 'Frontier imaginings and subversive Indigenous spatialities', *Journal of Rural Studies* 25: 396–403. doi.org/10.1016/j.jrurstud.2009.05.006

Reynolds, Henry 2003, *The Law of the Land*, Penguin, Ringwood.

Russell, Penny 2010, *Savage or Civilised? Manners in Colonial Australia*, University of New South Wales Press, Sydney.

Scott, Ernest 1940, 'Taking possession in Australia—the doctrine of terra nullius (no-man's land)', *Journal and Proceedings, Royal Australian Historical Society* XXVI(1): 1–19.

Seuffert, Nan 2011, 'Civilisation, settlers and wanderers: Law, politics and mobility in nineteenth-century New Zealand and Australia', *Law Text Culture* 15(1): 10–44.

Shellam, Tiffany, Maria Nugent, Shino Konishi and Allison Cadzow (eds) 2016, *Brokers and Boundaries: Colonial Exploration in Indigenous Territory*, ANU Press, Canberra. doi.org/10.22459/BB.04.2016

Standfield, Rachel 2012, *Race and Identity in the Tasman World, 1769-1840*, Pickering and Chatto, London.

Strzelecki, P.E. De 1845, *Physical Description of New South Wales and Van Diemen's Land. Accompanied by a Geological Map, Sections, and Diagrams, and Figures of the Organic Remains*, Longman, Brown, Green and Longmans, London.

3

Mobility, Reciprocal Relationships and Early British Encounters in the North of New Zealand

Rachel Standfield

From the establishment of the European settlement at Port Jackson, Māori travelled to the Australian colonies and beyond. The kidnapping of Tuki and Huru and their forced journey from Muriwhenua to Norfolk Island in 1793 began a process whereby Māori took advantage of new connections and transport and developed connections via overseas travel.[1] Men like Tuki and Huru, as well as other travellers such as Ruatara and Te Pahi, have become well-known names in New Zealand history, with historians and anthropologists documenting their journeys.[2] However, this history of Māori movement is not simply one of intrepid individuals who travelled, but also signals a system of mobility borne out of and enabling further 'world enlargement' for Māori communities.[3] This world enlargement not only affected local Māori, it also exerted influence on British imperial relations. This chapter focuses on communities rather than individuals, and on the ways that Māori mobility brought Māori ideas and cultural values to bear on relations with Europeans.

---

1   Tuki-tahua and Ngahururu (better known in histories as Tuki and Huru) were kidnapped from the Cavalli Islands, north of the Bay of Islands, to teach convicts how to weave flax. See Binney 2004: 215–32; Ballantyne 2014: 42.
2   Salmond 1997; Binney 2005.
3   Hau'ofa 1993: 6.

I use the New South Wales colonial chaplain Samuel Marsden's journal of his first voyage to New Zealand in 1814–15 as both a source of evidence about Māori mobility and its effect 'at home' in the north of the North Island, and as a window to consider how Māori mobility influenced the chaplain's travels. The first of seven journeys made by Marsden, this journey was designed to introduce communities in the north of the North Island to the idea of a mission; it finished with Marsden concluding the land transaction for the mission station at Hohi, overlooked by Rangihoua pā, on the Purerua Peninsula in the Bay of Islands.[4] While the voyage was a 'first' for Marsden, he was accompanied by seven Māori men returning home: five Ngā Puhi Chiefs from the Bay of Islands—Ruatara and his uncle, the warrior chief Hongi Hika, Hongi's rival Korokoro and his brother Tuai, as well as Tuatara—and two Māori men who were working as sailors on the *Active*. All had been in New South Wales and were making the journey home.[5]

Marsden had established relationships with these men and other Māori who had made the journey to Port Jackson. His prior connections with these travelling Māori meant that he was already widely known in the Bay of Islands. The Bay of Islands communities' embrace of the mobility of individual iwi (people or nations) members prior to Marsden's first visit is investigated in this chapter. The effect of Marsden's integration into reciprocal relationships with Bay of Islands' Māori is also explored. Māori mobility ensured that Māori values were applied beyond the shores of New Zealand; here I argue that Marsden benefited from the positive application of utu to his relationships with Māori communities via the connections that he had already established with mobile Māori. Utu is defined by Sidney Mead as 'compensation, or revenge, or reciprocity'; he understood it as the principle of reciprocity or equivalence that is used to maintain relationships.[6] Raymond Firth considered utu to be the '"underlying mechanism" of all Māori exchange … the understanding that "for every gift another of at least equal value should be returned"'.[7] Anne Salmond defined utu as 'the principle of equal return, often expressed in revenge' and noted the importance of utu as a 'main theme' in Māori society, alongside mana (prestige) and tapu (sacredness).[8]

---

4   Ballantyne 2014: 48.
5   See Ballantyne n.d. See also Ballara 1990a; Cloher 2003: 23, 66; Ballara 1990b. Korokoro and Tui are identified as Ngaati Manu by Salmond 1997: 455.
6   Mead 2003: 31.
7   Metge 2002: 312.
8   Salmond 1975: 12.

By 1814, Marsden was already an important part of Māori networks that extended to Australia and beyond. By the first decades of the nineteenth century, the Australian colonies, especially Sydney, were becoming a 'node' for mobile Māori, operating as a crucial site for Māori interaction with the British and a first stop for some Māori before they travelled further afield.[9] As perhaps the most central European figure in Māori travel during this early imperial period, Marsden was vital to this 'node'. In the period before and after his first voyage to New Zealand, he offered accommodation, support and an introduction to elite New South Wales colonial society for Māori journeying to Port Jackson. Many travellers, like the men accompanying him back home on the *Active,* had stayed with his family at their farm in Parramatta. Marsden was also a strong voice in shaping discourses that promoted Māori as people to be engaged with—as able, active and intelligent Indigenous people who were capable of being 'civilised'. In doing so, he developed implicit, and occasionally explicit, comparisons with Aboriginal people, who he derided as racially inferior and unable to be saved.[10] Alice Te Punga Somerville pointed out that by the time of Marsden's arrival in New Zealand in 1814, 'Māori, New Zealand, and the rest of the world were already inextricably tangled'. Indeed, she argued that New Zealand histories would look very different if they began in New Zealand Street, Parramatta (named after the site of the Māori seminary established in 1819), rather than New Zealand itself.[11] Starting in New Zealand Street would 'affirm the mobility of Māori: our enthusiasm, our curiosity, our adaptability, our agency' and the relationships that were established there.[12] Marsden's journey to New Zealand at the end of 1814 might have been the first for the chaplain—it may have been unknown territory for him—but it was territory where he was already well known. Māori mobility meant that when Marsden travelled to New Zealand for the first time, he brought into being a number of relationships that Māori communities had anticipated since their people had first encountered him in New South Wales—in this sense, he was returning 'home', even though he was setting foot in New Zealand for the first time. Marsden's first journey to New Zealand was not simply about him as an individual; it was about his relationships with Bay

---

9   Lambert and Lester 2006: 10.
10   For discussion of Marsden's developing interests in New Zealand in the period before his first voyage, and the comparisons he drew to Aboriginal people and their effect on developing racial thought in the region, see Standfield 2012a: 109–12.
11   Somerville 2014: 655–69. See also Standfield 2012b.
12   Somerville 2014: 663.

of Islands Māori. Therefore, rather than focus on Marsden himself, his perspectives on the voyage, his reactions to the visit and his engagement with other travelling Europeans on the *Active* (which Sandy Yarwood provides in his biography of Marsden), this chapter considers Māori reactions, responses and agency in shaping Marsden's journey.[13]

Recent scholarship on early encounters in New Zealand and the Pacific has stressed the importance of relationships for understanding and analysing the nature of imperial contact. In their book *He Kōrero: Words Between Us*, New Zealand scholars Alison Jones and Kuni Jenkins argued that a desire for relationships drove Māori engagement with Europeans. Countering the commonly held view that, in engaging with Europeans, Māori were primarily interested in access to guns, Jones and Jenkins asserted that:

> It is primarily the *social relationships*, whether friendly or hostile, that form the shifting lines of power along which desirable objects move … So, as well as being captured, Pākehā needed to be understood, fed and looked after, and drawn into an educational and social as well as an economic exchange.[14]

Examining another Pacific context—that of early encounters between Tahitians and the British—Vanessa Smith's *Intimate Strangers* similarly aimed to broaden the focus of historical scholarship to include a serious analysis of friendship as a form of cross-cultural exchange. Emphasising the translation required to understand different, culturally inflected concepts of friendship that shape encounters, Smith argued for a focus on friendship to help counter what she viewed as an excessive concentration on violence in contemporary historical scholarship.[15] Likewise, in their work examining imperial networks, Magee and Thompson claimed that trust must be considered vital to network formation, as it plays a crucial role in the structure of networks through creating mutual obligation.[16] Extending this field of study on imperial networks, scholars such as Smith, and Jones and Jenkins, have emphasised the cultural factors that shape relationships on both sides of cross-cultural encounters.

---

13   Yarwood 1996 [1977]: 168–80.
14   Jones and Jenkins 2011: 63 (original emphasis).
15   Smith 2010.
16   Magee and Thompson 2010.

Pacific histories can offer a model for examining how cultural values have shaped patterns of movement. Mobility and the wider cultural and community drivers for Indigenous travel are key considerations in the work of a number of historians considering both pre-colonial and colonial periods of history in the Pacific. Paul D'Arcy emphasised the place of movement in pre-colonial society, exploring mobility in the regional exchange of goods and knowledge, as well as travel for social purposes. Operating with the 'sea as a highway', D'Arcy showed how Pacific peoples moved throughout the Pacific and were mobile to an exceptionally high degree in the Tonga, Fiji and Samoa triangle.[17] Debate over the relationship between individuals and communities has also inspired histories of colonial mobility in Pacific scholarship, in which questions of Indigenous agency surrounding mobility are problematised, even in the coercive regimes of indentured labour.[18] In 'Travel-Happy Samoa', Damon Salesa analysed Samoan travel in the late nineteenth and early twentieth centuries; he argued that although the 'rewiring of the Pacific' was 'coincident with the arrival and actions of Papalagi (non-Indigenous people), it was a process that complicated agency, a process necessarily both shared and contested' and 'a work crafted by both islanders and Papalagi'.[19]

Salesa's study is informed by Epeli Hauʻofa's seminal paper that placed mobility at the heart of Pacific cultural and community life. Hauʻofa responded to views of the Pacific Islands as 'tiny' by calling for a return to the idea of the Pacific as a 'sea of islands'. Hauʻofa theorised that the:

> 'World enlargement' carried out by tens of thousands of ordinary Pacific islanders … [made a] nonsense of all national and economic boundaries, borders that have been defined only recently, crisscrossing an ocean that had been boundless for ages before Captain Cook's apotheosis.[20]

Hauʻofa's emphasis on the interdependent relationships between static communities and travellers provides an important lens for viewing not just contemporary but also historical travel in Pacific societies.

Hauʻofa made a strong case for considering the role of reciprocity as a core cultural value for Pacific peoples. With this in mind, this chapter focuses on communities and their role in travel, and examines how Marsden was

---

17 D'Arcy 2006: 50–69.
18 Banivanua Mar 2007: 43–69; Shineberg 1995.
19 Salesa 2003: 172.
20 Hauʻofa 1993: 6.

treated during his first voyage to New Zealand through the lens of utu as a key cultural driver for Māori. Utu is commonly imagined in 'everyday discourse' as applying only in a negative sense; it is accorded a meaning closer to revenge than reciprocity, and historical scholarship too focuses much more strongly on its negative aspects.[21] The most well-known and, indeed, most archetypal example of utu in New Zealand historical scholarship is the burning of the colonial ship the *Boyd* by Māori in 1809.[22] Marsden's first voyage to New Zealand and his discussions with Whangaroa Māori, which are outlined later in this chapter, came to form a key part of the *Boyd's* narrative, which stressed European fault and Māori motivation as revenge for wrongs done against them. This discourse acted as a counter to earlier emphasis on Māori savagery and cannibalism, and of New Zealand as 'retaliatory and damaging'.[23] However, Māori communities today have a much more complex understanding of utu, which embraces both negative and positive meanings.[24] This extension of utu into cross-cultural relationships was a function of the significant numbers of Māori who were travelling across the Tasman to visit New South Wales. Utu, and the range of meanings associated with it, had a significant effect on cross-cultural encounters in both New Zealand and New South Wales prior to Marsden's first visit to the Bay of Islands. Indeed, Tony Ballantyne argues that 'personal connections and forms of reciprocity enabled the establishment of the mission, and they provide an often-neglected social context for understanding the mission's foundation'.[25]

Māori community attitudes towards travel appear to have undergone an important shift since the first colonial settlement in Australia. The development of personal relationships and trust seem to have shaped changing community attitudes to overseas travel when Māori began to travel to New South Wales. Accounts from the earliest Māori journeys overseas suggest that home communities may not have been happy, or may have had a mixed response, to individuals' decisions to travel. However, by the time of Marsden's arrival in the Bay of Islands, communities were strongly involved in decisions to travel and in choosing who would travel, and were vying to send people on journeys. The journeys of early travellers—such as the Ngā Puhi man Te Mahanga, and Te Pahi, a senior

---

21 Metge 2002: 314.
22 See Wevers 2002: Chapter 1.
23 Wevers 2002: 27, 24.
24 My thanks to Lachy Paterson and Mike Stevens for this point.
25 Ballantyne 2014: 59.

chief of the north-western Bay of Islands—were reported in European records in terms that suggested that their communities did not want them to travel.[26] Te Mahanga, known as Moyhanger in John Savage's writings, left the Bay of Islands in 1806 and travelled with Savage to London.[27] Savage reported both the reaction of Moyhanger's community, and the grief of his whānau (extended family) at his departure. According to Salmond, 'some' of Te Mahanga's 'relations' approved of his adventure, and others disapproved, but he was unshaken in his resolve.[28] Te Pahi, visiting Sydney in 1805, was reported by Philip Gidley King as stating that he had 'long designed' a visit to the British colony, having been encouraged not only by Tuki and Huru's experiences, but also by 'the request of his father'. Although his travel was 'much against the wishes of his dependants', the chief felt that their objections were 'much outweighed by the probable advantages that would derive from his visit'.[29] Te Pahi travelled with the explicit objective of increasing his mana, having strategically decided that visiting New South Wales would allow him access to goods and connections that would improve his community standing, even if was against the wishes of his family. As Ballantyne has demonstrated, Māori were keen to embrace European technologies due to the particular features of their history. Long-distance migration from Polynesia had created a history of 'radical cultural adaptation', and long-distance trade was a feature of relationships between Māori communities. These features of Māori society meant that 'Māori had by the late eighteenth century developed a strong interest in the opportunities that might be presented by cross-cultural contacts, as well as in the novel technologies and ideas that they might access from strangers'.[30]

Māui, known as Mowhee in European sources, and also known as Tommy Drummond, gave an account of his departure for Port Jackson in 1806, which shows how community attitudes towards travel changed from the initial reticence that people such as Te Mahanga and Te Pahi encountered.[31] Māui described to Basil Woodd how, in 'about the year 1806, one of the Natives had gone to Port Jackson in New South Wales, and staid [sic] there some time'. This person informed the community of the 'fine place

---

26   Ballara 1990c; Walrond 2005.
27   Salmond 1997: 343.
28   Salmond 1997: 343.
29   King 1898: 3.
30   Ballantyne 2014: 60.
31   Salmond 1997: 466; Marsden 1814: volume 6, frame 31.

the English people had' and, according to Woodd, also relayed news of Christianity. This unnamed Māori traveller had a significant influence—he or she was credited with having 'persuaded many of the Natives to wish to send their children thither'.[32] Soon after, ships arrived, and one of the captains struck up a friendship with Māui's father, leading him to 'earnestly entreat' a place on the ship for Māui, who was about nine years old. On the day that he was destined to leave, he met a Māori man, Hiari (known as 'Hearry' in European sources), on one of the ships:

> With whom he was acquainted who had been to visit the English Settlements, and was going back again with the Captain. He spake [sic] highly of the kindness of the Captain, and of the English people; and persuaded Mowhee to persevere in his intention'.[33]

Māui's tale of his departure from New Zealand suggests that community attitudes towards journeys to the colony were changing. It also highlights the vital role of prior relationships and personal connections with both Europeans and with Māori experienced in travel to the new British colony. Māui's experience suggests that, while it was individuals who travelled, their communities played strong roles in the decision to do so; even as early as 1806, a cohort of Māori travellers was influencing decisions around mobility, so that mobility encompassing New South Wales and further afield was being viewed positively.

By the time Marsden arrived in 1814, Māori travel to the colony was well established. Indeed, Marsden arrived accompanied by five chiefs and two Māori men working as sailors on the *Active*—all had been in New South Wales and were making the journey home. In fact, the chiefs had been in Port Jackson specifically to collect Marsden and accompany him to the Bay of Islands. In March 1814, Marsden had sent a letter to Ruatara, 'writing of their friendship' and sending gifts to reinforce his message.[34] The letter, 'possibly the most significant document in the history of early New Zealand', according to Ballantyne, announced Marsden's plans to establish a mission. In it, Marsden 'framed his relationship with the chief primarily in the idiom of reciprocity'. He acknowledged Ruatara's mana by referring to him as 'Duaterra King', sent news of each member of Ruatara's circle in New South Wales and also sent gifts, including one from his wife Elizabeth 'to Ruatara's wife, Rahu: a red gown, red being

---

32   Woodd 1817: 2.
33   Woodd 1817: 2. Hiari is identified in Jones and Jenkins 2011: 48.
34   Jones and Jenkins 2011: 57.

a colour prized by Māori and associated with chiefly status'.[35] Marsden had sent the letter in the care of Tuai, younger brother of Korokoro, leader of the Ngare Raumati confederation in the eastern Bay of Islands.[36] Tuai had been living with Marsden in Parramatta. Hongi Hika, the great warrior chief of the northern alliance of Ngā Puhi, and Ruatara's matua or 'uncle', decided to travel to New South Wales to collect Marsden himself, and insisted that Ruatara, with his English language skills, accompany him as his interpreter.[37] This was Hongi's first overseas trip. He is better known for his journey to England in 1820, which Ballantyne considers in his chapter in this volume. Korokoro, Hongi's rival, was a late addition to the party.[38] Jones and Jenkins have described Ruatara, Hongi and Korokoro's journey to 'collect Marsden' as being highly significant.[39] The act of collecting an important visitor constituted a mutual recognition of mana; a protection of mana through ensuring the safe arrival of the visitor that simultaneously enhanced the visitor's status. While each chief had his individual motivations for travel, making the journey as a group was a particularly important form of culturally based mobility, and one that was to place Marsden in a position of esteem when he arrived in New Zealand.[40]

The vital role that the community played in mobility, and the community's clear interest in, and commitment to forging connections with, the British in New South Wales, was apparently not something Marsden anticipated when he ventured to New Zealand for the first time in late 1814. He did not expect to be already embedded in relationships with Māori communities, but, rather, to require introductions as he travelled along the coast. When the *Active* first arrived at North Cape, he sent 'all the chiefs [he] had on board' ashore, 'but no Europeans, so that they might open an intercourse between us and the Natives, and bring us some supplies'.[41] The boat in which they travelled 'was well armed, that they might defend themselves'.[42] The preparation for this journey ashore

---

35   Ballantyne 2014: 58.
36   'An uneasy truce prevailed between the related peoples of the Bay of Islands: the northern alliance (Hongi, Ruatara, Te Pahi, and others), the southern alliance (Tara, Tupi, Te Morenga and others) and the Ngare Raumati confederation (Korkor, Tuai and others) of the eastern alliance'. Jones and Jenkins 2011: 67.
37   Sissons, Hongi and Hohepa 1987: 13–14.
38   Jones and Jenkins 2011: 67.
39   Jones and Jenkins 2011: 72.
40   Jones and Jenkins 2011: 72.
41   Marsden 1814: 57 and transcript 42.
42   Marsden 1814: 57 and transcript 42.

suggests that there was fear, perhaps among the Māori travellers as well as the chaplain, for the safety of the party. However, arriving ashore in a boat laden with weaponry may well have increased the mana of the returning chiefs, as they displayed the bounty that came from travel to the newly established colony.

While the party was ashore, a chief and his son came out to the ship in a waka (canoe), with 'some very fine looking men'.[43] When Marsden asked whether the chief had seen Ruatara ashore, he replied that he had not, but to show the strength of his relationship with Ruatara he produced a 'pocket knife … given to him by Duaterra a long time before', which he valued highly. Marsden was pleased to meet people connected to Ruatara, believing that it bolstered his chances of a successful voyage. He was surprised to find that these people knew who he was; everyone on board the canoe 'seemed well acquainted' with Marsden's name. Marsden noted that they:

> Immediately enquired after a young man belonging to that place, who had lived with [him] some time previously; [that man's] brother was in the Canoe and greatly rejoiced he was to see me [Marsden]. He made the most anxious enquiries after his brother, and I [Marsden] gave him every information I could.[44]

Marsden had arrived in a place that already had strong relationships with European goods and people, and in which he himself was known. In this sense, his first journey became for him also a kind of reunion or homecoming, as he entered relationships already established or anticipated because of connections he had with mobile Māori. Tellingly, he wrote, 'we were now quite free from all fear, as the Natives seemed desirous to shew [sic] their affection by every means in their power'.[45] Marsden's place in Māori relationships ensured his safety, which in turn played a crucial role in ensuring his sense of comfort on the voyage, and his subsequent feeling that the voyage was a success. Fear of Māori violence had constituted an overriding concern in early British imperial relationships with New Zealand and, indeed, because of the sacking of the *Boyd,* had delayed Marsden's first voyage to the country. Clearly, both European and Māori mobility was affecting entire communities in the Bay of Islands area. Europeans arriving on the shores of New Zealand were bringing

---

43 Marsden 1814: 57 and transcript 42.
44 Marsden 1814: 57 and transcript 43.
45 Marsden 1814: 58 and transcript 43.

goods, knowledge and connections, but this was being matched by Māori travel, with the result that iwi were becoming enmeshed in relationships that spanned the Tasman and further afield. These were relationships that Marsden was not necessarily aware of before he first came to New Zealand, but these relationships had a significant impact on his journey.

While it seemed that Marsden was not yet aware of how utu operated to reciprocate good deeds as well as bad, utu may well have played a key role in the first formal introduction between him and the Bay of Islands chiefs. Korokoro, his brother Tui and Ruatara brought a group of chiefs out to the *Active* to be introduced to the visiting Europeans. Korokoro arrived dressed, painted and flanked by warriors; after introductions, which included a 'war song' by the Māori and the 'discharge of thirteen small arms' from the ship, the group came on board. The introduction also included giving the visitors 'several presents in the most polite manner'.[46] After introducing the chiefs 'from other districts' to those onboard the *Active*, Korokoro:

> Commented on the particular attention they had shown to him when at Port Jackson; and lamented that the poverty of his country prevented [him] from returning their kindness according to his wishes.[47]

Korokoro's actions appear to accord to the gift exchange that formed a vital part of utu—that is, to reciprocate gifts that had accrued to individuals (and hence the whole community) in the past. By explaining how each European person present had treated him at Port Jackson as he presented gifts, Korokoro reciprocated the 'kindness and hospitality' that had been shown to him while travelling. His concern for the 'poverty of his country' was probably driven by the importance placed on reciprocal relationships for the 'repayment of obligations', as these tended to be 'more lavish than the original gift for the reason of enhancing a group's social reputation and prestige or its mana'. Further:

> [A] gift beyond the recipient's ability to reciprocate could humiliate them, place them in your debt or even subtly subordinate them. Thus the more one gave, the greater one's mana, and an unequal response meant loss of mana.[48]

---

46 Marsden 1814: 86 and transcript 62.
47 Marsden 1814: 86 and transcript 62.
48 New Zealand Ministry of Justice 2001.

Only after this introduction did Korokoro explain to the assembled chiefs the role that the missionaries had come to perform, and their intention to stay in New Zealand.[49]

Thus, it would appear that utu shaped the reception given to Marsden and the accompanying missionaries when they arrived in the Bay of Islands. Marsden's investigation of the circumstances surrounding the burning of the *Boyd* meant that he also gained increased understanding of the negative potential of utu. On hearing that the chiefs and warriors of the Whangaroa people were nearby, visiting the mainland opposite the Cavalli Islands for the funeral of 'some great Warrior', Marsden travelled to meet them, protected by Ruatara, Hongi, guns and warriors.[50] Marsden met with Te Ara, 'known to the Europeans by the name of George', chief of the Ngāti Uru hapū, a man who had travelled extensively, 'spoke tolerable English' and had been central to the *Boyd* incident. Te Ara had also 'been at Parramatta and knew me', Marsden wrote.[51] Te Ara, who, with his brother Te Puhi, was the 'leading rangatira [chief] of the Whangaroa hapū Ngāti Pou', explained to Marsden that the situation that had led to the capture of the *Boyd* was a consequence of cross-cultural encounters arising from Māori mobility. According to Te Ara, the crew of the *Boyd* had treated him without respect and thus slighted his mana; they had also refused to listen to warnings that their actions would have consequences in New Zealand.[52]

As Marsden met with the assembled Whangaroa people, he asked them 'how they came to cut off the *Boyd* and massacre the crew'. Two people who had travelled on the *Boyd*, having been sent home on the ship by Sydney merchant Simeon Lord, came forward. They explained how Te Ara had become ill and 'unable to do his duty as a common sailor'. For this he was 'severely punished—was refused provisions'; he was told he would be put overboard and was subjected to 'many other indignities'.[53] Te Ara 'remonstrated' with the master of the ship and 'begged that no corporal punishment might be inflicted on him'. At the same time, he tried to explain 'that he was a Chief in his own country', a fact that would be apparent when he arrived in New Zealand. However, he was not believed;

49   Marsden 1814: 86 and transcript 62.
50   Marsden 1814: 72 and transcript 53.
51   Marsden 1814: 74–75 and transcript 55. Ballara 1990b.
52   Sissons, Hongi and Hohepa 1987: 15.
53   Marsden 1814: 74–75 and transcript 55.

he was 'told he was <u>no</u> Chief'.[54] Te Ara was subsequently abused in terms
that Marsden recognised as being 'too commonly used by British seamen'.
Returning to Whangaroa with a lacerated back from the punishment
inflicted on him, Te Ara's 'friends and people were determined to revenge
the insult which had been offered to him'. Te Ara explained that 'if he had
not been treated with such creulty [sic] the *Boyd* would never have been
touched'.[55]

Marsden used the meeting with Te Ara's people to encourage them to
embrace peace and reconciliation with communities in the Bay of Islands,
to 'lay aside all sorts of war and murder' and to 'become a great and
happy people'. Te Ara replied that 'he did not want to fight any more,
and was ready to make peace'.[56] The focus of the discussion shifted, and
'much conversation then passed chiefly respecting New Zealand and Port
Jackson, which George [Te Ara] had visited'.[57] Marsden capitalised on the
Whangaroa people's interest in Port Jackson to encourage their acceptance
of missionaries, stressing that missionaries would facilitate access to the
material goods that Māori had seen in the New South Wales colony.
Marsden compared the current conditions that Māori lived in with the
advantages of 'civilisation' to convince Te Ara to accept missionaries:

> I endeavoured to impress upon his mind the great degree of comfort we
> enjoyed as compared with his countrymen's enjoyments—our mode of
> living, Houses &c. which he had seen, and that all these blessings might be
> obtained by them, by cultivating their land, and improving themselves in
> useful knowledge, which they would now have an opportunity to acquire
> from the European settlers. He seemed sensible of all these advantages,
> and expressed a wish to follow my advice.[58]

In their conversation, Te Ara and Marsden placed Māori mobility and
experiences in New South Wales at the centre of both the explanation
of cross-cultural conflict in the *Boyd* massacre and the future of the
Whangaroa people who, it was understood, could access the 'advantages'
they knew from their travels by accepting missionaries. In this way,
Marsden was involved in a process whereby knowledge of the New South
Wales colony ultimately filtered through whole communities as 'the other

---

54   Marsden 1814: 75 and transcript 55 (original emphasis).
55   Marsden 1814: 75 and transcript 55.
56   Marsden 1814: 79–80 and transcript 58.
57   Marsden 1814: 80 and transcript 58.
58   Marsden 1814: 80 and transcript 58.

chiefs and their people stood around us'.[59] Marsden, like the increasingly large cohort of Māori travellers returning to their communities, conveyed what interaction with the British at Port Jackson could offer to Māori communities.

Crucially, this conversation was a prelude to Marsden spending his first night sleeping onshore in New Zealand surrounded by the people who had cut off the *Boyd*.[60] This scene was to become a key part of how Marsden was (and is) remembered. Importantly, his confidence derived from his knowledge of why the *Boyd* had been attacked and his nascent understanding of the principles of utu. Marsden was coming to appreciate the way that reciprocity operated as revenge for negative behaviour and, as he travelled along the coast, he began to derive benefits from the positive application of utu.

While the visiting Europeans as a group were beneficiaries of hospitality and gifts resulting from reciprocal relationships, Marsden received particularly special treatment. At times on his first voyage, these relationships were crucial to the success of his journey. He was anxious to access timber for building houses for the mission at Rangihoua but found himself with dwindling stocks of iron goods. Marsden noted that he was:

> Much distressed for want of axes, and other articles of trade, as the presents I had made at the North Cape and along the coast, had very much reduced my stock.[61]

Deciding to set up a smith to produce more ironwork, and needing access to timber, he travelled to the timber districts on the Kawakawa River at the southern end of the Bay of Islands.[62] During this trip, Marsden became very concerned, as they had 'omitted to bring coals with us from Port Jackson':

> I hardly knew how to remedy these defects—As nothing could be done in our mechanical operations, nor could we purchase provisions from the natives without carpenters tools; Such as axes &c.[63]

---

59   Marsden 1814: 80 and transcript 58–59.
60   Marsden 1814: 81 and transcript 59.
61   Marsden 1814: 92 and transcript 67.
62   McNab 1914: 177.
63   Marsden 1814: 92–93 and transcript 67.

At Kororāreka, Marsden met with Tara, the 70-year-old chief known as 'Terra' in his journal, to gain permission to take timber.[64] He did this, he wrote, to 'prevent any misunderstanding'.[65]

Marsden was accompanied by Māui, 'a young man about seventeen years of age, who was related to the Chief' and who had been in New South Wales for nine years, the latter part of which had been spent with Marsden. Māui's departure from New Zealand was discussed earlier in this chapter.[66] Accompanied by Māui, Marsden noted that Tara 'received us very cordially, and wept much on account of the young man's return, as did many others, some of whom wept aloud'. The chief refused to accept Marsden's gifts of iron, saying 'he did not want any present from me, but only my company, as he had heard so often of me, from his own people and others'.[67] Tara's oldest son, Kawiti Tiitua, had visited Māori in Parramatta in 1811 and, hearing that Ruatara had been working on Marsden's Parramatta farm, had marked out an area of land by notching trees, planning to use this as his own farm and promising to send 100 men to work the land. Jones and Jenkins argued that this visit, and Marsden's generous offer of land, formed 'the basis of ongoing collaboration … between Europeans and the people of the southern Bay of Islands'.[68] It is clear that Māui and Kawiti had established a relationship with the chaplain, and that Marsden's arrival in Tara's community allowed the senior rangatira to meet his obligations and extend the relationship.

During Marsden's visit to Kororāreka, Tara expressed his desire for Marsden's missionaries to come and live with his people. He showed Marsden his plantation of wheat from a previous visit from the *Active* and gave permission for the chaplain to take as much timber as he needed.[69] Not only would Tara not take Marsden's gifts, but he refused to let Marsden continue travelling, instead ordering baskets of kumara to be roasted for the visiting Europeans, and more to be presented to them for their travels.[70] Marsden's role in Māui's long stay in New South Wales,

---

64   McNab 1914: 177; Salmond 2007: 466; Sissons, Hongi and Hohepa 1987: 39.
65   Marsden 1814: 93 and transcript 68.
66   Marsden 1814: 93–94 and transcript 68. In his memoir, Māui credited Marsden with helping him to leave his employment as a shepherd in Australia by arranging 'an exchange' with his original host. This transpired after Māui had expressed his 'earnest desire to quit the farm, and gratify his curiosity in seeing more of the world'. See Woodd 1817: 3.
67   Marsden 1814: 94 and transcript 68.
68   Jones and Jenkins 2011: 59.
69   Marsden 1814: 94 and transcript 68–69.
70   Marsden 1814: 95 and transcript 69.

as well as the attention paid to Tara's son in Parramatta, had established a reciprocal relationship that Tara could repay when Marsden arrived seeking assistance. Tara's repayment of this obligation, and his desire for deeper connections with Marsden and the Europeans associated with him, helped to ensure the smooth continuation of the voyage. The timber Tara provided gave Marsden the means to make iron tools, which in turn provided Māori with the goods they desired from Europeans. Marsden's ability to restock his supply of iron tools meant that he could extend his relationships with Māori communities, and not be seen to be favouring one group over another.

Thus, part of the success of Marsden's journey is attributable to Tara who, though he had never travelled, was drawn to assist Marsden as part of reciprocal relationships that existed despite their never having met. As Catherine Hall has demonstrated, empire came to have a significant effect on the identities and subjectivities of those who never travelled, including Indigenous peoples.[71] Lester and Lambert have explained how:

> Even if one experiences places only through travelling discourses, such as texts, tales, conversations and the viewing of images, each such encounter with place involves engagement—each produces 'the need for judgement, learning, improvisation'.[72]

Added to this, it is important to recognise that Indigenous cultural concepts were vital to cross-cultural encounters in imperial and colonial situations and to take these concepts into account as well.

As Marsden continued on his journey, he fielded regular requests from people who wished to travel with him back to New South Wales. By the time the *Active* was preparing to sail for Australia on 24 February 1815, Marsden had 'given permission for ten New Zealanders to accompany [him] to Port Jackson, eight of whom were chiefs or sons of chiefs, and two servants'.[73] Marsden received so many requests to join him on the journey to New South Wales that, while turning the majority down 'partly because [he] had not room in the vessel' and partly because of the expense, he:

---

71   Hall 2006.
72   Lambert and Lester 2006: 15.
73   Marsden 1814: 159 and transcript 112.

Told them [he] would at all opportunities permit a few to have a passage at a time and that they should come in turn by rotation, and with these prospects—they were satisfied.[74]

The manoeuvres Marsden made around the choice of Māori voyagers provides insight into the effect that mobility was having on Bay of Islands communities, and the types of decisions that were being made about travel.

Before the *Active* left New Zealand, Marsden made a final visit to a chief at North Cape, who had a 'quantity of flax dressed and ready for me'.[75] When the 'principal native' of this iwi requested to travel to Port Jackson, Marsden turned him down.[76] However, when he received the same request from the chief's son, he consented. It is not clear whether this is because the young man was the son of a senior chief, or because his appearance signalled that he was embracing certain European goods that had been presented to him by Marsden. The chaplain wrote:

We met the chief's son dressed in the India print I had given to his father, when on my way to [the] Bay of Islands. The edges of his garment were ornamented by a white hog's skin with the hair on, which looked tolerably handsome the Print being red and white gave it a tasteful effect—He was an exceeding fine youth.[77]

According to Marsden, the young man carried 'wrapt up and covered with great care' the 'printed Orders of Governor Macquarie'.[78]

The community's internal negotiations about who would travel are also apparent in Marsden's journal. As Marsden left the North Cape, he was sent 'a boy whom the chief wished me to take to Port Jackson'. Another man, Jem, would accompany the boy and then return to New Zealand. Marsden wrote: 'I was unwilling to disappoint the wishes of this chief who placed such confidence in me—and I therefore gave my consent for them both to remain in the vessel'. Jem relayed the story of the iwi's negotiations about who would travel to the British colony. The chief's eldest son—of the India print cloak—had wanted to make the journey,

74   Marsden 1814: 183 and transcript 114.
75   Marsden 1814: 165 and transcript 115; McNab 1914: 185.
76   Marsden 1814: 165 and transcript 115–116.
77   Marsden 1814: 167 and transcript 117.
78   Marsden,1814: 167 and transcript 117.

but 'his mother would not consent at this time'.[79] Thus, it is clear that travel was not an individual decision, but subject to the wishes of the iwi, and that women possessed the power to influence these decisions.

Upon leaving New Zealand, Marsden deemed the voyage a success. It filled him with 'the most heartfelt satisfaction' to state that 'I had not met with the slightest accident, provocation or insult—I had fully accomplished the object of my voyage'.[80] Marsden's integration into reciprocal relationships with Bay of Islands Māori ensured the 'success' of his voyage. However, it was Māori 'world enlargement' that created the conditions for success— Bay of Islands communities had embraced the mobility of individual iwi members by the time of Marsden's visit and, as he left, were vying to send people across the Tasman. This system of Māori mobility ensured that Māori values were applied beyond the shores of New Zealand. Marsden's important role as a contact for mobile Māori in Australia meant that he was drawn into reciprocal relationships with Māori communities in the Bay of Islands. These relationships, established well before he arrived in New Zealand, meant that communities used his arrival in New Zealand to balance their relationships with him via reciprocation—Marsden was the beneficiary of the operation of utu. When Marsden left New Zealand accompanied by 12 Māori travellers and with a promise to provide passage to others in turn, he was provided with the opportunity to repay gifts he had received, extend obligations into future years and develop reciprocal relationships with new Māori communities.

References

Ballantyne, Tony n.d., 'Cast of Characters', Marsden online archive, marsdenarchive.otago.ac.nz/about/people

Ballantyne, Tony 2014, *Entanglements of Empire: Missionaries, Maori and the Question of the Body,* Duke University Press, Durham. doi.org/ 10.1215/9780822375883

Ballara, Angela 1990a, 'Ruatara', *Dictionary of New Zealand Biography: Te Ara—the Encyclopedia of New Zealand,* www.teara.govt.nz/en/ biographies/1r19/ruatara

---

79 Marsden 1814: 170 and transcript 118–19.
80 Marsden 1814: volume 6, frame 106–07 and transcript 19.

Ballara, Angela 1990b, 'Hongi Hika', *Dictionary of New Zealand Biography: Te Ara—the Encyclopedia of New Zealand,* www.teara.govt.nz/en/biographies/1h32/hongi-hika

Ballara, Angela 1990c, 'Te Pahi', *Dictionary of New Zealand Biography: Te Ara—the Encyclopedia of New Zealand,* www.teara.govt.nz/en/biographies/1t53/te-pahi

Banivanua Mar, Tracey 2007, *Violence and Colonial Dialogue in the Australian-Pacific Indentured Labor Trade,* University of Hawaii Press, Honolulu.

Binney, Judith 2004, 'Tuki's universe', *New Zealand Journal of History* 38(2): 215–32.

Binney, Judith 2005, *The Legacy of Guilt: A Life of Thomas Kendall,* third edition, Bridget Williams Books, Wellington. doi.org/10.7810/9781877242335

Cloher, Dorothy Urlich 2003, *Hongi Hika: Warrior Chief,* Viking Press, Auckland.

D'Arcy, Paul 2006, *The people of the Sea: Environment, Identity and History in Oceania,* University of Hawaii Press, Honolulu.

Hall, Catherine 2006, 'Imperial careering at home: Harriet Martineau on empire', in *Colonial Lives Across the British Empire,* David Lambert and Alan Lester (eds), Cambridge University Press, Cambridge: 335–59.

Hauʻofa, Epeli 1993, 'Our Sea of Islands', in *A New Oceania: Rediscovering Our Sea of Islands,* Eric Waddell, Vijay Naidu, and Epeli Hauʻofa (eds), School of Social and Economic Development, University of the South Pacific, and Bleake House, Suva: 2–6.

Jones, Alison and Kuni Jenkins 2011, *He Kōrero—Words Between Us: First Māori-Pākehā Conversations on Paper,* Huia publications, Auckland.

King, Philip Gidley 1898, 'King papers: The legality of Government and General Orders: 2 January 1806', in *Historical Records of New South Wales: Volume 6, King and Bligh, 1806–1808,* Government Printer, Sydney: 1–9.

Lambert, David and Alan Lester 2006, 'Introduction: Imperial spaces, imperial subjects' in *Colonial Lives Across the British Empire*, David Lambert and Alan Lester (eds), Cambridge University Press, Cambridge. doi.org/10.1484/m.seuh-eb.4.00082

Magee, Gary B. and Andrew S. Thompson 2010, *Empire and Globalisation: Networks of People, Goods and Capital in the British World, c. 1850–1914*, Cambridge University Press, Cambridge. doi.org/10.1017/CBO9780511805868

Marsden, Samuel 1814, Journal: Reverend Samuel Marsden's First Visit to New Zealand in December 1814, marsdenarchive.otago.ac.nz/MS_0176_001#page/1/mode/1up

McNab, Robert 1914, *From Tasman to Marsden: A History of Northern New Zealand from 1642 to 1818*, J. Wilkie and Company, Dunedin.

Mead, Sidney M. 2003, *Tikanga Maori: Living by Maori Values*, Huia Publishers, Wellington.

Metge, Joan 2002, 'Returning the gift—"utu" in intergroup relations: In memory of Sir Raymond Firth', *The Journal of the Polynesian Society* 111: 4.

New Zealand Ministry of Justice 2001, 'Part 1: Traditional Maori concepts—utu', in *He Hinatore ki te Ao Maori A Glimpse into the Maori World: Maori Perspectives on Justice*, Ministry of Justice, Wellington, www.justice.govt.nz/publications/publications-archived/2001/he-hinatore-ki-te-ao-maori-a-glimpse-into-the-maori-world/part-1-traditional-maori-concepts/utu

Salesa, T. Damon I. 2003, '"Travel-happy Samoa": Colonialism, Samoan migration and a "brown Pacific"', *New Zealand Journal of History* 37(2): 171–88.

Salmond, Anne 1975, *Hui: A Study of Maori Ceremonial Gatherings*, A.H. and A.W. Reed, Wellington.

Salmond, Anne 1997, *Between Worlds: Early Exchanges between Maori and Europeans, 1773–1815*, Viking Press, Auckland.

Shineberg, Dorothy 1995, '"The New Hebridean is everywhere": The Oceanian labor trade to New Caledonia, 1865–1930', *Pacific Studies* 18(2): 1–22.

Sissons, Jeffrey, Wiremu Wi Hongi and Pat Hohepa 1987, *The Pūriri Trees are Laughing: A Political History of the Ngā Puhi in the Inland Bay of Islands*, Polynesian Society, Auckland.

Smith, Vanessa 2010, *Intimate Strangers: Friendship, Exchange and Pacific Encounters*, Cambridge University Press, Cambridge. doi.org/10.1017/CBO9780511763021

Somerville, Alice Te Punga 2014, 'Living on New Zealand street: Maori presence in Parramatta', *Ethnohistory* 61(4): 655–69. doi.org/10.1215/00141801-2717813

Standfield, Rachel 2012a, *Race and Identity in the Tasman World*, Pickering and Chatto, London.

Standfield, Rachel 2012b, 'The Parramatta Maori seminary and the education of Indigenous peoples in early colonial New South Wales', *History of Education Review*, 41(2): 119–28. doi.org/10.1108/08198691311269493

Walrond, Carl 2005, 'Māori overseas—18th- and 19th-century travellers', *Dictionary of New Zealand Biography: Te Ara—the Encyclopedia of New Zealand*, www.teara.govt.nz/en/maori-overseas/page-1

Wevers, Lydia 2002, *Country of Writing: Travel Writing and New Zealand, 1809–1900*, Auckland University Press, Auckland.

Woodd, Basil 1817 (1 February), 'Memoir and Obituary of Mowhee, a young New Zealander, who died at Paddington, Dec. 28, 1816', *Missionary Register* (London): 71.

Yarwood, A.T. 1996 [1977], *Samuel Marsden: The Great Survivor*, Melbourne University Press, Carlton South.

4

'A Defining Characteristic of the Southern People': Southern Māori Mobility and the Tasman World

Michael J. Stevens

Historians—especially historians interested in identifying and recovering 'native' agency—assume that Asia, America, Australasia, and Africa are populated by 'indigenous people' whose activity consists in their expression of authentic cultural idioms tied to their 'native' place. Such a perspective makes migration and mobility seem an inauthentic and unnatural form of economic and cultural expression.

Jon E. Wilson[1]

We [Ngāi Tahu] are essentially southern both in geography and disposition and that is a reflection of our history. Since the early nineteenth century when we first learnt about muskets, potatoes and whaleboats and that fabled place Poi Hakena—Port Jackson, Ngai Tahu have been crossing the Tasman to trade, to settle and to marry. The voyage west has always been more attractive to us than the journey north.

Tipene O'Regan[2]

1   This chapter forms part of a larger research project entitled 'Between Local and Global: A World History of Bluff', which is supported by the Marsden Fund Council from New Zealand Government funding, administered by the Royal Society of New Zealand. I sincerely thank Rachel Standfield for patiently waiting for me to complete this chapter and David Haines for editing suggestions that improved it considerably. David, you were the 'best man' for the job; the tītī are in the post! Wilson 2008: 264.
2   O'Regan 2002: 36.

Introduction

In *The Welcome of Strangers*, archaeologist Atholl Anderson wrote that while mobility was common in pre-European Māori life, it was more frequent within the South Island's Kāi Tahu tribe, to which he and I belong.[3] Indeed, Anderson described mobility as 'almost a defining characteristic of the southern people'.[4] This chapter outlines the causes and consequences of Kāi Tahu mobility. In doing so, it focuses especially on Murihiku, an area south of the Waitaki River and the Foveaux Strait region.[5] It argues that pre-existing patterns of Māori mobility in this locale expanded in response to sustained European contact from the early 1800s that emanated out of Sydney and, from the late 1850s, Melbourne. Māori knew these places as 'Poihakena' and 'Poipiripi'—transliterations of Port Jackson and Port Phillip, respectively—names that speak directly to the maritime nature of the Tasman world in which large numbers of nineteenth-century Māori people moved.[6]

My chapter traces Kāi Tahu individuals who visited and lived in New South Wales and Victoria over the long nineteenth century. It considers how connections with these places affected southern Kāi Tahu families and communities who remained embedded in Murihiku and Foveaux Strait. According to Alan Lester and Zoë Laidlaw, their experiences were 'no less shaped by trans-imperial networks, and they were no less active participants in the new social assemblages' that emerged before and after formal colonisation, which began in southern New Zealand in 1848.[7] I support Lester and Laidlaw's view that an investigation of the relationship between in situ communities and trans-imperial networks is the next logical step for indigenous history.[8] Both Kāi Tahu individuals who directly engaged with trans-imperial networks by travelling beyond home shores, and those who participated in these networks from home

---

3   I mostly use the dialectical southern Māori 'k' instead of the diphthong 'ng' of North Island derived standardised Māori orthography. Therefore, unless I am quoting something to the contrary, Ngāi Tahu is expressed as Kāi Tahu and the likes of mahinga kai as mahika kai and rūnanga as rūnaka.
4   Anderson 1998: 118.
5   See Stevens 2011.
6   Georgie Craw estimates that 1,000 Māori individuals left New Zealand in European vessels in the early contact period. Many of them sailed to, or through, Poihakena, which 'quickly became an important site in the expanding Māori world'. Indeed, several 'made it their home for extended periods of time'. Craw 2014: 91.
7   Lester and Laidlaw 2015: 8. In 1848, the *John Wickliffe* and *Philip Laing* arrived at Port Chalmers with nearly 350 Scottish settlers who inaugurated the Dunedin settlement. See Olssen 1984: 33–39.
8   Lester and Laidlaw 2015: 9.

places, remained connected by genealogy and kinship practices. They were also connected by takata pora (ship people)—multiethnic and polyglot crews of sealers, traders and whalers, who were memorably, if somewhat problematically, termed 'Tasmen' by James Belich.[9]

Many takata pora entered into enduring relationships with Kāi Tahu women between the 1820s and 1860s, producing large families whose descendants have constituted the corpus of Kāi Tahu since the early twentieth century. Although these men opened up new avenues of Māori mobility, the familial ties forged with Kāi Tahu communities often circumscribed their own capacity for movement. As Bishop Selwyn noted during an 1844 visit to Foveaux Strait, 'the great hold upon these men is their love of their children'.[10] Itinerant and resident takata pora altered Māori life ways and senses of place in southern New Zealand. Many of the cultural elements they introduced were perpetuated and are now considered key components of southern Kāi Tahu culture. This includes circuits of mobility that encompass Australia, especially its eastern and southern seaboards, which this chapter illuminates.

Ka Nukunuku, Ka Nekeneke

Anderson, Aroha Harris and Bridget Williams have recently restated the centrality of migration and mobility in Māori experience, noting that these variables have been present 'from the earliest movements to the present day'.[11] From the time of Polynesian settlement of the New Zealand archipelago (c. 1200 AD), movement was at the core of the development of a distinctive Māori culture, especially its southern Māori variant.

As Anderson has shown, initial Polynesian settlement centred substantially on the South Island, where abundant moa (large flightless birds) and fur seals fuelled rapid population growth.[12] Once these protein sources were exhausted, settlement refocused on the warmer North Island and the cultivation of kūmara (sweet potato), the hardiest Polynesian crop.[13]

9   Belich 1996: 131–32. I say problematically because women often travelled on ships that operated between New South Wales and New Zealand in the first half of the nineteenth century.
10   Selwyn, 'Journal of the Bishop's Visitation Tour from December 1843 to March 1844, New Zealand. Part III —11 February 1844', cited in Irwin 1948: 151.
11   Anderson, Harris and Williams 2014: 10.
12   Anderson 2014b: 77.
13   Anderson 2014b: 85, 94–96.

Continued population growth during this martial period pushed some North Island–based genealogical groups in a southerly direction.[14] By such means, Kāti Mamoe kin groups shifted from the east coast of the North Island, across Cook Strait and into the east coast of the South Island, in the late sixteenth century. Kāi Tahu groups repeated this pattern in the early eighteenth century.[15] A key part of the Kāi Tahu strategy to hold and expand territory in the south was the development of a pā (fortified settlement) at Kaiapoi (c. 1700).[16]

Kūmara were grown at Kaiapoi Pā, near the southern limit, and valuable mahika kai (wild-foods) were located to the south. Millions of tītī (sooty shearwater/mutton-bird) that nest on islands clustered around Rakiura (Stewart Island) were especially important as a winter food source and valuable trade item. Groups from Kaiapoi made seasonal visits to these islands to harvest and pack pre-cooked juvenile tītī into bags made of cured bull kelp, called pōhā. Riches entered Kaiapoi from other directions, including pounamu (nephrite jade) from the South Island's west coast. Thus, the village functioned as a trading hub; as Tipene O'Regan has observed, it was to the wider Kāi Tahu resource economy as Singapore was to the British Empire.[17] Its name, Kaiapoi, reflects this, denoting a place where:

> 'Kai' must be 'poi' or swung to the spot … potted birds from the forests of Kaikoura in the north; fish and mutton birds from the sea-coasts of the south; kiore [Polynesian rat] and weka [small flightless birds] and kauru [cabbage tree stem] from the plains and mountain ranges of the west.[18]

Seasonal harvesting of mahika kai and trade between horticultural and non-horticultural zones, centred on Kaiapoi, were important ways in which Kāi Tahu kin groups maintained connections across a massive tribal area. Marriage was another way. Whakapapa (genealogy) shows how marital unions were used to bind together widely dispersed people and resource sites. This can be seen in the truce negotiated by Kāi Tahu and Kāti Mamoe in the late eighteenth century at Poupoutunoa:

---

14   Anderson 2014b: 116–19.
15   Anderson 2014b: 119.
16   Anderson 1998: 36–37.
17   O'Regan 1990: 12.
18   Locke Travers and Stack 1971: 182.

The first [marriage] was between Raki-ihia of Ngāti Māmoe and Hinehākiri, the cousin of Ngāi Tahu's leading chief, Te-hau-tapunui-o-Tū. The second union was between Honekai, the son of Te-hau-tapunui-o-Tū, and Kohuwai, the daughter of Raki-ihia. These marriages were arranged at Kaiapoi and confirmed at Taumata in Otago.[19]

Likewise, in the 1820s and 1830s, Te Pahi and his brother, Te Marama, were regionally prominent chiefs who were married to Wairua and Piki, sisters of the Upoko Ariki Te Maiharanui.[20] Te Marama and Wairua appear to have lived mainly at Kaiapoi; Te Pahi and Piki were based in the Foveaux Strait region. Both couples participated in the annual tītī harvest. A third brother, Tahatu, was a leading chief at Ōtākou, near the present-day city of Dunedin.[21] While there are differing views regarding the extent of regional cooperation and unity at this time, these ties demonstrate the dispersed, yet interconnected, nature of Kāi Tahu tribal leadership and seats of political power. They also reveal the constant back and forth of communication and return visits between the tribe's dominant families.

Kāi Tahu authority prevailed over Kāti Mamoe in Murihiku and Foveaux Strait at the time takata pora visited southern New Zealand, partly through these marriages.[22] Anderson suggested that the arrival of takata pora from the 1790s drove Kāi Tahu and Kāti Mamoe to maintain peace with one another.[23] Certainly, the ethnographer Herries Beattie was told that when the two peoples ceased fighting they did not necessarily live 'in perfect trust together'. However, this underlying 'latent suspicion was mitigated when the white men came sealing and later whaling on the coasts, and died out completely when the white settlers came'.[24] Moreover, several Kāi Tahu people and families were pulled south, curious about the newcomers and desirous for trade with them.[25] This pattern was accelerated from 1830 with the capture and killing of Te Maiharanui by Ngāti Toa chief Te Rauparaha, the subsequent destruction of Kaiapoi Pā in 1832 and the death and capture of many Kāi Tahu people.[26] This left Kaiapoi, and much of the wider region, largely deserted.[27]

---

19 Tau 2006: 124. See also Anderson 1998: 51.
20 Anderson 1998: 92–94.
21 Anderson 1998: 94.
22 Anderson 1998: 92.
23 Anderson 1998: 75.
24 Beattie 1916: 96.
25 Anderson 1998: 207.
26 Anderson described Ngāti Toa invasions as a 'demographic disaster' and estimated they left a fifth of the population killed or captured. Anderson 1998: 206. See also Dacker 1994: 10–11.
27 Anderson 2014a: 184–85; Tau 2006: 127–28; Anderson 1998: 90; Dacker 1994: 11.

Kāi Tahu communities emerged and expanded in Murihiku at the time of their transformative encounter with takata pora. Ships and men from Port Jackson engaged with southern Māori *in* these places and it was *from* these places that Kāi Tahu people first travelled to Sydney, thereby expanding physical and mental horizons. This pattern of compounding mobilities brings to mind Epeli Hau'ofa's often-quoted notion of 'world enlargement', which refers to the way in which European interest in the Pacific extended pre-existing circuits of indigenous mobility.[28] To frame that argument in southern Māori terms, from the 1820s, Kāi Tahu entered a process of 'poi' enlargement, one in which a Kaiapoi-centred world was replaced by a Murihiku-centred one that expanded to include Poihakena and Poipiripi as key nodes.

Ōtākou me Ruapuke

Two places were central to Murihiku being integrated into the Tasman world: the village of Ōtākou, which is located on the eastern side of Otago Harbour, just inside its entrance, and Ruapuke Island in Foveaux Strait. Ōtākou was discovered and occupied soon after the Polynesian discovery of New Zealand, and a Kāi Tahu community was living there by the dawn of the nineteenth century. Cross-cultural encounters with sealers and other Tasman world travellers began shortly thereafter. Then, in 1831, two Kent-born, Sydney-based brothers, Edward and Joseph Weller, landed at Ōtākou and negotiated with local chiefs to establish a shore whaling station.[29] One of these chiefs, Tahatu, used a traditional technique to secure the agreement: marriage. His daughter, Paparu, was married to Edward and the couple had a daughter whose many descendants are now located on both sides of the Tasman Sea, including at Ōtākou.

The Weller brothers' settlement, which mixed whaling with shipbuilding, and farming with trading in flax, fish and preserved Māori heads, came to employ as many as 85 men. Rebuilt after it was destroyed by fire in 1832, the station sat at the 'centre of a network of seven stations from Banks Peninsula to Foveaux Strait'.[30] When Tahatu died from introduced measles in 1835, the high-born cousins, Karetai and Taiaroa, filled any leadership vacuum. The latter was born at Banks Peninsula but migrated

---

28 Hau'ofa 1994.
29 Entwisle 1990.
30 Entwisle 1990.

south to Ōtākou and was highly mobile within and beyond southern New Zealand. He was at Rakiura and Ruapuke at various times throughout the 1820s (at least 300 kilometres south of Ōtākou) and was active in fighting northern Māori at various South Island battles in the 1830s (e.g. Kaiapoi about 400 kilometres north of Ōtākou). He also made multiple trips to Sydney during that decade and continued to represent Kāi Tahu interests at key Māori events in the North Island into the 1860s.[31] After Edward Weller's wife Paparu died in 1836, Taiaroa's daughter, Nikuru, became his second wife. She died three days after giving birth to their daughter, Nani, who went on to marry Raniera Erihana/Daniel Ellison, giving rise to the notable Ellison family.[32]

Edward Weller took over the running of the Ōtākou station after his brother Joseph died in 1835; however, following declining catches from 1837, he handed over control to his sister's husband in 1840. He then returned to Sydney and lived alone as 'a Victorian colonial squire in up-country New South Wales'.[33] One of Edward's grandsons was Thomas Rangiwahia Ellison (1867–1904), best known in New Zealand for suggesting a playing kit featuring a black jersey with a monogrammed silver fern at the inaugural meeting of the New Zealand Rugby Football Union in 1893. Ellison, whose wife was also Kāi Tahu—a daughter of John Howell who established a shore whaling station at Riverton in 1837 and later switched to farming—toured New South Wales en route to England as a member of the New Zealand Natives Team in 1888. During this visit it is said that he visited his grandfather, Edward, who had left Ōtākou almost 50 years prior.[34]

Taiaroa's cousin, Karetai, was similarly mobile. He commonly visited settlements in Foveaux Strait; took part in inter-tribal musket wars in the northern South Island; and made several trips to Sydney, including for up to a year in 1834, when he and one of his wives were guests of Reverend Samuel Marsden in Parramatta. The couple possibly introduced measles to Ōtākou upon their return from New South Wales in 1835. Karetai, who

---

31 Oliver 1990.
32 A large number of Raniera and Nani's 12 children and numerous grandchildren achieved considerable educational, commercial and sporting success in colonial New Zealand and advanced numerous Māori causes, including redress from the New Zealand Government for Te Kerēme, the Ngāi Tahu Claim. See Edward and Ellison 1998: 148–49.
33 Entwistle 1990.
34 Edward and Ellison 1998: 149.

is estimated to have had eight wives, has numerous descendants and many of them continue to be based at Ōtākou; they are also found in Bluff, Southland's industrial port town and a number of Australian settings.[35]

As with Ōtākou, Ruapuke Island assumed great importance on New Zealand's pre-colonial frontier. Significant numbers of Kāi Tahu began settling in the Foveaux Strait region between 1810 and 1820, by which time Ruapuke probably began to be densely occupied.[36] Powerful Kāi Tahu chiefs based themselves on the island, not only because it was a staging post for the Tītī Islands and its seasonal bounty, but also to be closer to, and trade with, takata pora. Its value also lay in its connections with another nearby island, Whenua Hou, which is located on the west side of Rakiura. From the mid-1820s, Whenua Hou was home to a community of sealers and whalers who mostly came to southern New Zealand via Sydney and their Kāi Tahu wives and children.[37] It is unclear whether Kāi Tahu groups settled on Ruapuke before or after the Whenua Hou community emerged, but, either way, the latter was a central means by which takata pora were incorporated into this Māori polity.

Ruapuke was the main residence of the chief Te Whakataupuka, son of Honekai and Kohuwai; later, of his nephew, Tuhawaiki; and, later still, of Topi Patuki, son of the aforementioned Wairua and Te Marama. Some, including O'Regan, credit Te Whakataupuka's father, Honekai, with grasping the island's strategic importance. According to O'Regan, 'he took them out there because of its trade possibilities—it was [like] Rauparaha and Kapiti [Island]'.[38] The trade possibilities O'Regan referred to centred in part upon harakeke, so-called New Zealand flax, especially whitau, the dressed fibre or 'hemp' that Māori women expertly extracted from it and which literally held Māori villages together.[39]

Harakeke and whitau were key drivers of British imperial and colonial interest in Murihiku. In late 1822, the New South Wales Government contracted Captain Edwardson to take the *Snapper* to southern New Zealand and secure samples of hemp and information about it. Edwardson found an abundance of harakeke at Ruapuke and negotiated for two Kāi

---

35 Evison 1990.
36 Anderson 1998: 68, 207.
37 Anderson 1998: 76. See Middleton 2007.
38 O'Regan, 12 September 2007, interview by the author.
39 Captain Edwardson stressed the centrality of harakeke for Māori and explained that 'it furnishes clothing, roofs for the huts, cordage, the largest nets and the string with which to attach the pieces of wood of which the canoes are composed'. McNab 1909: 317.

Tahu women to extract whitau near the ship 'with the promise of fish-hooks, nails, knives, scissors, hatchets, razors, glass beads and trinkets'.[40] In arranging this and subsequent trade encounters, Edwardson was aided by the chief Te Pahi and the Pākehā–Māori James Caddell (c. 1794–1826), a former ship's boy whose life had been spared by southern Kāi Tahu during a violent encounter with sealers from the *Sydney Cove* led by Honekai at or near Rakiura in 1810.[41] The *Snapper* also 'shipped a large quantity of potatoes for Sydney' and visited Bluff. A cordial meeting there with the chief Te Wera resulted in Edwardson taking one of his 'relatives' back to Port Jackson. It is highly likely that this person, referred to as 'Jacky Snapper', was Tuhawaiki (c.1805–44). Caddell and his wife Tokitoki, a niece of Honekai's, were also on board.[42]

Edwardson arrived in Sydney in March 1823. The *Sydney Gazette* reported that the *Snapper* brought 'about a ton of prepared flax'; however, the paper was mostly interested in its passengers—'two chiefs, one of whom is accompanied by his wife'.[43] Confident in Edwardson's assertion that systematic trade was possible, the colonial government sponsored further expeditions to Murihiku, continuing to utilise chiefly relationships and Caddell's services as interpreter. The records created by these journeys, especially the writings of Captain John Rodolphus Kent, provide unique insight into the regional and trans-Tasman mobility of Kāi Tahu at this time. Kent's observations of the seasonal tītī harvest, including the drowning of Te Pahi and many of his people in 1823 while returning from the Tītī Islands to Ruapuke, are of enduring value to the tribe.[44] This is especially true for my own Bluff-based family, as we are direct descendants of Te Pahi and continue to harvest tītī through rights inherited from him. Kent also recorded a party of Kāi Tahu tītī harvesters at Ruapuke who had travelled by sea from 'about the lookers on [Kaikoura] of Cook's chart … for the purpose of procuring winter food', demonstrating the extent to which genealogy entitled people to resources far from their usual places of residence and the great value, as well as the considerable risks, attached to the southern tītī harvest.[45]

---

40 McNab 1909: 310.
41 See Hall-Jones 1990.
42 Beattie 1919: 158–59.
43 McNab 1909: 317.
44 Transcript of Extracts of Journal kept by John Rodulphus Kent, MS-0440/13, Hocken Library, University of Otago: 18.
45 Transcript of Extracts of Journal kept by John Rodulphus Kent, MS-0440/13, Hocken Library, University of Otago: 19.

In 1824, during another flax trading voyage, the *Elizabeth Henrietta* was wrecked in Foveaux Strait. Named after the wife of Governor Lachlan Macquarie, the 150-ton government brig broke free from two anchors and was blown ashore at Ruapuke. As well as causing a major headache for colonial mariners and administrators—requiring two further voyages from Sydney to refloat the vessel—the wreck had the ecological consequence of releasing mice onto Ruapuke. This is the earliest record of their arrival in New Zealand, a full six years before the second recorded invasion at the Bay of Islands. The mice were given the name 'hinerata', a Māori transliteration of Henrietta.[46] Mice are still known by that name by the owners of Ruapuke, who maintain homes there and are all descendants of the nineteenth-century chiefs mentioned in this chapter.[47]

Sydney also introduced other undesirable things to southern Kāi Tahu, including diseases. There is no evidence of introduced epidemics among Kāi Tahu before 1830; however, by the end of that decade, they had well and truly left their mark.[48] In mid to late 1835, the *Sydney Packet* visited Preservation Inlet and 'found the measles very bad among the Maoris'. A year later, the same vessel again called into Ruapuke. The ship's crew had been badly affected by a strain of influenza long present at Sydney and resident Kāi Tahu 'threatened to kill the steward for introducing this new disease among them'.[49] The impact of measles, which killed Te Whakataupuka in 1835, was not confined to either Ōtākou or Foveaux Strait; the peripatetic nature of Kāi Tahu individuals and families meant that the disease spread—and spread quickly. Despite their awareness of the threat of epidemic disease, Kāi Tahu individuals, including chiefs, continued to visit Sydney and engage with its agents on home shores after the mid-1830s.

Alongside Taiaroa, Karetai and another regional chief, Tuhawaiki, who succeeded his uncle Te Whakataupuka, 'sold' large tracts of land to Sydney-based speculators in 1838. In January 1840, a group of 10 Kāi Tahu chiefs, led by Tuhawaiki, visited Sydney and met with Governor

46   Houghton 1895: 209.
47   See Searle, Jeremy, Jamieson, Gündüz, Stevens, Jones, Gemmill and King 2009. See also blog. tepapa.govt.nz/2013/01/08/hunting-henriettas-on-ruapuke-island-on-the-tail-of-new-zealands-first-mice/
48   Anderson 1998: 76.
49   McNab 1913: 175. Pybus claimed that this event occurred at Ōtākou: 'In 1836, the *Sydney Packet* arrived at Otakou with a few influenza cases on board. Immediately the disease attacked the Maori, and the people died in hundreds, reducing the population to an alarming degree.' Pybus 1954: 56. See also Anderson 1998: 193.

Gipps who asked them to sign a treaty at Government House; they refused.[50] By this stage, the Māori presence in Sydney had been common for more than a decade and visits like this were no longer necessarily reported in newspapers.[51] As well as rejecting Gipps' treaty, Tuhawaiki ignored his subsequent proclamation against land sales by purporting to sell the South Island to the currency lad turned whaling magnate John Jones (c. 1808–69) and his associate, William Charles Wentworth—the so-called Wentworth–Jones Deed.[52] However, at Ruapuke in June 1840, Tuhawaiki signed a copy of the agreement subsequently known as the 'Treaty of Waitangi', which purported to uphold Māori property rights and chiefly authority while simultaneously ceding sovereignty to the British Crown.

In mid-1844, the trajectories of convergence between Ruapuke and Ōtākou were highlighted when Tuhawaiki oversaw the New Zealand Company's purchase of the Otago Block, paving the way for a Wakefield-inspired settlement, eventually known as Dunedin.[53] After introducing cattle to Ruapuke on his return from Sydney, Tuhawaiki spent the early 1840s focused on the sea, ferrying goods and passengers around southern New Zealand and co-owning several vessels.[54] However, during the protracted negotiations for the Otago Block, he reputedly made a stirring speech in which he reflected critically on events of the past 10–15 years, especially the connections with colonial Australia:

> We were once a numerous people … We are but a poor remnant … dotted in families … where formerly we lived as tribes … We had a worse enemy than Te Rauparaha and that was the visit of the pakeha with his drink and disease … the very scum of Port Jackson shipped as whalers or landed as sealers on this coast. They brought us new plagues, unknown to our fathers, till our people melted away.[55]

---

50 Dacker 1994: 18; Craw 2014: 88–89.
51 Craw 2014: 93, 95, 95–100.
52 Evison 2006: 44; Dacker 1994: 18.
53 Evison 2006: 51–60.
54 Anderson 1990a.
55 Pybus 1954: 56–57. Without denying that Tuhawaiki made a speech, or its general thrust, David Haines points out that it was recollected by George Clarke Jnr and put into writing by him 43 years after the event. It cannot therefore be considered what Tuhawaiki said word for word; it was, rather, a 'retrospective dramatisation of events'. Haines 2003: 49–50.

Tuhawaiki's comments recognise the critical place of engagement with Poihakena for the prospects of southern Kāi Tahu. While it is possible that his description of the impacts of disease and alcohol may have been exaggerated for effect, there is little doubt that, in this period, Kāi Tahu confidence in meeting the challenges of European expansionism was severely strained by depopulation.[56] Confronting this challenge was made much harder when, a few months after the Otago Deed was signed, Tuhawaiki drowned near Timaru en route to Wellington.

Kāi Tahu and the Tasman World After 1844

Georgie Craw has recently re-examined the 'considerable Māori engagement with Australia' between 1793 and 1839 and concluded— quite rightly—that 'Māori actively helped to cultivate a Tasman World in the early nineteenth century'.[57] I agree with Craw that the movement of southern Kāi Tahu individuals and families to and from Australia's southern and eastern seaboards was inaugurated by the pre-colonial frontier, but it was not limited to this time period. Kāi Tahu, on Ruapuke and in other communities around Foveaux Strait, continued their mobile existence and connections with colonial Australia during the era of large-scale South Island land purchases by the Crown, between the 1840s and 1860s. In many ways, this process grew stronger between the 1860s and the 1930s, when shipping networks linked the southern port of Bluff, my hometown, with colonial ports on both sides of the Tasman and more distant points across and beyond the English-speaking world. Such traffic persisted throughout and beyond the nineteenth and twentieth centuries, and is a key component of contemporary Kāi Tahu life. The 'world beyond the waters', as Craw put it, forever became part of our Kāi Tahu world. Not only have we never stopped operating within it, we commonly continue to do so in maritime ways.

The persistence of mobile and expanding southern Māori life ways can be seen in the Kāi Tahu chief Topi Patuki (c. 1810–1900). Topi was born in South Otago when his parents, Te Marama and Wairua, returned to the Canterbury region after the annual tītī harvest in Foveaux Strait. He later shifted to Foveaux Strait and Ruapuke sometime before Ngāti

---

56   Montgomerie 1993: 50.
57   Craw 2014: 90.

Toa destroyed Kaiapoi Pā. In 1838, as mentioned above, he accompanied Tuhawaiki to Sydney and worked on the whaling station established in Bluff.[58] During the colonial encounter, he and his children were present at events such as land sales, sittings of the Native Land Court, political meetings, Māori hall openings, regattas, horse races, weddings and tangi, which occurred across the Kāi Tahu domain.[59] However, his primary residence was on Ruapuke, where he 'became the effective leader' after Tuhawaiki died, as Tuhawaiki's son and heir apparent, John Frederick Kihau, was in his early teens.

An expert whaler who spoke good English and 'dressed in the style of the better class of English sailor', it was Topi who welcomed Reverend J.F.H. Wohlers of the North German Mission Society, Foveaux Strait's first foreign resident missionary, to Ruapuke in 1844. When Kihau drowned in 1852, Topi became the acknowledged chief in Foveaux Strait, albeit at a time when chiefly authority was rapidly eroding. Four years later, he took Kihau's widow, Madeline Kurukuru, as a second wife.[60] She bore him sons whose descendants have been, and still are, active participants in the region's seasonal tītī harvest and commercial fishing in Foveaux Strait, as well as in Australian waters.

Underlining Ruapuke's networked existence in the maritime world of pre-colonial and early colonial New Zealand, in May 1845, Wohlers explained to his mission superiors in Germany that:

> For the time being this island … remains the most suitable place for the mission, because it is a kind of gathering place, where everybody, native or European who crosses through these waters comes ashore.[61]

However, Wohlers added that 'in the future it cannot maintain any significance for cultivation, because even for agriculture it is too rocky'.[62] Wohlers worked hard to teach the residents to grow crops, including wheat that could be ground into flour. He also introduced sheep to Ruapuke.[63]

---

58   Anderson 1990b; Anderson 1998: 100.
59   See, for example, 'News of the Week', *Otago Witness*, 7 November 1874: 14; *Evening Star*, 3 July 1879: 2; 'MIDDLE ISLAND NATIVE LAND PURCHASES ROYAL COMMISSION', *Akaroa Mail and Banks Peninsula Advertiser*, 16 March 1880: 2; 'The Tangi at Moeraki', *Otago Daily Times*, 18 April 1881: 3; 'MAORI HALL AT LITTLE RIVER', *Star*, 20 April 1885: 3; *Otago Daily Times*, 8 January 1895: 2.
60   Anderson 1990b.
61   Wohlers 1845.
62   Wohlers 1845.
63   Wohlers 1895: 193.

However, his efforts did not effect the social changes he anticipated and a suite of pre-existing resource practices, most of them sea-based, prevailed. The tītī harvest is a case in point: early on in his mission, Wohlers found himself 'rather lonely on this island', almost all the residents having left to 'gather some fat meat for the winter'.[64] The harvest, and the mobility it required, persisted throughout Wohlers' 40-year residence on Ruapuke and is still a central activity for many southern Kāi Tahu families today, including mine.

Aside from having maritime rather than terrestrial inclinations, Ruapuke-based Kāi Tahu families did not focus their efforts on growing crops and livestock for trade because, despite finding a market among initial colonists on the Southland plains in the late 1850s, this declined as soon as these newcomers became self-sufficient. This was a familiar story. When 'settlers increased in numbers and confidence, they found fewer uses for native expertise', as Montgomerie put it.[65] A partial exception to this rule was the rural labouring sometimes available to Kāi Tahu workers on the mainland. Sheep shearing, in particular, employed many people, which arguably resembled an aspect of the traditional Kāi Tahu economy, in that the work was peripatetic, communal, intergenerational and gender inclusive.[66] Its seasonal nature also meant it could be worked in with the tītī harvest.[67]

Much of Wohlers' published writing focused on the widely debated question of the 'dying Māori', which he considered to be mainly a consequence of tuberculosis and interracial marriage in southern New Zealand.[68] Wohlers strongly supported the colonial ideal of a racially amalgamated New Zealand and thus endorsed interracial marriage. He additionally saw mixed-race households as offering protection against tuberculosis. On this basis, he correctly predicted that Foveaux Strait's 'half-castes', as he termed them, would be the region's surviving 'natives'.[69]

---

64   Wohlers 1845: 037.
65   Montgomerie 1993: 17.
66   Wohlers 1895: 193.
67   A similar state of affairs defined Kwakwaka'waka life in late nineteenth-century British Columbia. Despite colonial prescriptions against it, they, like southern Kāi Tahu, used wage labouring to underpin mobile rather than sedentary lifestyles. Both benefitted from the fact that the 'timing of the … wage labor cycle conveniently matched the older migrations for food and resource collection'. Raibmon 2005: 27.
68   See Wohlers 1870: 229–34; Wohlers 1881: 123–34. See also Stenhouse 1996: 124–40.
69   See Stevens forthcoming [2018].

However, to paraphrase Te Maire Tau, while interracial marriage certainly transformed Kāi Tahu as a tribe, it did not lead to its anticipated disappearance.[70] In the case of Ruapuke, a key driver of depopulation was simply young inhabitants moving their primary residence away from the island, especially by the late 1860s.[71] Wohlers wrote that:

> The young men [who had] grown up with the sound of the roaring sea singing in their ears, had little taste for agriculture and cattle raising, but they were so much the bolder sailors, saw something of the wide world and gained experience.[72]

Although, according to Wohlers, most of them returned, 'married the young girls, and built little vessels', they 'came to the conclusion that the little island of Ruapuke … was not adapted for them'.[73] In 1857, the island's population was 127; however, by 1887, two years after Wohlers died, only 16 people remained. Many of its residents had relocated to Rakiura or joined relatives on the mainland, especially in Bluff.[74]

An Australian-based descendant of marriages between Kāi Tahu women and various tākata pora has accurately described colonial-era Bluff as 'a halfway house between [Foveaux Strait's mixed-race] island communities and the Europeanised mainland'.[75] James Spencer, an ex-sealer and whaler whose life and family are discussed in more detail in the next section, established a store in Bluff in the mid-1830s. He was joined by William Stirling, a whaler who established a shore whaling station in Bluff in 1836 on behalf of (or at least with assistance from) John Jones, the aforementioned whaling merchant.[76] Both Spencer and Stirling married Kāi Tahu women and had families. In contrast to Ruapuke, the colonial town of Bluff was described as having a large native population

---

70 Tau 2008: 204.
71 Wohlers 1895: 199. The island's role as refuge in the context of Ngāti Toa invasions ended as early as 1839, when hostilities formally ceased and its function as a base to interact and trade with newcomers did not carry over into the colonial encounter. Accordingly, many Kāi Tahu people on Ruapuke whose primary residences had earlier been in Otago or Canterbury returned north to these regions. Those from, or who remained in, the south commonly shifted to whaling stations or colonial towns that grew out of some of them such as happened at Riverton and Bluff. See *Southland Times*, 21 February 1887: 2.
72 Wohlers 1895: 198–99.
73 Wohlers 1895: 198–99.
74 *Southland Times*, 21 February 1887: 2.
75 McDonald 2016.
76 See Stirling 1936: 11.

in 1863;[77] similar observations were made periodically throughout the later nineteenth and twentieth centuries. In 1955, an elderly West Indian seaman, who settled in the port in the 1890s, recalled that 'there were a lot of Maoris'. A female visitor in 1937 likewise noted that 'Maoris are plentiful', but added that 'few of them ... do not show some admixture of pakeha blood'. Nevertheless, she observed the ongoing presence of Kāi Tahu material traditions: 'On the outside walls of all their houses may be seen hanging the kelp bags in which the mutton-birds ... are stored'.[78]

Shipping routes connecting Sydney and Melbourne to New Zealand from the 1860s meant that many colonists or visitors arrived at, or departed from, Auckland or Bluff. In 1887, the Bostonian writer and publisher Maturin M. Ballou visited Bluff, then officially known as Campbelltown, and recorded that 'among the spectators of the ship's arrival who had come to the pier were a score of half-breeds—Māori girls and men, laughing and chattering like little monkeys'.[79] The 'young women of this descent' were described as having fine eyes and rich brown complexions and as answering 'to our quadroons of the Southern States in appearance'.[80] However, Bluff's Kāi Tahu residents were not the immobile playthings of racialising American visitors—as another encounter, reported in a local newspaper, powerfully illustrates:

> Two citizens of the United States of America were in Bluff and were desirous of visiting Ruapuke [and] asked a Ruapuke native what he would charge to take them across in his boat'.[81]

The answer they received was £3.

> [The] Yankees, always with an eye on the almighty dollar, haggled over the fare until they had it reduced to £1 and were chuckling over their cleverness in beating the 'ignorant savage'.[82]

77 Bassett 1993a: 6.
78 'Felix Devalon, who has sailed seven seas, celebrates his 90th birthday next Sunday', 5 October 1955, cited in *Early Bluff: The Newspaper of the Bluff History Group*, October 2009, 16: 4; Wiseman 1937: 32.
79 Ballou 1888: 286–87.
80 Ballou 1888: 288.
81 'Reminiscences of Topi' in 'Ruapuke: Random Recollections and Reminiscences' undated newspaper clipping, Rata Harland Scrapbook Collection, access courtesy of Maurice Skerrett (hereafter Harland Collection).
82 'Reminiscences of Topi' in 'Ruapuke: Random Recollections and Reminiscences' undated newspaper clipping, Harland Collection.

However, once their visit to Ruapuke had concluded, and the Americans asked to be returned to Bluff:

> [They] were at once told that the return fare … would be £5 down before leaving the Island. The Yanks blustered and bounced but it was of no avail, the Māori would not come down; so after waiting another day they had to pay over the five pounds demanded and probably left New Zealand with a more respectful knowledge of the reasoning powers of the Maori.[83]

Sea transport and commercial links between southern New Zealand and southern Australia were further consolidated from 1875 with the rise of the Union Steam Ship Company, a large and powerful corporation that grew out of the estate of John Jones, who moved from Sydney to North Otago in 1843 and became an influential figure in colonial Dunedin.[84] In 1883, Melbourne's *Argus* observed that the company's boats were an 'important factor in the trade and prosperity' of southern New Zealand, and that the 'commercial interests of [the lower] South Island are closely allied to Victoria, so the arrival of the Melbourne boats one would imagine would be anxiously looked for'.[85] Meanwhile, many Kāi Tahu men on the shores of Foveaux Strait turned to inshore fishing for employment in the mid to late nineteenth century.[86] This became increasingly the case from the mid-1880s when a freezing works was established on Bluff's foreshore that enabled fish to be frozen and exported, along with oysters, to Melbourne on Union Steam Ship vessels.

In the early twentieth century, a retired Bluff fisherman, 'Old Bill', recalled oystering in Foveaux Strait in this era, before engines allowed boats to 'run to timetable like a train'.[87] In earlier days, he explained, there was one company of oyster merchants, the Bluff Oyster Company, which was owned and operated by 'Captain Anglem, Tom Gilroy, Joey Ward an' I think old Charley Bradshaw'[88]—all individuals who were (by birth

---

83   'Reminiscences of Topi' in 'Ruapuke: Random Recollections and Reminiscences' undated newspaper clipping, Rata Harland Scrapbook Collection, see fn 81, Harland Collection.

84   McLean 1993; Tapp 1990.

85   'Roundabout New Zealand. The Bluff to Dunedin', *Argus*, 26 May 1883: 13.

86   Wohlers 1895: 199.

87   'Oystering Then and Now. Stirring Sailing Days Recalled. 'Old Bills' Reminiscences [sic]', undated newspaper clipping, Harland Collection.

88   Charles Bradshaw married the Kāi Tahu woman Rena Lahey. Their first-born child, also Charles (or its transliteration, Taare), is Tipene O'Regan's Pōua. Tipene O'Regan, 26 March 2015, email message to author.

or marriage) from Kāi Tahu families, with the exception of Ward who became the local member of the House of Representatives and, later, New Zealand's Colonial Treasurer and Premier.[89] Old Bill remembered that:

> A lot of oysters were sent to Melbourne in cement casks. I've seen the decks of … the Union Company's boats fair stacked up with casks … You don't see that nowadays … those were good days.[90]

According to other reports, it was in 1896–97 that Foveaux Strait's fishing industry boomed, 'owing to the export trade to Melbourne'. Growth was so phenomenal that Bluff-based merchants negotiated to establish a station, with cleaning and packing sheds and accommodation, on Māori-owned Ruapuke. 'At the height of the station's prosperity there were from 60 to 80 men engaged in cod and net fishing'; the little settlement was described as resembling a mining camp, due to its 'roughly built shacks … and a good sprinkling of run-away sailors … of many nationalities'. Cleaned and cased fish were sent to Bluff by regular cutter and 'conveyed to the Freezing Works' and then to Melbourne.[91] Unfortunately, overfishing brought declining catches and the station was abandoned by 1903. Yet, a fine spell of winter weather in 1917, during which plenty of oysters and fish were landed in Bluff, meant that an 'intercolonial boat' was 'badly wanted to place a big consignment … now held in cool store on the Australian markets'.[92] The Melbourne service ended in 1930 but its memory lived on. Nearly two decades later, a visitor to Southland wrote that 'one is constantly reminded that Bluff is actually nearer to Hobart than Auckland and the people sigh for the restoration of the Bluff–Melbourne steamer service'.[93]

With respect to the colonial period, I have thus far referred only to Kāi Tahu males who travelled to and from Australia and further beyond. However, Kāi Tahu females also travelled. A case in point is Iwa Skerrett.[94] Iwa's great-niece, Angela Skerrett-Tainui, recalled that, as a child, there was a photograph of 'a beautiful Maori maiden looking regal in a feather cloak' on the wall of her grandfather's house in Bluff. She asked him

---

89   Bassett 1993b.
90   'Oystering Then and Now. Stirring Sailing Days Recalled. 'Old Bills' Reminiscences [sic]', undated newspaper clipping, Harland Collection.
91   'When Fishing Boomed' in 'Ruapuke: Random Recollections and Reminiscences' undated newspaper clipping, Harland Collection.
92   *Southland Times*, 12 July 1917: 4.
93   'Land of Promise', *Nelson Evening Mail*, 11 December 1947.
94   Also known as Evaline, or Eva Skerrett, but also the full transliteration Iwa Kereti.

who the woman was, and he replied: 'That is my sister, Iwa. She went to England for the coronation of King George V with a Maori concert party and never returned'.[95]

Born on Rakiura in 1890, Iwa and her parents relocated to Bluff to join her maternal grandparents when she was two years old. She told a Sydney reporter that in about 1900—when, probably because of kin connections, she was living with my great-great-great-grandparents[96]— the Premier, Richard John Seddon, 'visited our little town … and we children sang a song of welcome. The big man called me to him and told me I had a glorious voice'. She later joined the choir at St Matthew's Anglican Church in Bluff and was invited to sing at concerts.[97] In late 1909, Iwa competed in a musical competition in Dunedin in which she placed second; its judge, Mr Orchard of Sydney, described her as 'a contralto with a future'.[98] Thereafter, she was offered singing lessons and asked to join a Te Arawa–based Māori concert party being assembled by Maggie Papakura, who had accepted invitations to perform in Australia and London.[99] The group's tour began with an outdoor performance for 6,000 people in Melbourne. It subsequently performed in Sydney—a place Papakura reportedly had an 'an undying love for'—then Adelaide and Perth.[100]

Described as a 'Maori mezzo-soprano', Iwa delighted her audience and it was predicted that she 'should become a great favourite in Sydney'.[101] She also found favour in the UK, where she remained after performing at the Festival of Empire and Coronation Exhibition in 1911. Finding fame as 'Princess Iwa', she joined and became a lead singer in the Royal Carl Rosa Opera Company, performing 'at top halls and theatres from London to Glasgow to Paris', often in Māori attire with backdrops of New Zealand scenes.[102] She represented New Zealand at an Anzac ceremony and entertained troops in World War I training camps. She married

---

95   Crean 2015.
96   The Bluff Public School Register for 1900 lists John Haberfield, of Greenhills, as Eva Skerrett's guardian. Eva's Aunt Elizabeth (née Honor, formerly Newton) was married to John. Their only son, William, is my grandfather's great-grandfather. Stevens 2015.
97   'Iwa, the Maori Singer', *Sunday Times*, 1 January 1911: 20.
98   'Stage Gossip', *Otago Witness*, 10 November 1909: 68.
99   Northcroft-Grant 1996.
100 'The Maori Village', *Sydney Morning Herald*, 26 December 1910: 3.
101 'The Maori Village', *Sydney Morning Herald*, 26 December 1910: 3.
102 Crean 2015.

a principal tenor with the Royal Carl Rosa Opera Company and had a circle of friends that included Australian soprano Dame Nellie Melba, actor Mary Pickford and Charlie Chaplin.[103]

Iwa planned to visit southern New Zealand in 1915, but this did not eventuate. Her brother George, who served at Gallipoli, attempted but failed to meet her when he was in London recovering from injuries. Iwa, who had children, neither saw George nor returned to New Zealand, before her death in 1947.[104] Other Kāi Tahu women who went to Australia or further abroad in the late nineteenth or early twentieth century also never returned to their Kāi Tahu communities. For instance, Kuini Lahey and her two children; essentially evacuated from Moeraki to New South Wales to escape a difficult marriage, Lahey remarried there, had further children and is buried there. According to Tipene O'Regan, a higher *proportion* of these Australian-based Kāi Tahu, many into their second or third generation in Australia, are in more 'regular communion' with tribal affairs than those in New Zealand. Evidence of this is found in tangihanga (funerals) on our marae (communal Māori meeting complex) in Bluff where, as O'Regan has stated, 'it is not uncommon to find significant numbers of Australians gathering over our dead. These are 'Ngāi Tahu Australians, yes, but still Ngāi Tahu'.[105] Further examples of these trajectories and enduring connections are commonly found in our tribe's monthly newsletter, *Te Pānui Rūnaka*, and Invercargill's main newspaper, the *Southland Times*.

In October 2014, *Te Pānui Rūnaka* noted the recent death of Harry Taiaroa Pene in Tasmania. His children explained that 'his ashes were brought back … to be buried with our mother Gwen, daughter of Puhi Taiaroa-Royal in Rotorua' and that they—his children—came from Darwin, Melbourne and Tasmania to accompany him to Te Mangungu Marae in Naenae, where a tangihanga took place. The family then travelled northward, 'stopping off to pay our respects to our tūpuna [ancestors] at Kikopiri Marae and Kererū Marae'.[106] Two years earlier, the Kāi Tahu community at Ōnuku, near Akaroa on Banks Peninsula, recorded that George Tainui ('Butch') Robinson had died in a truck accident at Mareeba near Cairns,

---

103 Crean 2015.
104 See Schultz 2016: 62–76.
105 O'Regan 2002: 37.
106 *Te Pānui Rūnaka*, Ono/October 2014: 30.

Australia, and that his whānau (family) had passed on their thanks to Ōnuku and the nearby Kāi Tahu settlement of Wairewa for the koha (gifts and donations) they sent.[107]

Conversely, some Kāi Tahu 'Mossies'[108] have lost touch with their Kāi Tahu families and communities; some are like 'Tai te Kiteraki and Toi te Uatahi', two boys who 'went to sea and never returned' but were believed to have settled in New South Wales.[109] Yet, many of these people are willing and able to reconnect with their Kāi Tahu side, as a story from *Te Pānui Rūnaka*, published in mid-2014, illustrates:

> And here we sit in the wharenui [meeting hall] at the marae. [We] are told we affiliate to Arowhenua [near Temuka, in South Canterbury]. Our ancestral grandmothers Potete Ashwell and her daughter Rebecca Lewis and all our kaumātua [elders] now passed on, being represented by we 13 'very blond' Ngāi Tahu Ozzies.

This visit was described as the culmination of 30 years of 'journeying to reconnect with our whakapapa'. Although their marae host, Uncle Joe Waaka, was not sure of their genealogical connection and much remained 'clouded in mystery', they noted that 'those here, who keep the home fires burning, have big wide, open spaces in their hearts'.[110]

The group was attempting to retrace the steps of their tipuna (ancestor), 'Dadda Lewis', who left his whānau, the Ashwell family, in the late 1890s, and travelled to Goondiwindi, a town in south-east Queensland, where he worked as a shearer. Here he met and married a first generation Australian, Mary Ellen Ursula Hammill, whose parents had come from Ireland. The couple had a family of four boys and four girls, whose descendants have spread out across the globe.[111] Other members of the Ashwell family have more recently relocated to Queensland, as the 'socio-economic destruction of far southern New Zealand proceeds apace'. In O'Regan's words, 'young Ngai Tahu leave and they do not head North. They do what Ngai Tahu have always done and they head for Australia'.[112] This was evident in Brisbane—now possibly the fourth largest urban concentration

---

107   *Te Pānui Rūnaka*, Whā/August 2012: 8.
108   Common Tasman world slang term meaning 'Maori Aussies'. Some New Zealand-based Maori grandparents also refer to Australian-based mokopuna (grandchildren) as 'moko-roos'.
109   Beattie 1994: 464.
110   *Te Pānui Rūnaka*, Mātahi-ā-Te Tau/May 2014: 17–18.
111   *Te Pānui Rūnaka*, Mātahi-ā-Te Tau/May 2014: 17–18.
112   O'Regan 2002: 37.

of Māori in the world[113]—during its 2011 floods. In an article entitled 'Skipper from Bluff saves boat', the *Southland Times* reported that Roy Ashwell, a skipper on one of Brisbane's CityCat ferries, narrowly managed to move his houseboat before the marina it was tied to was washed down the Brisbane River. Speaking to a reporter while motoring up the coast to Scarborough after a night moored near St Helena Island, Ashwell, a former meat inspector at Bluff's Ocean Beach Freezing Works, commented that although he had been in Brisbane for 30 years, Bluff was still home.[114]

Bluff's Spencer Family[115]

The story of Dublin-born James Spencer (c. 1790–1847) and his Kāi Tahu descendants is an apt case study that draws attention to the enduring place of mobile Māori livelihoods in southern New Zealand, particularly Bluff, as well as ongoing connections with the Tasman world, including travel to—and work within—the Australian colonies.

Spencer first appears in the southern South Island's historical record in the mid-1820s as a sealer. A Peninsula War veteran, he ventured to Australia upon the conclusion of the Napoleonic Wars and, by 1832, was at the Preservation Inlet whaling station in south-west New Zealand. There he witnessed the first land sale in southern New Zealand.[116] In 1835, Edward Weller's Sydney-based brother, George, referred to Spencer as 'one of the Codfish mob', suggesting he was part of the Whenua Hou community.[117] Spencer purchased land in Bluff from Tuhawaiki at around this time and established a store that bought excess provisions from American whale ships and onsold them. One of his sons later noted that 'French and English whalers used to put in to the Bluff ... so there was more traffic than one might think'. James also collected and sold whalebone and traded in 'feetow' (whitau) that he sold in Sydney.[118]

---

113 Heather 2012.
114 Morgan 2011.
115 This section draws on research from a Māori Summer Studentship hosted by the Department of History and Art History co-funded by the Division of Humanities at the University of Otago and Te Rūnanga o Ngāi Tahu in 2015–16, which was undertaken by Rosie Welsh (nō Kāi Tahu).
116 Beattie [1935].
117 Middleton 2007: 24–25.
118 Beattie [1935].

In early 1841, James married a Kāi Tahu woman, Meri Te Kauri (1816–76)—also known as Tinirauwaho, Mary Jane Spencer and Jane Shepard—in Waikouaiti (present-day Karitane); this was the first Christian marriage conducted in the South Island.[119] Meri hailed from Ōtākou but relocated south to the Foveaux Strait area, specifically Ruapuke Island, possibly in response to Te Rauparaha and Ngāti Toa.[120] James and Meri had two children, James (1842–1903) and William Te Paro (1844–1938).[121] Their lives, as with most of their Kāi Tahu contemporaries, were shaped by a confluence of southern Māori customs and European maritime traditions. Though based primarily in Bluff, their father, James, continued to travel to Sydney for business transactions and to make good on pre-colonial land purchases in the port. A trip to Sydney in late 1846 was occasioned by illness rather than commerce and he died at sea on the return voyage in March 1847.[122] Captain Stirling and another whaler, the Isle of Mann–born John 'Jack Tiger' MacGibbon, who came to Bluff with Stirling, were trustees of James' estate. His will, made in 1846, specified that funds be put towards the maintenance and education of his two sons, who would inherit his real estate and personal property when William, the youngest, reached the age of 21.[123]

Both James and William married women like themselves—people from Foveaux Strait with Kāi Tahu mothers and European sailor fathers. James married Charlotte Ann Kure Whenua Edwards (1844–1900), who was born on Whenua Hou, and William married Louisa Te Memeke Coupar (1846–1930), who was born at The Neck, on Rakiura. Louisa's mother was Te Mahana and her father was Stewart Coupar, originally from Dundee, Scotland.[124] Aside from two years spent in Temuka, William and Louisa spent most of their time in Bluff.[125]

---

119 Ellis 1998: 19.
120 Ellis 1998: 19.
121 According to William Spencer, his father, James, whose middle name was either Power or Powers (Te Paro being a transliteration), had three younger brothers, two of whom were named William and John. Beattie [1935]: (2).
122 Beattie [1935]: (6).
123 Ellis 1998: 14–15.
124 Ellis 1998: 67. Both Meri Te Kauri and Te Mahana are represented in the large carved pou-wāhine inside the whare-tipuna, *Tahu-potiki* on Bluff's Te Rau Aroha Marae. See Christensen 2013: 160–71.
125 Beattie [1935]: (11). See Mikaere 1998.

William worked at a number of occupations during his lifetime and in a number of places. In his youth, he drove sheep from Bluff into the developing agricultural hinterland. In late 1861, aged 17, he travelled on the ship carrying the first cargo from the Invercargill wharf to Australia.[126] Leaving the vessel in Melbourne, William worked and travelled his way inland, shearing in sheds across Victoria, before spending two seasons shore whaling at Twofold Bay in southern New South Wales.[127] He returned to Bluff in May or June 1864, at around the same time as the negotiation and signing of the Rakiura Deed. This document formally extinguished native title to Stewart Island but safeguarded the Tītī Islands for Kāi Tahu individuals and families genealogically entitled to them.[128]

William found employment shearing on Southland farms and constructing gold dredges throughout the lower South Island.[129] He also helped to construct the Waipori power station, south of Dunedin, during which time he visited the nearby Kāi Tahu settlement, Maitapapa, whose residents included individuals and families from Whenua Hou and Rakiura.[130] William also took part in sealing expeditions in Fiordland and went gold prospecting on the South Island's west coast. From his Bluff home, which was located very close to his brother's, William fished, oystered and spent numerous seasons engaged in the tītī harvest.[131] This took place on Te Poho o Horomamae, a Tītī Island located on the east side of Rakiura near the entrance to Lord's River, to which Louisa had beneficial rights through her mother.[132] A large number of William and Louisa's descendants, many of them primarily Bluff based, continue to maintain houses and harvest tītī on this island. One of them, who is New Zealand's Ambassador to Chile, flew from Santiago with her daughter to take part in the harvest in 2017.

Before James and William could succeed to their father's land at Bluff, a neighbouring property owner, George Green (1810–72), an English-born Sydney boat builder, later based in Dunedin, cajoled their mother into signing their interests over to him.[133] This was done in collusion

---

126 Ellis 1998: 66.
127 Ellis 1998: 66; Beattie [1935]: (5).
128 Stevens 2014.
129 Beattie [1935]: (11).
130 See Wanhalla 2009: 10–11.
131 Beattie [1935]: (11).
132 Ellis 1998: 157. The island is commonly known as Horomamae but is also sometimes referred to as Owen Island.
133 'THE LATE MR GEORGE GREEN', *Otago Witness*, 7 September 1872: 10.

with the local constable and other Bluff residents who stood to materially benefit.[134] However, when William turned 21, he and James were able to access their father's sealed papers in Sydney, including his land deeds, Crown Grants and a duplicate of his will. With the assistance of an Invercargill solicitor, this evidence was presented to the Commissioner of Crown Lands and legal proceedings were commenced against Green. It was found that Green had obtained Meri's and William's signatures by deception and, in 1868, New Zealand's Legislative Council passed special legislation to cancel a land grant made to him and instead award a 200-acre block to James and William. However, it seems that legal expenses forced them to subdivide and sell-off part of the land.[135]

Soon afterwards, James became embroiled in Bluff's so-called newspaper races, which were triggered by the Franco-Prussian War and Bluff's proximity to the Australian colonies where updates of the conflict originated. The Franco-Prussian War was Australia's biggest overseas news story of 1870 and updates about it entered Adelaide from P&O mail ships. These updates were then telegraphed throughout the eastern colonies.[136] Bluff performed a similar function when it received mail from Melbourne.

Speaking from the port in 1930, William recalled that 'people here were deeply interested in the conflict, in particular those who had come from the Old Country'.[137] Bluff had two shopkeepers at the time, each representing rival Invercargill-based newspapers, to whom they telegraphed the most important overseas news.[138] 'The agent whose paper

---

134 Ellis 1998: 28; Beattie [1935]: (6).

135 Ellis 1998: 28; Beattie [1935]: (6).

136 Putnis 2007: 6.2–6.3.

137 'The Newspaper Race: Mr W. Spencer's Narrative', undated newspaper clipping, c. 1930, Harland Collection.

138 'The Newspaper Race: Mr W. Spencer's Narrative', undated newspaper clipping, c. 1930, Harland Collection. In 1865, the New Zealand Government built an electric telegraph in the South Island and the prominent Christchurch businessman and politician James Edward FitzGerald, who owned the Christchurch *Press* and had been Canterbury Agent in London, arranged for his brother Gerard to use the telegraph to transmit news from Bluff under the name of the New Zealand General Telegraphic Agency. Its first telegram, sent to Christchurch in May 1865, 'was a summary of news prepared in Melbourne'. O'Neill 1966: 865. Long-running advertisements for the Telegraphic Agency noted that Bluff Harbour, where its Head Office was based, 'occupies as the first port of arrival and last of departure for the steamers carrying Her Majesty's English and Australian Mails, as well as its growing importance as a port of call for sailing vessels of large tonnage'. It listed the company's principle agencies as being Melbourne, Adelaide, Sydney, Brisbane, Launceston, Gallo, Suez Alexandria, Malta, Marseilles Paris and London. See, for example, *Southland Times*, 5 January 1866: 1; *Nelson Examiner and New Zealand Chronicle*, 2 March 1867: 4.

arrived first', explained Spencer, 'naturally had the first use of the wire. Therefore the race for this privilege was always keenly waged'.[139] Both agents had a boat and crew of top oarsmen to row out and meet any approaching vessel. William's brother, James, rowed in one of these boats. One agent had a light whaleboat fitted out for the purpose, while the other responded by 'getting a strong four-oared boat of a racing pattern specially built for the service in Hobart'. The two crews 'were as keen in rivalry as their employers' and met ships past Stirling Point, 'even into the Straits', to retrieve copies of Melbourne and Sydney newspapers. Racing for Stirling Point, each boat would deliver their respective parcels to waiting horsemen and 'the race by horse from the point was often more exciting than the boat race'. The race ended at the post office 'with cheers for the winner'.[140]

William and James Spencer's histories illustrate how Bluff's rhythms and the lives of its Kāi Tahu residents continued to be shaped by their proximity to Australia, well after formal colonisation began in southern New Zealand. Through them, we can see that Kāi Tahu linkages with Australia, which began on New Zealand's pre-colonial frontier, did not end—or perhaps even wane—during the colonial encounter.

Conclusion: Three Thousand Miles from 'Home'?

In July 2015, two months after I returned to Dunedin from Bluff following that year's tītī harvest, conducted on our family's island in Foveaux Strait, I travelled to Sydney for the annual meeting of the Australian Historical Association. The conference theme, fittingly, was 'Foundational Histories'. During my stay, I wandered along the city's Foveaux Street and located archival material relating to Bluff and Ruapuke in the Mitchell Library. My wife and I also arranged to meet a childhood friend from Bluff. She was an ex-neighbour who I last saw in London, almost a decade earlier. She too, is Kāi Tahu; in her case, one of the many descendants of the Sydney-born Nathaniel Bates (1819–87), a whaler and brother-in-law

---

139 'The Newspaper Race: Mr W. Spencer's Narrative', undated newspaper clipping, c. 1930, Harland Collection.
140 'The Newspaper Race: Mr W. Spencer's Narrative', undated newspaper clipping, c. 1930, Harland Collection.

of the aforementioned George Green.[141] Bates 'had three wives—two Ngai Tahu women on the Foveaux Strait coast and one in Hobart' and, as O'Regan put it, 'the regularity of his trans-Tasman travel is attested by an extraordinary number of children'.[142]

My friend's Kāi Tahu father was raised near Kaiapoi and did his apprenticeship as a carpenter before moving to Bluff where he had extended relatives. He went to sea and eventually skippered an oyster boat, the *Ranui*, owned by Otakou Fisheries, a cooperative based in Ōtākou that is owned and operated by descendants of chief Taiaroa, particularly its Ellison branch.[143] My friend's parents moved to Sydney in the late 1980s in response to Bluff's falling economic fortunes and this is where their two children, and now grandchildren, all live. When my wife (who comes from the Ellison branch of the Taiaroa family) and I met my friend in Sydney, it was mainly to give her an unused oyster sack, stamped 'RANUI 86'. The significance of this gift, aside from its rarity because the boat had not been oystering in over 20 years, was that my friend had recently given birth to a daughter whose middle name was Ranui. Our gift, handed over in a cafe near the University of Sydney, provoked a short tangi (cry) and hugs, followed by a visit to a picture framer. This oyster sack now hangs in the lounge room of an inner-city Sydney home, a combined statement about Bluff, the persisting maritime nature of the Tasman world and the diverse trajectories of Kāi Tahu lives within it.

---

141 George married Nathaniel's sister, Maria, at St Phillip's Church, Sydney, in April 1830. See Broad n.d. For more, see 'THE LATE MR GEORGE GREEN', *Otago Witness*, 7 September 1872: 10.

142 O'Regan 2002: 36. Bates reportedly fathered between 31 and 33 children, see 'Accidents and Fatalities', *Otago Daily Times*, 15 July 1887; 'The Drowning Accident at Riverton', *Southland Times*, 18 July 1887: 2. Angela Wanhalla noted that Bates first entered into a customary marriage with Hinepu and the couple had three children before she died. In 1848, he married Harriet Watson, a daughter of fellow whaler Robert Watson and his wife Parure. Bates later moved a married woman, Ann Pauley, also a daughter of a whaler and a Kāi Tahu woman, into his and Harriet's household in Riverton after she became pregnant with his child. Their relationship lasted 23 years. Wanhalla 2009: 49, 51.

143 The *Ranui* was built over eight years from 1928 by a Norwegian boatbuilder at the southern end of Rakiura very close to where, in 1826, Taiaroa had met members of an expedition intent on delivering the first planned British settlers to New Zealand. My grandfather was transported to and from our family's Tītī Island as a young child on the *Ranui* with its first owner, Captain Billy Thompson, just before the vessel was taken over by the New Zealand Navy in 1941. During World War II it serviced sub-Antarctic Islands but also ventured as far north as the Solomon Islands. The *Ranui* remained in the central Pacific after the war, acting as a supply ship to remote islands and as a Royal Yacht for Queen Salote of Tonga. In 1954, it was purchased by George Ellison (1907–91) and brought back to southern New Zealand. The *Ranui* was then based mainly in Bluff and used for crayfishing and oystering until the early 1990s when the Foveaux Strait oyster fishery collapsed. See Rakiura Museum Book Committee 2008: 121.

A few years earlier, in mid-2012, Tahu Potiki, the Ōtākou representative to Te Rūnanga o Ngāi Tahu (who is married to a granddaughter of George Ellison and whose father-in-law's first two names are Edward Weller), reflected on the migration of tens of thousands of Māori to Australia and its 'influence on the evolution and expression of Maori identities'. His thoughts were triggered both by the death of an elderly relative and by six of the latter's grandsons returning to Ōtākou to attend his tangihanga. He observed that these young men, all descendants of chief Taiaroa, worked in physically demanding jobs and earned good money, and that 'all of them were able to afford to fly home with their young families'. Moreover, 'they are all browned up and most bear quality Maori tattoos and when their grandfather was carried from the house they and their cousins performed a rousing haka'.[144] Echoing O'Regan's sentiments observed earlier, Potiki noted that, despite living in Australia, 'their lives are still heavily influenced by a Maori upbringing and they have strong identities'. Potiki quite rightly wondered if this would continue following the death of their patriarch and the 'three thousand miles distance between them and home'. In his opinion, these young men were 'in new territory'.[145]

My assessment, based on historical evidence, is that the territory that these young Kāi Tahu men and their families are in is not especially new, but, rather, that they are following in the footsteps of their ancestors. That said, as O'Regan has acknowledged, the recent movement is more dramatic. Writing in 2002, O'Regan noted that the fastest growing geographic locations on our tribal register are second and third generation Australians; he observed that a 'steady stream of young adults from the south are migrating there and a noticeable group of retiring parents are moving to be closer to their grandchildren'. However, fundamentally, this is not a new phenomenon; instead, it is one in which 'the old pattern continues stronger than ever'.[146]

As for those of us Kāi Tahu who remain 'in place' in southern New Zealand, our lives continue to be shaped by patterns cast by early nineteenth-century connections to Australia. Our disproportionate involvement in southern New Zealand's inshore fishing industry, our seascapes, our places of work and play, and our everyday conversations include placenames like

---

144 Potiki 2012.
145 Potiki 2012.
146 O'Regan 2002: 37.

Foveaux, Henrietta, Paterson, Lord, Bunker and Bungaree. Many of us, as I have shown, are active participants in the annual mutton-bird harvest, a word—if not a practice—that came to us from Norfolk Island.[147] Moreover, many of the commercial boats owned and operated by Kāi Tahu families in places like Bluff, Rakiura, Riverton and Ōtākou—boats that frequently run families to and from our Tītī Islands—have been purchased in Australia. For instance, in June 1954, Tasmania's *Examiner* noted that 'Mr. Charlie Waitiri, of The Bluff, New Zealand' purchased the Launceston fishing vessel, *Buccaneer*, built in Hobart in 1946. In making the five–seven-day, 1,368-kilometre trip from Flinders Island to Bluff, the newspaper noted that, in addition to four men from Launceston, Waitiri's crew included his daughter, the aptly named Moana McQuarrie. Waitiri, who purchased the vessel 'for crayfishing off The Bluff', commented that 'New Zealand fishermen thought highly of Tasmanian-built boats', and that, since October, 'Bluff fishermen had purchased nine boats from Australia, the majority of which had been built in Tasmania'.[148]

Reflecting on the longevity of Sydney as one of New Zealand's most important cities and—for a century—New Zealand as one of Sydney's most important hinterlands, James Belich memorably concluded that throughout the nineteenth century 'the Tasman Sea was more bridge than barrier'.[149] In a later assessment of Australasian circuits of people and money, Belich argued that, prior to Australian federation in 1901, 'most of the people crossing the Tasman probably did not see themselves as migrating, but shifting and wandering within a single system, a linked constellation'.[150] This chapter's description and assessment of southern Kāi Tahu communities supports Belich's claims. However, the way these patterns persisted beyond the colonial encounter calls into question his claim that New Zealand abandoned the Tasman world when it chose not to federate.[151] At the very least, if 'New Zealand' did indeed abandon it, we southern Kāi Tahu did not; to paraphrase Ralph Waldo Emerson—a sea, once stretched, never returns to its original dimensions.[152]

---

147 Anderson 2001: 6.
148 'Rough Tasman Crossing Avoided By Mail Delay', *The Examiner*, 8 June 1954: 4.
149 Belich 1996: 134.
150 Belich 2001: 47–48.
151 Belich 2001: 48.
152 After 'the mind, once stretched by a new idea, never returns to its original dimensions', attributed to Ralph Waldo Emerson among others. See Makowsky 2013: 1.

References

Anderson, Atholl 1990a, 'Tuhawaiki, Hone', *Dictionary of New Zealand Biography: Te Ara—the Encyclopedia of New Zealand*, www.teara.govt. nz/en/biographies/1t110/tuhawaiki-hone

Anderson, Atholl 1990b, 'Patuki, Topi', *Dictionary of New Zealand Biography: Te Ara—the Encyclopedia of New Zealand*, www.teara.govt. nz/en/biographies/1p11/patuki-topi

Anderson, Atholl 1998, *A Welcome of Strangers*, Otago University Press, Dunedin.

Anderson, Atholl 2001, 'The Origins of Muttonbirding in New Zealand', *New Zealand Journal of Archaeology* 22: 5–14.

Anderson, Atholl 2014a, 'Old ways and new means, AD 1810–1830', in *Tangata Whenua: An Illustrated History,* Atholl Anderson, Judith Binney and Aroha Harris, Bridget Williams Books, Wellington: 138–63.

Anderson, Atholl 2014b, 'Pieces of the past, AD 1200–1800, in *Tangata Whenua: An Illustrated History*, Atholl Anderson, Judith Binney and Aroha Harris, Bridget Williams Books, Wellington: 75–76.

Anderson, Atholl, Aroha Harris and Bridget Williams 2014, 'Introduction', in *Tangata Whenua: An Illustrated History*, Atholl Anderson, Judith Binney and Aroha Harris, Bridget Williams Books, Wellington: 10–12.

Ballou, Maturin M. 1888, *Under the Southern Cross, Or Travels in Australia, Tasmania, New Zealand Samoa and Other Pacific Islands*, Ticknor and Company, Boston.

Bassett, Michael 1993a, *Sir Joseph Ward: A Political Biography*, Auckland University Press, Auckland.

Bassett, Michael 1993b, 'Ward, Joseph George', *Dictionary of New Zealand Biography: Te Ara—the Encyclopedia of New Zealand,* www.teara.govt.nz/ en/biographies/2w9/ward-joseph-george

Beattie, Herries 1916, 'Traditions and legends. Collected from the natives of Murihiku. (Southland, New Zealand)', *Journal of the Polynesian Society* 25: 89–98.

Beattie, Herries 1919, 'Traditions and legends collected from the natives of Murihiku. (Southland, New Zealand)', *Journal of the Polynesian Society* 28: 158–59.

Beattie, Herries [1935], 'The veteran talks. Born in Bluff 1844. Interviews with Wm. Spencer' in 'History collected to write a book about Bluff. Never printed. 1935', Hocken Library, University of Otago, HJ-582/I/7: 3.

Beattie, Herries 1994, *Traditional Lifeways of the Southern Maori*, Atholl Anderson (ed.), University of Otago, Dunedin.

Belich, James 1996, *Making Peoples: A History of the New Zealanders—From Polynesian Settlement to the End of the Nineteenth Century*, Penguin Press, Auckland.

Belich, James 2001, *Paradise Reforged: A History of the New Zealander—From the 1880s to the Year 2000*, Penguin Books, Auckland.

Broad, Michael, n.d. www.cemeteries.org.nz/stories/greengeorge230412 version50512.pdf

Christensen, Ian 2013, *Cliff Whiting: He Toi Nuku, He Toi Rangi*, He Kupenga Hao i te Reo, Palmerston North.

Craw, Georgie 2014, 'A world beyond the waters: Māori travel in the Tasman world, 1793–1839', MA thesis, University of Auckland.

Crean, Mike 2015, 'Troops adored Maori "nightingale"', *Southland Times*, 28 February: A17.

Dacker, Bill 1994, *Te Mamae me te Aroha—The Pain and the Love: A History of Kāi Tahu Whānui in Otago, 1844–1994*, Otago University Press, Dunedin.

Edward, Matapura and Shaun Ellison 1998, 'Ellison family', in *Southern People: A Dictionary of Otago Southland Biography*, Jane Thomson (ed.), Longacre Press, Dunedin: 148–49.

Ellis, Georgina 1998, *Time and Tide: Ramblings, Recollections and Reminiscences of the Spencer Family*, Georgina Ellis, Invercargill.

Entwisle, Peter 1990, 'Weller, Edward', *Dictionary of New Zealand Biography: Te Ara—the Encyclopedia of New Zealand*, www.teara.govt. nz/en/biographies/1w13/weller-edward

Evison, Harry C 1990, 'Karetai', *Dictionary of New Zealand Biography: Te Ara—the Encyclopedia of New Zealand*, www.teara.govt.nz/en/ biographies/1k1/karetai

Evison, Harry C. 2006, *The Ngai Tahu Deeds: A Window on New Zealand History*, Canterbury University Press, Christchurch.

Haines, David 2003, 'Te Kai a te Rakatira: Kai Tahu Leadership, 1830–1844', BA (Hons) thesis, University of Otago.

Hall-Jones, John 1990, 'Caddell, James', *Dictionary of New Zealand Biography: Te Ara—the Encyclopedia of New Zealand*, www.teara.govt. nz/en/biographies/1c1/caddell-james

Hauʻofa, Epeli 1994, 'Our sea of islands', *The Contemporary Pacific* 6(1): 148–61.

Heather, Ben 2012, 'Maori turn Australian towns into "little NZs"', *Dominion Post*, 30 October: A3.

Houghton, John 1895, 'The Translator's Visit to Ruapuke', in J.F.H. Wohlers, *Memories of the Life of J. F. H. Wohlers, Missionary at Ruapuke, New Zealand. An Autobiography*, John Houghton (trans.), Otago Daily Times and Witness Newspaper Company, Dunedin.

Irwin, Cecil H. 1948, '"The whalemen of Foveaux Strait". 1829–1850', MA (Hons) thesis, University of Otago, Dunedin.

Lester, Alan and Zoë Laidlaw 2015, 'Indigenous sites and mobilities: Connected struggles in the long nineteenth century', in *Indigenous Communities and Settler Colonialism: Land Holding, Loss and Survival in an Interconnected World*, Alan Lester and Zoë Laidlaw (eds), Palgrave Macmallan, Basingstoke: 1–23. doi.org/10.1057/9781137452368_1

Locke Travers, W. T. and James West Stack 1971, *The Stirring Times of Te Rauparaha (Chief of the Ngatitoa)*, Wilson & Horton, Auckland.

Makowsky, Veronica 2013, 'Editor's introduction: New perspectives on Puerto Rican, Latina/o, Chicana/o, and Caribbean American Literatures", *MELUS* 38(2): 1–4. doi.org/10.1093/melus/mlt021

McDonald, Susan 2016, 'I met the ghost of my Maori great-grandfather on a wild and lonely track', *The Guardian*, 1 February, www.theguardian. com/commentisfree/2016/feb/01/i-met-the-ghost-of-my-maori-great-grandfather-on-a-wild-and-lonely-track

McLean, Gavin 1993, 'Mills, James', *Dictionary of New Zealand Biography: Te Ara—the Encyclopedia of New Zealand*, www.teara.govt.nz/en/biographies/2m48/mills-james

McNab, Robert 1909, *Murihiku: A History of the South Island of New Zealand and the Islands Adjacent and Lying to the South, from 1642 to 1835*, Whitcombe & Tombs, Wellington.

McNab, Robert 1913, *The Old Whaling Days: A History of Southern New Zealand from 1830–1840*, Whitcombe and Tombes, Christchurch.

Middleton, Angela 2007, *Two Hundred Years on Codfish Island (Whenua Hou): From Cultural Encounter to Nature Conservation*, Department of Conservation, Wellington.

Mikaere, Buddy 1998, *Te Maiharoa and the Promised Land*, Reed, Auckland.

Montgomerie, Deborah 1993, "Coming to terms: Ngai Tahu, Robeson County Indians and the Garden River band of Ojibwa, 1840–1940. Three studies of colonialism in action", PhD diss., Duke University.

Morgan, Jared 2011, 'Skipper from Bluff saves boat from 'floating missiles' Brisbane torrent', *Southland Times,* 17 January: 4.

Northcroft-Grant, June 1996, 'Papakura, Makereti', *Dictionary of New Zealand Biography: Te Ara—the Encyclopedia of New Zealand*, www.teara.govt.nz/en/biographies/3p5/papakura-makereti

Oliver, Steven 1990, 'Taiaroa, Te Matenga', *Dictionary of New Zealand Biography: Te Ara—the Encyclopedia of New Zealand*, www.teara.govt. nz/en/biographies/1t2/taiaroa-te-matenga

Olssen, Erik 1984, *A History of Otago*, John McIndoe, Dunedin.

O'Neill, Reginald Brian (co-creator) 1966, 'Historical development', in *An Encyclopaedia of New Zealand*, A. H. McLintock (ed). *Te Ara—the Encyclopedia of New Zealand*, www.teara.govt.nz/en/1966/press-association/page-2

O'Regan, Tipene 1990, 'A Kai Tahu History', *Te Karanga* 6: 1.

O'Regan, Tipene 2002, 'The dimension of kinship', in *States of Mind: Australia and New Zealand 1901–2001*, Arthur Grimes, Lydia Wevers and Ginny Sullivan (eds), Institute of Policy Studies, Victoria Universiy of Wellington, Wellington.

Potiki, Tahu 2012, 'TV show has huge potential to explore identity of expat Maori', *The Press*, 11 May: A17.

Putnis, Peter 2007, 'Overseas news in the Australian press in 1870 and the colonial experience of the Franco-Prussian war', *History Australia* 4(1): 6.1–6.19.

Pybus, T. A. 1954, *The Maoris of the South Island,* Reed Publishing, Wellington.

Raibmon, Paige 2005, *Authentic Indians: Episodes of Encounter from the Late-Nineteenth-Century Northwest Coast*, North Carolina, Duke University Press, Durham. doi.org/10.1215/9780822386773

Rakiura Museum Book Committee, 2008, *Stewart Island Boats*, Rakiura Heritage Trust, Stewart Island.

Schultz, Marianne 2016, *Performing Indigenous Culture on Stage and Screen: A Harmony of Frenzy*, Palgrave Macmillan, New York.

Searle, Jeremy B., Paul M. Jamieson, İslam Gündüz, Mark I. Stevens, Eleanor P. Jones, Chrissen E.C. Gemmill and Carolyn M. King 2009, 'The diverse origins of New Zealand house mice', *Proceedings of the Royal Society of London B: Biological Sciences* 276(1655): 209–17. doi.org/10.1098/rspb.2008.0959

Stenhouse, John 1996. '"A disappearing race before we came here"— Doctor Alfred Kingcome Newman, the dying Maori, and Victorian scientific racism', *New Zealand Journal of History* 30(2): 124–40.

Stevens, Michael J. 2011, '"What's in a name?": Murihiku, colonial knowledge-making, and "thin-culture"', *The Journal of the Polynesian Society* 120(4): 333–47.

Stevens, Michael J. 2014, 'Te Hopu Tītī ki Rakiura: "Fat meat for the winter"', in *Tangata Whenua: An Illustrated History*, Atholl Anderson, Judith Binney and Aroha Harris, Bridget Williams Books, Wellington: 316–17.

Stevens, Michael J. 2015, '"Pōua's cloak": The Haberfield family kahu kiwi', in *The Lives of Colonial Objects*, Annabel Cooper, Lachy Paterson & Angela Wanhalla (eds), Otago University Press, Dunedin: 253–58.

Stevens, Michael J. forthcoming (2018), '"A lasting benefit for a new race"? Rev. J.F H. Wohlers and racial amalgamation in southern New Zealand', in *Pacific Futures: Past and Present*, Miranda Johnson, Warwick Anderson and Barbara Brookes (eds), University of Hawai'i Press, Honolulu.

Stirling, R. J. 1936, 'Who was the founder of Bluff," *Auckland Weekly News,* 30 December, in Herries Beattie, 'Scrapbook about Bluff and Gore', MS-582/D/6/K, Hocken Library, University of Otago: 11.

Tapp, E. J. 1990, 'Jones, John', *Dictionary of New Zealand Biography: Te Ara—the Encyclopedia of New Zealand*, www.teara.govt.nz/en/biographies/1j4/jones-john

Tau, Te Maire 2006, 'Ngāi Tahu', in *Māori Peoples of New Zealand: Ngā Iwi o Aotearoa*, New Zealand Ministry of Culture and Heritage (ed.), Bateman, Auckland: 122–31.

Tau, Te Maire 2008, 'Epilogue', in *Ngai Tahu: A Migration History: The Carrington Text*, Te Maire Tau and Atholl Anderson (eds), Bridget Williams Books, Wellington: 201–03.

Wanhalla, Angela 2009, *In/visible Sight: The Mixed-Descent Families of Southern New Zealand,* Bridget Williams Books, Wellington. doi.org/10.7810/9781877242434

Wilson, Jon E. 2008, 'Agency, narrative, and resistance', in *British Empire: Themes and Perspectives,* Sarah Stockwell (ed.), Blackwell, Oxford.

Wiseman, Dorothy 1937 (1 January), 'Our southern coast: Off the beaten track in the South Island', *New Zealand Railways Magazine* 11(10): 32.

Wohlers, J.F.H. 1845 (1 May), 'To the Committee of Administration of the North German Missionary Society, Report No. 4', Papers relating to the Reverend J.F.H. Wohlers and the Ruapuke Island Station, Adele Schafer and Felix Schafer (trans.), MS-0967/014, Hocken Library, University of Otago: 037, 045.

Wohlers, J.F.H. 1870, 'On the dying out of the natives of New Zealand', *Evangelist*, 1 August: 229–34.

Wohlers, J.F.H. 1881, 'On the conversion and civilization of the Maoris in the south of New Zealand', *Transactions and Proceedings of the New Zealand Institute* 14: 123–34.

Wohlers, J.F.H. 1895, *Memories of the Life of J. F. H≠. Wohlers, Missionary at Ruapuke, New Zealand. An Autobiography*, John Houghton (trans.), Otago Daily Times and Witness Newspaper Company, Dunedin.

5

Entangled Mobilities: Missions, Māori and the Reshaping of Te Ao Hurihuri

Tony Ballantyne

The intersections between the forms of mobility that were integral to the functioning of imperial systems and established patterns of Indigenous movement and circulation offer crucial insights into both the power and limits of empire. Empires have historically operated as highly uneven systems of extraction, appropriation and incorporation, which have been geared towards enhancing the resources, wealth, power and status of the empire-building state. Their functioning has been dependent on creating new connections between peoples and territories, drawing them into circuits of transportation, communication and exchange that enable commodities, capital and labour to be moved from place to place. However, the reach of empires was never complete. Even if the connective networks that gave empires shape were expansive and, in the case of the modern British Empire, world spanning, they were not all encompassing. While, in some regions, various agents of empires were able to fashion a host of thick and strong connections, there were gaps within these networks that allowed the persistence of key aspects of Indigenous life ways. In other territories ostensibly under British control, the empire had limited reach in the face of difficult terrain, resistant or insurgent 'native' communities, or because of the relative absence of marketable resources.

Thus, even as British imperial networks became more extensive as the nineteenth century progressed, 'native spaces' were entangled within the work of empire to varying degrees. Some spaces integral to the lives of Indigenous communities were firmly woven into the fabric of empire and this required profound shifts in the social organisation, material framework and cultural outlook of Indigenous communities; other spaces were only lightly touched by the reach of the various globalising forces that extended the formal power and informal influence of Britain. Voluntary associations created by British evangelicals committed to the project of bringing the Gospel to native communities created a host of such connections, even though evangelicals could, at times, be fierce critics of what they saw as the immorality or excesses of certain forms of colonialism. The British Protestant 'global overlay' created by missionaries—made up of mission stations, schools, hospitals, shipping and transportation networks, print shops and a seemingly ceaseless flow of texts—was a powerfully integrative force that provided a range of novel technologies, ideas and practices that were often reworked by Indigenous and colonised communities at the edge of empire, forming key elements of emergent modern cultural formations.[1]

My recent monograph, *Entanglements of Empire,* argued that thinking through the metaphor of 'entanglement' allows us to gain greater insights into the operation of empire in the Pacific and the abiding consequences of empire building than thinking of cross-cultural engagements as 'meetings' or 'encounters'. 'Entanglement' stresses both the mutually constitutive nature of these relationships that took shape at the edge of the empire and their transformative power, highlighting how they reshaped cultural formations, often in ways that were unpredictable and unexpected.[2] To gauge the impact of these entanglements, it is crucial to not only map pre-existing Indigenous cultural patterns, but to be aware of how those dynamics changed prior to (and during) the onset of cross-cultural engagement.[3]

With these aspirations at its heart, this chapter explores some of the entanglements that resulted from the extension of British missionary activity into Māori communities in Te Ika a Māui, New Zealand's

---

1   The notion of a 'global overlay' comes from Adshead 1997: 244.
2   Ballantyne 2014b: 16–18, 251–52, 257. An important earlier use of 'entanglement' in the Pacific was Thomas 1991. Other key works that have demonstrated the usefulness of 'entanglement' as a heuristic tool are Hamilton 1998: especially 3–4; Nuttall 2009.
3   Ballantyne 2005: 447–49.

North Island. It particularly focuses on the first decade of the Church Missionary Society (CMS) mission to New Zealand and the ways in which Māori engagement with the mission created new patterns of trade, catalysed new forms of movement and recalibrated and redirected long-established traditions of mobility. The analysis developed here is anchored in Mimi Sheller and John Urry's argument that reconstructing shifting forms and patterns of movement offers crucial insight into the changing shape and meaning of social formations.[4] New mobile orders were fundamental to the routine operations of missionary work, and mission stations—beginning with Hohi in 1823, then Kerikeri in 1819 and Te Puna and Paihia in 1823—reshaped the ways in which pathways and connections operated in the region. I particularly emphasise the connections between the motion of Indigenous people and the mobility of things, highlighting how novel technologies and media enabled and shaped new forms of travel, innovative ways of thinking about movement and new mechanisms for recording and explaining those experiences. Central to this argument is the notion that the mission immersed Māori in a world of paper—a paper empire—where paper was not only a key cultural material that was integral to the operation of missionary activity, but where it more broadly underpinned and directed the routines of administration, trade and mobility.[5]

The essay begins by briefly exploring some recent historical writing on Indigenous mobility before sketching how missionary activity reordered, at least partially, the ends, experiences and meanings of mobility on the New Zealand frontier. The final section focuses on paper—its importance in the mission and its connections to the kinetic new social formations that took shape in northern New Zealand from the 1810s. Here I suggest that, as a particular type of thing or artefact, paper was crucially important in an emergent new order because, like other types of objects, it could create connections between people.[6] However, unlike other objects, such as an adze, fishhook or hoe, the creation of connections between people was one of paper's primary functions and, because of its lightness and portability, it was able to do so over long distances.

***

---

4   Sheller and Urry 2006: 213.
5   I have developed my arguments about the connections between paper and empire in an arc of essays: Ballantyne 2011a; Ballantyne 2013; Ballantyne 2014a; Ballantyne 2016.
6   Hahn and Weis 2013.

Work on mobility is often structured by an assumption that movement has been a defining characteristic of modernity. Such arguments, of course, are themselves grounded by a series of dichotomised understandings that imagine Indigenous or colonised communities as place bound, local and traditional, as opposed to the open, global and dynamic nature of Western societies.[7] In the last decade or so, several scholars have challenged the old imperial equation of native and Indigenous with 'local' and 'fixed', and the world of European empires with 'global' and 'mobile';[8] they have suggested that native or Indigenous peoples could and did possess what James Clifford famously dubbed 'traveling cultures'.[9] In the Pacific, Damon Salesa has written about 'travel-happy Samoa', arguing that long before the European 'discovery' of Samoa in 1722, the people of those islands had created expansive worlds by voyaging, visiting and trading, as well as various exchange relationships. The rise of European empires and the consolidation of successive and competing colonial regimes in the Pacific certainly reshaped and redirected the 'circuitry' of mobility and social relations within the islands; however, Samoans and other Pacific peoples actively bent those pathways to their own purposes while continuing to move in ways that were largely outside or beyond the purview of colonial states.[10] More recently, Salesa has discussed the entangled histories of Fiji, Tonga, Samoa, Rotuma, Uvea, Futuna, Niuafo'ou and Niuatoputapu prior to the arrival of Europeans through the lens of a 'native sea'—an Indigenous complex of maritime movement and connection. Salesa's arguments are important because they demonstrate the weakness of old colonial assumptions that Pacific peoples were stable and fixed— both in terms of cultural development and physical location—prior to the intrusion of the British into Oceania. The long and deep history of mobility that Salesa draws our attention to shows that mobility predated modernity in the region, and that Europeans did not suddenly 'activate' the island communities.[11]

In a similar vein, I have demonstrated the need to recognise the importance of mobility in shaping the life ways of the Polynesian communities that settled in New Zealand from the thirteenth century.[12] It was only in

---

7   Ballantyne and Burton 2009; Salesa 2003; Ballantyne 2014c.
8   For one useful discussion of this within the Pacific, see Jolly 2001.
9   Clifford 1992.
10   Salesa 2003.
11   Salesa 2013a; Salesa 2013b.
12   Especially in Ballantyne 2011b.

the half century after sustained contact with Europeans following the arrival of Cook's *Endeavour* in 1769 that these peoples began describing themselves as 'tāngata Māori' or 'Māori': 'the normal people'. Even after this epistemological shift, the life of these communities continued to be structured around smaller functional units, whānau (extended family units) and hapū (sub-tribes or clans). For larger-scale economic activities and war making, hapū could be mobilised into the larger unit of the iwi (tribe).

The histories of hapū and iwi are typically understood as firmly anchored in space, being tied to specific rohe. Rohe are traditionally understood as the domain over which rangatira (hereditary leaders) of the allied kin groups that made up iwi exercised mana (authority). Such a political interpretation can also be complimented by a more geographically inflected reading. Rohe were the domains produced by the routine patterns and pathways of mobility of allied kin groups—groups that travelled regular circuits to source, process and trade food items and other valued resources, who travelled to meeting-up places for rituals and meetings, and who came together in times of conflict to form taua (war parties). These communities were linked not only by genealogical ties, but also shared pathways across the land and water and had strong ties to place, especially attachments to papa kāinga (home villages) and key landmarks such as maunga (mountains) and awa (rivers).

The apparent fixity of these referents is a modern phenomenon. Prior to the incursions of Europeans, mobility was integral to life ways and the territories that communities occupied often shifted significantly over time. As I have already suggested, mobility was at the core of daily life and the seasonal cycle of economic and social routines. Groups of kin would traverse the landscape to visit relatives, to engage in rituals or to gather together for major economic initiatives, such as large-scale harvesting, the bringing of new land into cultivation or construction projects. Movement also had important political dimensions as it was integral to the maintenance of the equilibrium between social collectives; taua muru (plundering parties) enabled kin groups to seek redress when social infractions impugned on their mana or created an intolerable imbalance. Given the manifold significance of motion and movement in the life ways of these groups, it is not surprising that one of the ways in which Māori describe the human world is 'te ao hurihuri': the world of motion, the ever-moving world. Thus, even though the direct connections from Te Ika a Māui to the rest of Oceania had become attenuated and atrophied long before Europeans arrived, complex circuits and pathways linked places and peoples, underscoring Sheller and Urry's insistence on the fundamental importance of mobility as an aspect of social organisation in all human societies.[13] Recent archaeological research has increasingly moved mobility to the centre of reconstructing the peopling of Te Ika a Māui and Te Wai Pounamu (New Zealand's South Island), and to understanding the development of pre-colonial social formations in these islands.[14]

The *Endeavour*'s careful circumnavigation of New Zealand in 1769–70 punctured the isolation of New Zealand from the rest of the Pacific world. However, it was not until the 1790s, when New Zealand's coasts began to effectively function as a frontier for the fledgling colony of New South Wales, that the place of mobility within the practices of kin groups in Te Ika a Māui was significantly reshaped. There has been surprisingly little work on these mobilities that transformed Māori life in the first half of the nineteenth century. There have been some studies of Māori travellers, but this work has largely been concerned with questions of 'experience' and has been driven by a desire to recover and document these life histories.[15] Rachel Standfield's chapter in this volume works to extend this scholarship beyond recovery of Māori experience to consider how Māori aspirations shaped mobility and early missionary travel in New Zealand. Less work has been undertaken on the reordering of Māori mobilities within the islands of New Zealand, especially in and around the 'musket wars' of the 1820s and 1830s, which fundamentally recalibrated the distribution of power and the geographies of settlement and kinship connections. This is not to suggest that this period has been neglected; rather, that it has primarily been approached through the lens of war and not the deep-seated geographic redistribution of tāngata/tākata whenua (people of the land).

This essay focuses on an even earlier period, exploring some of the mobilities that developed in association with the early years of the CMS mission that was formally established in the Bay of Islands in 1814, some six years after Samuel Marsden first began to formulate a plan for the evangelisation of Māori. Questions of mobility are prominent, albeit in an often analytically implicit way, in some recent work on the early

---

13   Sheller and Urry 2006.
14   Most notably, Walter, Jacomb and Bowron-Muth 2010.
15   Especially O'Malley 2015.

development of the mission. Several scholars, including Anne Salmond, Vincent O'Malley, Rachel Standfield, Alice Te Punga Somerville, Alison Jones and Kuni Jenkins, and Fred Cahir and Ian Clark, have drawn our attention to the significance of Māori travellers who played a key role in what James Belich has called the 'Māori discovery of Europe', but which would be better understood as the 'Māori discovery of the non-Polynesian world'.[16]

In many ways, these travels grew out of, and extended, the connections that developed out of Tuki and Huru's Norfolk Island sojourn following their kidnapping in April 1793.[17] A sequence of Māori men, including Te Pahi, Ruatara, Te Morenga, Māui, Titere and Tuai, travelled widely, and we have an increasing appreciation of their shifting apprehensions of the world. The stories of these pioneering voyages are very important; however, their experiences should not stand for 'Māori mobility' *tout court* in this period. Long-distance travel to the Australian colonies, Asia and Europe was one force that significantly reshaped the Māori world, but we need a broader apprehension of the importance of various forms of Māori mobility—both those that underwrote long-established traditions of war making and settlement, as well as those novel forms that developed in connection with the establishment of mission stations from 1814.

***

The CMS mission to New Zealand developed against a backdrop of acceleration, stretching and reshaping of Indigenous mobilities. Large-scale movements of kin groups became increasingly common in the period between the mid-1810s and 1840 as a result of shifting economic behaviour, warfare and a long and complex sequence of migrations and displacements. Even though New Zealand was not formally incorporated into the formal operation of British imperial sovereignty until 1840, the reach of British, Australian and Euroamerican traders was a powerful magnet, drawing individuals, trading parties and kin groups to sites of sustained cross-cultural trade, such as Kāwhia, Kerikeri, Kororāreka, Tāmaki, Mahia and Kāpiti. These commercial engagements—which were important vectors for the introduction of new weapons, technologies, animals and plants—were a significant catalyst that helped to energise

---

16   Belich 1996; Standfield 2012; Te Punga Somerville 2012; Jones and Jenkins 2011; Cahir and Clark 2014; Jones and Jenkins 2011.
17   Binney 2004.

a complex and sprawling sequence of military campaigns. From their base in the Bay of Islands and parts of the Hokianga, Ngāpuhi leaders initiated a series of devastating raids south to Tāmaki, Hauraki, Rotorua and down the east coast of Te Ika a Māui between 1819 and 1823. These raids were facilitated by Ngāpuhi's domination of cross-cultural trade. Ngāpuhi taua enjoyed a significant military advantage over their southern rivals as a result of their near monopoly on the musket trade (including with the rogue missionary Thomas Kendall), and their embrace of this new military technology allowed Ngāpuhi to seek utu (retribution, balance) for the various take (causes, issues) that underpinned this extended campaign of war making.

These increasingly extended raids to the south were further enabled by a significant shift in the material base of the tribe as a result of cross-cultural trade. By 1810, northern kin groups had embraced potato cultivation. Potatoes were much hardier than frost-sensitive kūmara (Polynesian sweet potato); this allowed rangatira to bring freshly cleared areas into cultivation to increase the output of production. Potatoes were also a key commodity in cross-cultural trade: they enabled groups in the Bay of Islands to access new tools and weapons from visiting European and American vessels. This encouraged rangatira to initiate large-scale potato cultivation that required a significant increase in labour inputs into production.[18] The connections between the shift to potato production and the intensification of inter-tribal warfare in Te Ika a Māui between the 1810s and 1830s remains contentious; however, there is some evidence to suggest that potatoes were the significant material base that sustained a protracted sequence of military campaigns and, further, that their cultivation encouraged the expanded use of war captives as a labour force.[19]

Ngāpuhi were not the only moving force in this age of hyperactive motion; further south, Ngāti Toa also launched a prolonged sequence of raids and campaigns. In the wake of ongoing conflicts over the rich resources and trading opportunities in the Kāwhia region with their Waikato and Maniapoto rivals, Ngāti Toa pushed south to the Kāpiti region in the south-west of Te Ika a Māui in 1821–22. After asserting their authority in the battle at Waiorua in 1824, Ngāti Toa then launched a sequence of

---

18   Salmond 1997: 422.
19   Ballara 2003: 397–98. Compare Ballara's cautious reading of the role of potatoes in providing the material base for the extension of Maori warfare—she suggests that they may have only become very significant in the 1830s—with Belich's more assertive reading: Belich 1996: 159.

long-distance raids from their Kāpiti stronghold into Te Wai Pounamu from 1831 that significantly impacted the demographics, settlement patterns and politics of the south. Four years later, Ngāti Toa's close kin, Ngāti Mutunga and Ngāti Tama, who had been displaced from northern Taranaki, travelled to Rēkohu (Chatham Islands), where they swiftly asserted their dominance over the Moriori people. Taken together, these campaigns, migrations and displacements redrew the demographic and political maps of Te Ika a Māui, Te Wai Pounamu and Rēkohu.

This intense period of accelerated and extensive movement was largely closed down by the formal assertion of British sovereignty over New Zealand in 1840. British rule constrained some traditional forms of Māori mobility, closing off some ways of moving across the landscape while simultaneously fashioning a new matrix of roads, markets, towns and ports that inflected both 'traditional' practices and the pattern of Māori engagement with the colonial economy and state institutions. At the same time, British power worked to calcify rohe as 'traditional' domains of the 'great chiefs' of the 'tribes' that loomed so large in the imagination of the colonial state.

***

In exploring the 'entanglement' of missionary and Māori mobilities, it is crucial to recognise the ways in which missionaries had to accommodate themselves to Māori ways of moving and the rules governing mobility. Missionaries, like the whalers, traders and sailors who frequented New Zealand's coastlines, were inhabiting landscapes that were encoded with meaning. Given both their long-term commitment to living among Māori and their desire to ultimately create native churches, missionaries had to grapple with the weight of traditional beliefs and practices in ways that marked them off from other newcomers. Tapu—things that were set apart and 'sacred' because they were connected to the workings of atua (supernatural powers, gods)—was a powerful challenge for missionaries eager to establish the authority of their god and cosmology. Many scholars, including, most recently, Angela Middleton, have argued that missionaries attacked tapu and discounted as profane Māori beliefs that tapu was manifest in the local landscape.[20] However, this argument is called into question by evidence of significant accommodations made on

20 Middleton 2008: 48–50. However, Middleton recognised that the missionaries were forced to make some accommodations to tapu in the early years of the mission.

mission stations to the power of tapu in the Māori world. For example, in 1817, Thomas Kendall explained to Samuel Marsden that the mission's relationships with local peoples and landscapes were constrained by tapu, especially those practices associated with death:

> In selecting a portion of land for a settlement, it would be advisable to take care that it be as clear as possible of what the natives call the wahhe taboo [wāhi tapu]. Wherever a person has breathed his last, or his bones have been laid for a time, there is always a piece of timber set up, if there is no tree already growing, to perpetuate his memory. This [wāhi tapu] is not suffered to be molested, and is held sacred both by friends and strangers. Amongst the natives, the least disrespect paid to their sacred relics or religious ceremonies and customs is considered a sufficient ground for a war by enemies and for a public debate by friends.[21]

As the Ngāpuhi elder and scholar Patu Hohepa has noted, traditional death ways had 'spread layers of tapu' over the terrain in the Bay of Islands. The region's landscape was studded with tapu sites where the deceased were prepared for display or burial, where exhumed bones were painted with ochre in preparation for secondary burial, and where bodies were buried and bones were finally interred.[22] Kendall's letter underscores the degree to which missionaries apprehended the power of these practices and felt constrained by tapu's presence and power.

Kendall noted that the pioneering cohort of missionaries had inadvertently violated tapu, triggering conflict:

> My colleague, Mr. Hall, and Mrs. Hall, suffered at Whitangee on account of the disrespect which had been paid by Warrakkee's people to some sacred relic, and not on account of any ill-will which the assailants entertained towards them.[23]

This referred to a taua muru (plunder party) that raided the Halls' new base at Waitangi in January 1816. The toa (warriors) threw William Hall to the ground and threatened him with weapons; they struck Dinah Hall in the face when she came to her husband's aid, temporarily blinding her. The party then plundered the mission house, stripping it of its bedding and taking tools, cooking utensils, an axe and two guns.[24] The plundering was a form of structured punishment. The Halls had unwittingly settled on land that had belonged to the recently deceased rangatira Waraki. It

---

21 Kendall 1817.
22 Hohepa 2007: 90.
23 Kendall 1817.
24 Hall 1816a. On taua muru see Ballara 2003: 103–11.

seems that Waraki's death, together with the vulnerability of the Halls, provided an occasion for a rival group to exact utu for an earlier infraction of tapu by Waraki's people.

Even as they were fiercely critical of tapu, missionaries recognised its cultural power; they were generally very careful to avoid any infractions on wāhi tapu. Grant Phillipson has noted that in negotiations for the purchase of land by the CMS, missionaries affirmed that they would respect wāhi tapu.[25] This understanding shaped how the missionaries ordered their own activity in the Bay of Islands, as they recognised that their own burials had to be undertaken with care. Essentially, the missionaries came to agree that burials at which they officiated had to occur within the boundaries of mission stations, thereby avoiding any implication that they were making claims to any other site through burials. This practice took shape from the winter of 1816, with the sudden death of Sarah Shergold.[26] Although the missionaries had witnessed many Māori deaths in the first 18 months of their work, Shergold was the first European to die since the establishment of the mission. William Hall spent a full day constructing a coffin and preparing the grave, which was dug at an unspecified location within the station at Hohi.[27]

Thus, quite quickly, the fledgling missionary community came to understand that they were living in a landscape brimming with history and meaning. In the early years of the mission, they felt very much under the control of their powerful chiefly patrons and that they had limited ability to move and act independently. The early mission stations were located at sites selected by their chiefly patrons. The first missionary settlement was established under the mantle of the rangatira Ruatara on narrow terraces at Hohi under the Ruatara's stronghold, the pā (fortified settlement) at Rangihoua. Ruatara was vital to the foundation of the mission: he had a close relationship with Samuel Marsden, he brokered amicable relationships for the mission with other northern kin groups and he guided Marsden on his travels in New Zealand. Ruatara also enabled the mission to be established in such a politically influential site as Rangihoua. The great rangatira, Hongi Hika, also had strong connections there. Ruatara and Hongi placed clear parameters and constraints on the development of the mission. The complex of simple buildings erected at

25 Phillipson 2007: 64.
26 Hall 1816b: 25 July 1816.
27 Hall 1816b: 25 July 1816.

Hohi was positioned so that the mission was under constant surveillance from the pā. Moreover, the narrow terraces they occupied provided limited productive land and no easily accessible space for future growth.

The pioneering missionaries Thomas Kendall and John King were all too aware of the implications of this arrangement; they could not be self-sustaining and were forced to rely on the CMS to provide them with goods to trade with local Māori. Kendall complained in 1815:

> We have now resided nearly two years at this place, and to all appearances there is no probability of our obtaining the necessaries of life in any other way than at the expense of the Society. The spot on which we live is barren, and … is so mountainous that it is quite unsuitable for the purpose of cultivation or for cattle.[28]

The inability of the missionaries to farm or garden meant that they remained heavily dependent on influential rangatira such as Hongi. From the very beginning of the mission, Hongi had tried to persuade Marsden that a missionary settlement should be established at Kerikeri, in the north-west corner of the Bay of Islands where the Kerikeri River flowed into a sheltered basin. Hongi's mana extended over this location, as his father, Te Hotete, had occupied the adjacent Kororipo pā in the 1790s.[29] This pā not only had commanding views of the basin and the bay, it also stood at the hinge between the ocean and the land, guarding the primary pathway to the significant centres of settlement and cultivation in the interior, including Hongi's great pā Ōkuratope. Kerikeri was at the heart of Hongi's growing power in the 1810s and 1820s. It provided access to excellent fishing and had excellent gravel-rich soils; it also served as a key military centre. It was the base from which Hongi launched his sequence of campaigns to the south and his taua returned to Kerikeri from war with their captives.[30]

Marsden and Hongi agreed in 1815 that the missionaries based at Hohi would be able to plant wheat at Kerikeri in the following spring, signalling that a formal connection was developing between the mission and the site.[31] Hongi worked hard to extend the relationship. During Marsden's second visit to Te Ika a Māui in 1819, Hongi took him and a group

---

28 Kendall 1816a.
29 Sissons 2007: 47.
30 Binney 2007: 10–12.
31 Sissons 2007: 47.

of missionaries up the Kerikeri River and formally offered the mission the right to use any lands that suited their purposes. The evangelical party was delighted by the site. Marsden observed that the soil was:

> Rich, the land pretty level, free from timber, easy to work with the plough and bounded by a fine freshwater river, and the communication by water free and open to any part of the Bay of Islands.[32]

The missionaries' desire to establish a permanent settlement at Kerikeri underlined, and further enhanced, the mana of Hongi. He rightly believed that having a mission station at Kerikeri would draw new flows of European goods into his domain and cement his domination over cross-cultural trade in the bay. Moreover, he knew this commercial advantage might enhance the military superiority of his kin, as controlling the reach of imperial trading networks into northern New Zealand would assist Hongi in sustaining the resource-hungry military actions he continued to launch against his rivals and competitors far to the south.

The implications of these shifts in the lines of trade were clearly understood by rival chiefs and kin groups. Korokoro, a Ngare Raumati chief whose authority rested in the coastal lands on the south side of the bay and in the islands in the east of the region, complained to Marsden about the impact of placing a mission station at Kerikeri. He explained that it was marginalising his people while consolidating Hongi's strategic advantage—a shift that was disrupting the relationships between kin groups in the region. Marsden noted that Korokoro believed that 'it was too great an affliction for all the Europeans to reside with Shunghee'. Marsden worked hard to placate Korokoro's concerns, visiting Korokoro's people near Paroa on the south side of the bay. Marsden promised to consider locating a mission near Paroa in the future, thereby rebalancing the circuitry of trade—a possibility that was never realised.[33]

In the 1820s, Hongi's relationships with the missionaries became increasingly tense as a result of his abiding links to the transgressive Thomas Kendall, who was removed from the mission in 1822. To Hongi's frustration, most missionaries, unlike Kendall, refused to engage in the musket trade or aid in having the weapons repaired. Nevertheless, a symbiotic relationship persisted between the great chief and the mission until Hongi's death in 1828, even if Hongi was less enthusiastic about Christian teaching than the benefits of trade.

---

32 Marsden 1819a.
33 Marsden 1819b.

By the end of the 1820s, Kerikeri and Hohi, especially the latter, had diminished as centres of Māori population and been eclipsed as primary trading centres. Ongoing missionary complaints about the limits of the Hohi site ultimately convinced the CMS to approve the mission on the north side of the bay to relocate a short distance to the west to Te Puna, a site that Kendall had preferred since 1815.[34] While Te Puna had greater agricultural potential, in reality, oscillations in the economic and social geography of the bay had made both Hohi and Te Puna relatively marginal. The pull of Hongi's power, especially inland at Ōkuratope, shifted the political geography of the region. At the same time, the prominence of Kororāreka (on the south side of the bay) as an anchorage and site of cross-cultural trade in weapons, tools, alcohol and sex meant that Te Puna was no longer the 'capital' of the bay, as it had been in the first decade of the nineteenth century under Te Pahi's influence.[35]

The north side of the bay was increasingly overshadowed as a consequence of the changing geography of missionary settlements and, in particular, the growing importance of the Paihia mission founded in the south-west. The mission's new leader, Henry Williams, was concerned at what he understood as the missionaries' dependence on, and subordination to, Māori powerbrokers. From the time of his arrival in New Zealand, Williams was also frustrated by the mission's reliance on the unreliable service provided by visiting ships and trade at Kororāreka. The station, established in 1823 at Paihia on the banks of the Kawakawa River in the south-west of the bay, put the mission on a more secure foundation. Chosen by Williams and Marsden, Paihia was a site that the missionaries saw as a new beginning for the mission. It was selected, in part, because of strong personal connections between Marsden and a key local rangatira, Te Koki. In Marsden's account of his visit to Paihia in August 1823, he noted that Te Koki, a 'very worthy man', had spent time with him at Parramatta.[36] Their personal bond was quite substantial; after Te Koki's son, Te Ahara, died at the Parramatta Native Institution, Marsden gave an undertaking that he would send a missionary to Te Koki and his people.[37] Williams understood the strength of the bond that underpinned the foundation of the missionary settlement at Paihia, for even as he hoped to secure more independence for the mission, he understood that 'the missionary

34   Kendall 1816a.
35   Middleton 2008: 69.
36   Marsden 1823a.
37   Rogers 1961: 31, footnote 1.

becomes one with the tribe with which he is connected'.[38] In addition to discharging this important personal obligation, the foundation of the mission at Paihia suggests that Marsden remained aware of the importance of balancing the interests of the kin groups on either side of the bay, even if he could not satisfy Korokoro's desire for a mission at Paroa. Te Koki was connected to Pomare, Tara and Te Morenga, important chiefs and key figures in the 'southern alliance' of hapū that controlled the southern and south-western sections of the bay.

It quickly became clear that the Paihia site was extremely advantageous, providing the mission with a secure material base that placed it at the centre of a new set of expansive networks. The mission was built on good, flat ground that sustained an excellent garden and orchard. It also had access to excellent local sites for fishing and gathering shellfish, a sheltered beach and good lines of sight across the bay.[39]

Given the importance of these maritime connections, it is hardly surprising that the extension of the mission's shipping capacity was a high priority. Soon after his arrival, Williams committed the mission to constructing its own New Zealand–based vessel in an effort to limit the mission's dependence on Māori and on the rhythms of trans-Tasman shipping. Under Williams' oversight, Māori workers played a key role in the construction of a schooner named the *Herald*. The vessel, which was constructed on the beach at Paihia, greatly enhanced the ability of the missionaries to initiate and directly control communications with New South Wales. It was equally significant in recalibrating social relations within Te Ika a Māui, as it enabled missionaries and their 'native teachers' to travel long distances with relative speed; it also allowed the mission to extend its influence down the east coast to Tauranga and the west coast via the North Cape.[40] As well as carrying the Gospel to new frontiers of evangelisation, the missionaries were able to exercise much more control over the movement of food, livestock, tools and trade goods that were the lifeblood of the mission. The *Herald* fundamentally reordered the economics of the mission, as it could now trade directly with more isolated hapū and iwi who accepted fishhooks as a medium of exchange rather than demanding muskets. The mission enjoyed greater security and its standing (mana) was enhanced, as the accumulation of food and

38 Williams 1823: 24 October.
39 Williams 1823: 13 November.
40 Middleton 2008: 225.

valued objects was a key marker of power and status in the Māori world. In 1825, Williams noted that the missionaries would no longer be at 'their wits' end for common necessaries', which meant that they would be much less dependent on Te Koki—who had effectively been their 'liege lord'.[41] Thus, the *Herald* allowed the mission to begin to temper the power of the chiefly patrons who exercised so much control over the mission's early development. The enhanced commercial capacity and confidence that flowed from it enabled the missionaries to become more assertive in emphasising the value of the Gospel, the power of the Christian God and the need for Māori to embrace 'new' ways of thought and action.

The establishment of a mission station inland at Waimate in 1831 marked a dilution of the mission's dependence on chiefly patrons and protectors. Even though the Waimate mission, like the one at Paihia, had its genesis in Marsden's connection with Hongi, the missionaries there had no 'liege lord'. It was a site where Hongi exercised power. Marsden and his party had been greatly impressed when Hongi showed them the pā's triple palisades and the 30 acres of potatoes and kūmara planted around the pā in 1815.[42] Marsden encouraged Hongi to develop this agricultural capacity; in an 1823 letter, he promised to provide Hongi with tools and seeds for new cultivations at Waimate. Marsden stressed that agricultural improvement should be the rangatira's priority, and that he should build his mana through cultivation and the provision of food, not raiding to the south: 'Then you will become a very great man and will be able to feed and clothe many people'.[43] In 1824, Marden sent the missionary farmer Richard Davis to New Zealand. He introduced Davis to Hongi as 'a gentleman who would be able to make a farm at Wymatte [sic]'.[44] A successful tenant farmer from Dorset, Davis taught Hongi's people how to use a plough and bullocks, cultivate wheat and produce flour. In the 1830s, the Waimate station developed in keeping with Davis' vision of a mixed English farm of some 250 acres. However, the mission had difficulty sourcing adequate labour, it was undersupplied with suitable tools and its livestock were vulnerable to attacks by dogs owned by local Māori. In the early 1840s, it was converted by the newly arrived Bishop Selwyn into an educational establishment.[45] Nevertheless, Waimate was

---

41 Williams, journal entry, 6 January 1825, cited in Fitzgerald 2011: 52–53.
42 Nicholas 1817: i, 333.
43 Marsden 1823b; Parsonson 1980.
44 Marsden 1824.
45 Hargreaves 1962.

a crucial experiment that demonstrated the ability of missionaries to pursue their own model of economic organisation—a degree of autonomy that increased the appeal of Christianity and the influence of missionaries as both peacemakers and agents of social change more broadly.[46]

***

While the development of missionary settlements was deeply embedded in the changing economic and social geography of northern Te Ika a Māui, and played a key role in shaping lines of trade and movement across and beyond the Bay of Islands, they also rerouted patterns of mobility on a smaller scale at a daily level. *Entanglements of Empire* emphasised the ways in which mobility structured the everyday relationships between missionaries, mission workers and Māori, underwriting the daily routines of missionary labour; the book also stressed the pivotal role that mobility played in shaping the nature of mission stations. Arguing against the tendency in the existing historiography to see the stations as enclosed European or British spaces separated from the Māori world by fences, it noted both the persistent insecurity of the stations and the regular pulses of movement that wove them into local society.[47]

Rather than focusing on fences as cultural boundaries and barriers, it is important to remember that the gates to the station enabled connection. The opening of the gates enabled and directed the quotidian mobilities of life on mission stations to unfold. Indeed, we might follow Anna Tsing's formulation and understand the mission's gates as channelling the 'friction' that was an integral part of these entanglement of cultures, shaping the 'grip of worldly encounter'.[48] Māori from local settlements or more distant communities would enter into missionary settlements to undertake work in, or around, the houses, in the workshops, at the sawyer's pit, blacksmith's shop or in the gardens and fields. Children, youths and adults would come into stations for school or more informal lessons, as well as for prayer and formal services. More irregular traffic brought influential visitors: chiefly patrons and Māori leaders from distant communities, British officials, European travellers and European and American sea captains.

---

46 Ballantyne 2014b: 76–77, 100, 136.
47 Ballantyne 2014b: 90–97; cf. Middleton 2008; Fitzgerald 2001.
48 Tsing 2004: 1.

Things also moved in and out of the gates. Māori brought fish and shellfish into the stations, providing an important food source for the mission. Kai moana (seafood) was just one element in a steady traffic of food and animals: poultry, livestock and horses came into the mission and went out again, as did seeds, seedlings and new food plants. While iron and building materials (timber, raupo and fern) were brought into the stations, nails, toki (adzes), and simple tools moved out of the smithy, as did sawn timber from the sawyers' pits and furniture from William Hall's workshop. In addition, many Māori carried beads, cloth, clothes, hats, soap, food and fishhooks—important gifts, rewards and payments given by missionaries—back to their communities, meaning that the material framework of the mission was increasingly woven into the life ways of Māori communities. The Gospel too moved in and out of the mission; missionaries and native teachers who travelled out to itinerate around the bay, or to visit new frontiers where missionaries were not yet formally established, carried printed texts, while many Māori who visited the mission left carrying printed portions of Scripture.[49]

These on-the-ground economic relationships were dependent on maritime connections that provided the mission with trade goods. Ships and shipping were the lifeblood of the mission; however, they were also a constant concern, both to missionary families and to Marsden who, over the long run, became adept at coordinating mail and the movement of goods and people through a patchy and irregular set of oceanic networks. Until 1830, all of the mission stations were littoral communities, reflecting the importance of shipping to their function. Missions were hubs visited by Māori waka, mission ships and other vessels that called at the Bay of Islands. After unloading their cargoes of tools, people, seeds, animals, foodstuffs, commodities, clothes, materials, shoes, books, mail and so on, European ships loaded letters, ethnographic artefacts, missionary travellers and their families, and Māori guides and political brokers (such as Ruatara and Te Morenga). In turn, this maritime traffic articulated with shipping and commercial networks centred on Port Jackson, expansive trans-Pacific trading networks and the global commercial traffic fashioned by the British Empire. These connections underwrote the governance of the mission through correspondence, and were crucial in allowing missionaries to maintain their own familial networks.

***

---

49   Ballantyne 2014b: 94.

Paper was one of the key instruments that came to shape social relations in and around the mission. Paper was central to the development of plans for the mission, underwriting its eventual foundation and directing its subsequent growth. The movement of paper framed the physical extension of evangelisation in the 1830s: north towards Kaitaia, south towards Manukau, the Waikato, the area around the Waihou River, Tauranga and to the East Cape, and further south to Otaki. Letters of persuasion and argument, committee minutes, and instructions and directives framed a strategy of expansion; these paper instruments moved expansively, by foot and on horseback, and on waka and ships within Te Ika a Māui and beyond to Port Jackson and London. The expansion of the mission was also pushed forward by Māori themselves; influential chiefs wrote beseechingly, requesting missionaries, teachers and schools, while native catechists carried the Gospel far beyond the frontiers of the mission's circuits of itineration, and new converts spread the Christian message through texts and oral conversation.

It is important to assess the connections between mobility, paper and literacy in the 1810s—a period that the historiography has characterised as long predating the formal impact of Christianity, literacy and the printed word. Paper is a recurrent concern in the early letters and journals of the missionaries, reflecting its importance to their daily practices. When Thomas Kendall wrote to the CMS in October 1816, he requested a bell for the school and outlined the various types of paper he required: 'Post & Letter Paper that will bear ink well. I am almost entirely without. The paper intended for me was used on account of the New Zealanders first Book at Port Jackson'. He also requested:

3 Doz copy Books Extra paper
3 Doz Foolsc for the Settlers Children & ciphering Books Extra paper ...
Quills & copy Books & Ink for the Native children.[50]

In a December 1818 letter, Kendall noted that he 'wanted for the Native Boys':

6 reams of writing paper that will bear ink well
6 Quires of paper for Copy Book covers
12 papers of ink powder
6 Lead Ink stands
1000 Quills.[51]

---

50 Kendall 1816b.
51 Kendall 1818.

Through the mission's writing exercises and its quills, ink, pencils, slates and paper, literacy became a significant component of the northern Māori world by 1820; its reach was extended, deepened and further democratised in the 1820s and 1830s.[52] There is some evidence that suggests that literacy was part of the novel, cultural package that made Christianity attractive to some Māori and that its accoutrements (i.e. paper and pens) were valued by those Māori who saw the mission primarily as an opportunity to access new technologies and skills (Hongi Hika is an excellent example of that dynamic). These new media and novel skills were woven into many aspects of Māori life, being used to communicate ideas and news across long distances; they were pivotal in concluding agreements of various kinds with missionaries, traders and other newcomers; they were woven into bodily adornment and decorative schema, sometimes functioning as talisman; and were intimately connected with the spread of Christian thought and teaching. As I have shown elsewhere, the chronological and geographical spread of the 'culture of paper' was regionally particular—the pattern in the far south diverged from the north in significant ways—but what is particularly important here is the distinctive materiality of paper when viewed against the media that underwrote the traditional Māori knowledge order.[53]

While it is commonplace to designate Māori culture as 'oral', in reality, the pre-European peoples of Te Ika a Māui and Te Wai Pounamu stored and encoded knowledge in a range of objects. Prior to the arrival of Europeans, the knowledge-bearing objects of the people of Te Ika a Māui were typically made out of wood, bone, or pounamu (jade), and their cultural value was underlined by their highly worked nature. Important knowledge was encoded into the elaborate carvings that decorated houses and meeting places, the ornamentation on treasured weapons and musical instruments, the forms of various worked figures used for architectural or personal ornamentation, and into rākau whakapapa (genealogical rods or staffs). Such objects often stored information about community history (especially key ancestors) or the connections between atua (supernatural powers or gods) and the human world. Often the physical form of these objects or decorative schema operated as a prompt, providing a starting point or framework for a narrative, rather than an entire narrative or body of knowledge. Rākau whakapapa did not provide the names and

---

52   Middleton 2008.
53   Ballantyne 2011a.

relationships of all ancestors; instead, their carved form provided a physical framework for the recitation of genealogy. Thus, they functioned as both an incitement to kōrero (speech) and a way of organising recall and recitation. They were tangible physical guides around which genealogical information could be recalled, organised and recited. The construction of these objects in hard-wearing materials meant that they were long lasting and could not easily be changed or revised; they were valuable because of their particularity and durability. As such, these objects were well suited to communicating knowledge across time. Within the analytical framework of Harold Innis' pioneering studies of media and communication, these objects were 'time-binding'; they enabled the transmission of knowledge between the generations, embodying the validity of traditional knowledge and the cultural authority of those who mastered such bodies of information and understanding.[54]

Conversely, the order championed by missionaries was expansive—it was geared to communication across space, connecting missionaries in New Zealand to the dispersed communities among whom they itinerated, to Marsden and the colonial authorities in New South Wales and to the CMS's secretaries in London. Generally speaking, the missionaries valued literacy, paper and printing; media and knowledge that were geared towards transcending physical space; and sharing news, information, knowledge and ideas over long distances.

Harold Innis termed these kinds of activities and aspirations 'space-binding knowledge practices'. As I have observed elsewhere, this incoming order tended to value the attainment of education over rank and celebrate exchange and debate rather than retention; it was oriented towards the expansiveness of a dispersed empire and global community of Protestantism over the confines of a local community defined by genealogical ties.[55] Fundamentally, the missionaries valued mobility, motion and the open movement of ideas—dynamics that were central to the British evangelical revival and that, as Joel Mokyr has shown, encoded British economic thought and practice in the early nineteenth century.[56] However, we must guard against seeing these knowledge orders as fixed, rigid and slow moving, for there is strong archival evidence to point to the ability of Māori to quickly deploy and rework new ideas, technologies

54   Innis 1950; Innis 1951.
55   Innis 1950; Innis 1951.
56   Mokyr 2009.

and skills on the mission stations—evidence that reinforces Michael Stevens' recent arguments about the porousness and flexibility of Māori mentalities and practices.[57]

The 'culture of paper' was more than the connective tissue of the mission, it was also central to the mission's ability to 'account'—a flexible verb that encompassed the provision of descriptive written narratives, the creation of records of stock, income and expenditure and, even more specifically, a particular type of bill. Missions were a type of bureaucratic regime and 'accountability' was a significant component of the mission's function. Accounting for the dispersal of gifts and items of trade was a constant concern within the archives of the CMS in New Zealand in the 1810s and 1820s.

Writing also was a way of keeping track of Māori, especially for the schoolteacher Thomas Kendall and his assistant, William Carlisle. Their roll for the Rangihoua school in October 1816 recorded the attendance of some 51 pupils. The document shows the extent to which the missionaries had to accommodate the rhythms of movement that were integral to Māori social and economic life. For example, 'A Hooia' missed school for the second half of the month as she was 'on a journey'; 'Ka dooa' left the school altogether having 'gone to Whitianga'; 'A Keena' missed a week of lessons while they were 'on a journey'; 'Taa hoo horo' did not attend in the middle of the month for the same reason; 'A Hoongha', 'Titeedoea', 'A Peeko' and 'A Too' were all absent for the entire month while they were 'at the sweet potato grounds'; and 'A Hei', 'A Kahou', 'A Moe', 'Na Motoo', 'Heena Hoodoo' and 'A Ranee' all missed instruction as they were recorded as being 'at work' for periods of time. The school records give a sense of motion and movement and the bustling rhythms of agriculture, trade and travel. Pupils moved in and out of the school and some, such as 'Ranghee Totto', whose 'residence' was noted as being at a 'great distance', travelled extensively to attend the school. Kendall and Carlisle noted:

> The weather being generally fine and pleasant during the present month and the Natives of Ranghee Hoo [being] busy in preparing the Grounds for the purpose of planting sweet Potatoes, many Scholars have been occasionally absent. We have been also under the necessity of following several of our pupils into the Bush, where we have taught them their

---

57   Stevens 2011; Stevens 2015; Ballantyne 2014b.

Lessons. We have promised to each Scholar a set of Beads as rewards with a view to prevent them leaving the School house as little as possible. The children are to attend one month for the Beads.[58]

On 19 August 1816, the missionaries noted that attendance at the school was low, as several students were 'absent procuring cockles'. Schooling was also interrupted by visitors. On 21 August, it was noted that 'interuptions [sic] from the Chief Werea and his party' were a distraction; three days later, the school was 'visited by the chief Toutaddee & family'. A brief note for 29 August—'Kumokuno, Shunghee & their party'—suggests that further interruptions followed. On 16 and 17 September, successive entries noted: 'A party of Scholars absent procuring cockles; Several Scholars in the Sweet Potato grounds in the day time'.[59] This suggests that, while mission stations redrew lines of connection within the northern Māori world as they became significant centres of trade (including muskets), they had little impact on the mobilities, large and small, that underwrote the predominant patterns of Māori labour until at least the early 1820s.[60]

Early printed texts, such as *A Grammar and Vocabulary of the Language of New Zealand* (1820), suggest that the foundation of the mission recalibrated some of the possibilities for mobility. Although traditionally attributed to Thomas Kendall in collaboration with the Orientalist linguist Professor Samuel Lee, recent work by Alison Jones and Kuni Jenkins has reframed the *Grammar* as a kind of co-creation or co-production strongly imprinted by Kendall's travelling companions, Hongi Hika and Waikato, and by Kendall's earlier Māori teachers.[61] The *Grammar* is shot through with movement: people come and go, meet, return and depart. One of the verbs used to illustrate various moods is 'aire' ('haere'): to travel, walk, continue, depart and, when followed by 'mai', to come.[62] Of course, 'to go' is a basic grammatical construction in many languages; however, the prominence of this perhaps reflects the mobility of missionaries and their Māori patrons, as well as the frequent meetings and encounters with new peoples that were integral to evangelisation—moments loaded with possibility and danger within te ao Māori (the Māori world). The *Grammar* features dialogues and vocabulary connected to ships, journeys, rivers, harbours and travel, both over short and long distances. One dialogue

---

58   Church Missionary Society 1816a.
59   Church Missionary Society 1816b.
60   Ballantyne 2014b.
61   Jones and Jenkins 2011.
62   Kendall 1820: 35–45.

discusses Hongi's departure for England and his planned return. New vocabulary related to European transportation technologies, such as 'a cabin of the ship' ('E páre-máta no te kaipúke'), were prominent.[63] So too was a sense of confidence and power. Another of the dialogues asks about the voyage of Hongi and his party to England: 'what are they going to do'? The answer is revealing:

> Ko te títiro átu óki ki te pai o te wenúa óki, kit e ánga o te pakeha óki, ki te tíni o te tángata óki.

> To see the goodness of the land, the occupations of the people, the number of the inhabitants.[64]

Here the imperial gaze was reversed. It was the powerful Māori rangatira who were crossing the world to assess and evaluate distant lands. While this journey allowed Kendall to shore up his relationship with Hongi, who had emerged as the most powerful of the leaders in the Bay of Islands, the two rangatira made their motivations for this trip clear. Soon after their arrival in England, Kendall recorded their demands. Kendall was to aid them in putting together a party of men to 'dig up the ground' in search of iron ore, and to gather more 'preachers' and 100 settlers to be taken to New Zealand. The missionary was also to furnish the chiefs with a large dog each as a marker of their mana, and to recruit a contingent of 20 soldiers accompanied by three officers.[65] With its references to 'Ingland' (England), 'Port Jákson' (Port Jackson) and 'Paramáta' (Parramatta), the *Grammar* captures the expansion of te ao Māori. If the human world is te ao hurihuri (the changing or turning world), then the establishment of the CMS mission, the engagement of Māori with the global reach of British missionary and imperial networks, and their growing interest in the Bible (as a deep and expansive store of stories), simultaneously stretched that world in range of ways. Books and ships, pens and paper, and Bibles and maps became important parts of Indigenous life, and proved to be central in reordering relationships within and between communities over the subsequent decades as Māori grappled with the opportunities and terrible dangers of an expanded te ao hurihuri—a mobile and connected world.

---

63   Kendall 1820: 69.
64   Kendall 1820: 97.
65   Church Missionary Society 1820.

References

Adshead, S.A.M. 1997, *Material Culture in Europe and China, 1400–1800: The Rise of Consumerism*, Macmillan, Basingstoke. doi.org/10.1007/978-1-349-25762-1

Ballantyne, Tony 2005, 'Religion, difference, and the limits of British imperial history', *Victorian Studies* 47(3): 427–55. doi.org/10.2979/VIC.2005.47.3.427

Ballantyne, Tony 2011a, 'Paper, pen, and print: The transformation of the Kai Tahu knowledge order', *Comparative Studies in Society & History* 53(2): 232–60. doi.org/10.1017/S0010417511000041

Ballantyne, Tony 2011b, 'On place, space and mobility in nineteenth-century New Zealand', *New Zealand Journal of History* 45(1): 50–70.

Ballantyne, Tony 2013, 'Indien und die globalisierung kolonialen wissens', in *Von Käfern, Märkten und Menschen: Kolonialismus und Wissen in der Moderne*, Rebekka Habermas and Alexandra Przyrembel (eds), Vandenhoeck & Ruprecht, Göttingen: 115–25. doi.org/10.13109/9783666300196.115

Ballantyne, Tony 2014a, 'Contesting the empire of paper: Cultures of print and anti-colonialism in the modern British Empire', in *Indigenous Networks: Mobility, Connections and Exchange,* Jane Lydon and Jane Carey (eds), Routledge, London: 219–40.

Ballantyne, Tony 2014b, *Entanglements of Empire: Missionaries, Maori and the Question of the Body*, Duke University Press, Durham. doi.org/10.1215/9780822375883

Ballantyne, Tony 2014c, 'Mobility, empire, colonisation', *History Australia* 14(2): 7–37.

Ballantyne, Tony 2016, 'Moving texts and "humane sentiment": Materiality, mobility and the emotions of imperial humanitarianism', *Journal of Colonialism and Colonial History* 17(1). doi.org/10.1353/cch.2016.0000

Ballantyne, Tony and Antoinette Burton 2009, 'The politics of intimacy in an age of empire', in *Moving Subjects: Gender, Mobility, and Intimacy in an Age of Global Empire*, Tony Ballantyne and Antoinette Burton (eds), University of Illinois Press, Urbana: 1–28.

Ballara, Angela 2003, *Taua: 'Musket Wars', 'Land Wars' or Tikanga?: Warfare in Maori Society in the Early Nineteenth Century*, Penguin Books, Auckland.

Belich, James 1996, *Making Peoples: A History of the New Zealanders: From Polynesian Settlement to the End of the Nineteenth Century*, Penguin, Auckland.

Binney, Judith 2004, 'Tuki's universe', *New Zealand Journal of History* 38(2): 215–32.

Binney, Judith 2007, 'Introduction', in *Te Kerikeri 1770–1850: The Meeting Pool*, Judith Binney (ed.), Bridget Williams Books, Wellington.

Cahir, Fred and Ian Clark 2014, 'Aboriginal and Maori interactions in Victoria Australia, 1830–1900: A preliminary analysis', *New Zealand Journal of History* 48(1): 109–26.

Church Missionary Society 1816a (October), 'List of School Children', Samuel Marsden Collected Papers, Hocken Collections, University of Otago, Dunedin, MS 0056/028.

Church Missionary Society 1816b, 'Monthly Account of the Attendance of the Native Children at the Church Missionary Society's School, Bay of Islands New Zealand commencing August 12th. 1816; For September 1816', Samuel Marsden Collected Papers, Hocken Collections, University of Otago, Dunedin, MS 0056/023.

Church Missionary Society 1820, 'Objects of Shunghee and Whykato in Visiting England', Church Missionary Society, Archives Relating to the Australian and New Zealand Missions, 1808–1884, Mission Books Containing Correspondence to the CMS, CN/M1, Hocken Collections, University of Otago, Dunedin.

Clifford, James 1992, 'Travelling Cultures', in *Cultural Studies,* Lawrence Grossberg, Cary Nelson and Paula Treichler (eds), Routledge, New York: 96–116.

Fitzgerald, Caroline 2011, *Te Wiremu—Henry Williams: Early Years in the North*, Huia, Wellington.

Fitzgerald, Tanya 2001, 'Fences, boundaries and imagined communities: Re-thinking the construction of early mission schools and communities in New Zealand 1823–1830', *History of Education Review* (30)2: 14–25.

Hahn, Hans Peter and Hadas Weis 2013, 'Introduction: Biographies, travels and itineraries of things', in *Mobility, Meaning and Transformations of Things*, Hans Peter Hahn and Hadas Weis (eds), Oxbow Books, London.

Hall, William 1816a (26 January), Letter to Samuel Marsden, Samuel Marsden Collected Papers, Hocken Collections, University of Otago, Dunedin, PC 0129.

Hall, William 1816b, Private Journal of William Hall, 1816–1838, Alexander Turnbull Library, National Library of New Zealand, Wellington, Micro-MS 0853.

Hamilton, Carolyn 1998, *Terrific Majesty: The Powers of Shaka Zulu and the Limits of Historical Invention,* Harvard University Press, Cambridge, MA.

Hargreaves, R.P. 1962, 'Waimate—pioneer New Zealand farm', *Agricultural History* 36 (1): 38–45.

Hohepa, Patu 2007, 'Kerikeri, Tapu, Wahi Tapu', in *Te Kerikeri 1770–1850: The Meeting Pool*, Judith Binney (ed.), Bridget Williams Books, Wellington. doi.org/10.7810/9781877242380_9

Innis, Harold 1950, *Empire and Communications*, Oxford University Press, Oxford.

Innis, Harold 1951, *The Bias of Communication*, University of Toronto Press, Toronto.

Jolly, Margaret 2001, 'On the edge? Deserts, oceans, islands', *The Contemporary Pacific* 13(2): 417–66. doi.org/10.1353/cp.2001.0055

Jones, Alison and Kuni Jenkins 2011, *Words Between Us—He Kōrero: First Māori-Pakeha Conversations on Paper*, Huia, Wellington.

Kendall, Thomas 1816a (6 November), Letter to Secretary of CMS, Samuel Marsden Collected Papers, Hocken Collections, University of Otago, Dunedin, PC 0130.

Kendall, Thomas 1816b (28 October), Letter to Reverend Josiah Pratt, Samuel Marsden Collected Papers, Hocken Collections, University of Otago, Dunedin, MS 0056/025.

Kendall, Thomas 1817 (25 July), Letter to Samuel Marsden, Samuel Marsden Collected Papers, Hocken Collections, University of Otago, Dunedin, PC-0131.

Kendall, Thomas 1818 (8 December), Letter to Reverend Josiah Pratt, Samuel Marsden Collected Papers, Hocken Collections, University of Otago, Dunedin, MS 0056/210.

Kendall, Thomas 1820, *A Grammar and Vocabulary of the Language of New Zealand*, Church Missionary Society, London.

Marsden, Samuel 1819a (17 August), Journal, 'Rev. S. Marsden's Journal of Proceedings at New Zealand from July 29 to Oct 19, 1819', Samuel Marsden Collected Papers, Hocken Collections, University of Otago, Dunedin, PC 0140.

Marsden, Samuel 1819b (18 August), Journal, 'Rev. S. Marsden's Journal of Proceedings at New Zealand from July 29 to Oct 19, 1819', Samuel Marsden Collected Papers, Hocken Collections, University of Otago, Dunedin, PC 0140.

Marsden, Samuel 1823a (7 August), Journal, 'Rev. S. Marsden's journal from July 2 to Nov 1, 1823', Samuel Marsden Collected Papers, Hocken Collections, University of Otago, Dunedin, MS 0177/003.

Marsden, Samuel 1823b (11 November), Letter to Hongi, in *Letters and Journals of Samuel Marsden*, J.R. Elder (ed.), Coulls, Somerville, Wilkie, Dunedin.

Marsden, Samuel 1824 (26 July), Letter to Hongi, in *Letters and Journals of Samuel Marsden*, J.R. Elder (ed.), Coulls, Somerville, Wilkie, Dunedin.

Middleton, Angela 2008, *Te Puna—A New Zealand Mission Station: Historical Archaeology in New Zealand*, Springer, London. doi.org/10.1007/978-0-387-77622-4

Mokyr, Joel 2009, *The Enlightened Economy: An Economic History of Britain, 1700–1850*, Yale University Press, New Haven.

Nicholas, John Liddiard 1817, *Narrative of a Voyage to New Zealand Performed in the Years 1814 and 1815*, James Black & Son, London.

Nuttall, Sarah 2009, *Entanglement: Literary and Cultural Reflections on Post Apartheid,* Wits University Press, Johannesburg.

O'Malley, Vincent 2015, *Haerenga: Early Maori Journeys Across the Globe*, Bridget Williams Books, Wellington.

Parsonson, Ann 1980, 'The expansion of a competitive society', *New Zealand Journal of History* 14(1): 45–60.

Phillipson, Grant 2007, 'Religion and land: The Church Missionary Society, 1819–50', in *Te Kerikeri 1770–1850: The Meeting Pool*, Judith Binney (ed.), Bridget Williams Books, Wellington.

Rogers, Lawrence M. (ed.) 1961, *The Early Journals of Henry Williams: Senior Missionary in New Zealand of the Church Missionary Society 1826–40,* Pegasus Press, Christchurch.

Salesa, Damon 2003, '"Travel-happy" Samoa: Colonialism, Samoan migration, and a "brown Pacific"', *New Zealand Journal of History* 37(2): 171–88.

Salesa, Damon 2013a, 'Pacific in Indigenous time', in *Pacific Histories: Ocean, Land, People*, David Armitage and Alison Bashford (eds), Palgrave, Basingstoke.

Salesa, Damon 2013b, 'Passages in a native sea: Some Indigenous histories of globalization in the Pacific', J.C. Beaglehole Lecture, New Zealand Historical Association Conference, Dunedin.

Salmond, Anne 1997, *Between Worlds: Early Exchanges between Maori and Europeans 1773–1815*, Viking, Auckland.

Sheller, Mimi and John Urry 2006, 'The new mobilities paradigm', *Environment and Planning A* 38: 207–26. doi.org/10.1068/a37268

Sissons, Jeffrey 2007, 'Hongi Hika', in *Te Kerikeri 1770–1850: The Meeting Pool*, Judith Binney (ed.), Bridget Williams Books, Wellington. doi.org/10.7810/9781877242380_5

Standfield, Rachel 2012, *Race and Identity in the Tasman World, 1769–1840*, Pickering & Chatto, London.

Stevens, Michael J. 2011, '"What's in a name?": Murihiku, colonial knowledge-making, and "thin-culture"', *Journal of the Polynesian Society* 120(4): 333–47.

Stevens, Michael J. 2015, 'A "useful" approach to Maori history', *New Zealand Journal of History* 49(1): 54–77.

Te Punga Somerville, Alice 2012, *Once Were Pacific: Maori Connections to Oceania*, University of Minnesota Press, Minneapolis.

Thomas, Nicholas 1991, *Entangled Objects: Exchange, Material Culture and Colonialism in the Pacific,* Harvard University Press, Cambridge, MA.

Tsing, Anna Lowenhaupt 2004, *Friction: An Ethnography of Global Connection*, Princeton University Press, Princeton.

Walter, Richard, Chris Jacomb and Sreymony Bowron-Muth 2010, 'Colonisation, mobility and exchange in New Zealand prehistory', *Antiquity* 84(324): 497–513. doi.org/10.1017/S0003598X00066734

Williams, Henry 1823, Journal, Alexander Turnbull Library, National Library of New Zealand, Wellington, Micro-MS 0209

6

'As Much as They Can Gorge': Colonial Containment and Indigenous Tasmanian Mobility at Oyster Cove Aboriginal Station

Kristyn Harman[1]

In 1803, the British began to expropriate Van Diemen's Land (now Tasmania) principally as a repository for convicts. They did this without prior negotiation with the estimated 6,000 Aboriginal people residing there, whose ancestors' custodianship of country dated back at least 40,000 years. As increasing numbers of free settlers arrived, the British settlements in the north and south of the island, and the pastoral frontier, expanded. Consequently, Aboriginal mobility became severely constrained. Conflict over space, mobility, bodies and resources led to sustained warfare between Aboriginal people and colonists throughout the latter half of the 1820s and the early 1830s. The Vandemonian War was ultimately resolved by the exile of Aboriginal survivors to islands in Bass Strait. This was achieved by diplomatic negotiations between Lieutenant

1   The author would like to acknowledge the generous support of a grant from the Plomley Foundation.

145

Governor George Arthur and Kickerterpoller (known to colonists as Black Tom), and by Conciliator of Aborigines George Augustus Robinson's 'friendly mission' in which Kickerterpoller was a participant.[2]

While there are any number of possible terms that could be used to describe this 'negotiated exodus' of Tasmanian Aboriginal people from the Tasmanian mainland in the 1830s, I have chosen to use the word 'exile' to encapsulate this process. I also refer to those who were removed from their homelands as 'exiles'. In doing so, I am following the example of Edward Said who defined exile as 'the unhealable rift forced between a human being and a native place, between the self and its true home'. This descriptor is particularly apt for those Tasmanian Aboriginal people who were removed to the Bass Strait islands.[3] In 1847, Lieutenant Governor William Denison decided to repatriate the exiles to mainland Tasmania. This decision was made to overcome the problem of the concentration of exiles at the Aboriginal Establishment on Flinders Island in Bass Strait having been 'delivered over to the caprice of a single individual' (a controversial commandant), and because of rising expenses and a falling Aboriginal population.

This chapter considers the role that ideas about, and practices of, Aboriginal mobility played in the second removal of Aboriginal people to Oyster Cove. It considers constraints on Aboriginal mobility as a key aspect of systems of control and surveillance. This mid–nineteenth century shift in the ways that nation states deployed power to manage their populaces has been theorised by Michel Foucault. According to Foucault, spectacles of power—such as the scaffold—were giving way to new disciplinary regimes that produced docile bodies. In this case, Aboriginal bodies were to be trained to internalise colonial society's norms with the aim that they would become self-governing through constant processes of self-surveillance. This would ultimately negate the perceived need for white protectors, overseers and instructors.[4]

---

2   Brodie 2015; Brodie 2017; Johnson and McFarlane 2015; Clements 2014; Lawson 2014; Ryan 2012; Harman 2009; Reynolds 1995. After being removed to several islands, the exiles were housed at the Aboriginal Establishment on Flinders Island, which has since become commonly known as Wybalenna, a Tasmanian language term that translates as black men's houses.
3   Said 2002.
4   Foucault 1991 [1977].

Colonial authorities not only managed Aboriginal mobility, they also orchestrated some Aboriginal travel to Hobart for colonial purposes. Initially, this was to show colonists that Aboriginal people were no longer a threat. Later, when viewed through a romanticised lens of a dying race, it became part of a valorisation of Aboriginal 'status'—in both instances a form of entertainment and spectacle for colonists to enjoy. This chapter also traces the relaxation of restrictions on the mobility of Oyster Cove residents in an attempt to mitigate the effects of mistreatment and cost cutting in relation to their health and wellbeing. It shows that, as the health of residents was declining and people were dying, the resumption of some mobility was a colonial strategy designed to improve health, and perhaps restore a degree of wellbeing to the ageing and infirm Oyster Cove residents.

In response to Denison's plan to repatriate the Aboriginal exiles, 'A Colonist' observed in a letter to the Launceston-based *Examiner* that the lieutenant governor 'intimates his resolution to fill up the cup of our calamities by the restoration of a horde of savages to these shores from whence it was naturally hoped that they had been forever most providentially removed'.[5] From a colonist's point of view, Tasmanian Aboriginal mobility was thus constructed as inherently dangerous and undesirable when placed in a mainland Tasmanian landscape that British colonists had expropriated for themselves.

On Thursday 30 September 1847, 200 colonists attended a public meeting in Launceston to discuss their opposition to the repatriation. They shared the *Examiner* correspondent's concern about Denison's proposal that Aboriginal people 'might be allowed to reassume their old habits of life without any risk to the colonists'. Attendees believed that allowing Aboriginal people to return to the Tasmanian mainland would be dangerous, not only to colonists, but also to the exiles. Within living memory, Tasmanian Aboriginal mobility had led to numerous encounters with colonists, some planned and others accidental, which had resulted in death. It was difficult for colonists to believe that those returning to the Tasmanian mainland would no longer pose the risks to property and person that had been a feature of the colony's Vandemonian War. Some colonists would also have remembered the risks posed to mobile Aboriginal people by armed colonists. The dangers considered inherent

---

5   'A Colonist', *Examiner*, 25 September 1847: 4.

in Aboriginal mobility stand as testament to the effectiveness of the Aboriginal campaigns waged a decade and a half earlier, the longevity of colonial memory of the Black War and the willingness of at least some colonists to shoot Aboriginal people on sight.[6]

Despite the settlers' mounting concerns, Denison was determined to forge ahead. In November 1847, a government notice announced the repatriation of the exiles to the mainland. In an accompanying editorial, the *Examiner* observed that while the exiled Tasmanian Aboriginal people had been allowed to 'roam without restraint at Flinders', on their return to Tasmania they would 'be subjected to a surveillance and constraint they have never before experienced'.[7] As Aboriginal mobility was clearly still feared within the colonial community, the newspaper was at pains to stress that, while Aboriginal life in exile may have been characterised by freedom of movement (albeit across a small island contained by the sea), at Oyster Cove those who returned would be subject to unprecedented surveillance and restraint. The Tasmanian Government was committed to taking extraordinary measures to contain the remnant population, in so far as was possible, within the boundaries of the Oyster Cove Aboriginal Station. Nevertheless, those who were repatriated gradually regained a measure of mobility. A coercive form of mobility occurred at the behest of colonial authorities who orchestrated a range of public appearances and staged events in which the repatriated Aboriginal people were key participants. Those Aboriginal people who returned also undertook numerous journeys of varying type and length at their own volition, re-establishing old networks and forging new ones. This practice received tacit colonial endorsement as the ageing Aboriginal population's health and numbers were seen to be in severe decline.

Oyster Cove is south of Hobart, adjacent to a small bay on the D'Entrecasteaux Channel. In 1844, it was chosen as a site for a female penitentiary that never eventuated. Approximately 120 male convicts were sent there to construct buildings and perform labour. When reporting on Oyster Cove to the Secretary of State for the Colonies in May 1847, Lieutenant Governor Charles La Trobe informed Grey that the decision had been made to 'break up the establishment', which had become

---

6   'Releasing the Aborigines: Public Meeting', *Examiner*, 2 October 1847: 4. On the apparent willingness of some colonists to shoot Aboriginal people on sight, see Harman 2009: 16.

7   'Editorial', *Examiner*, 17 November 1847: 3.

'expensive and unprofitable'.[8] The government sold the vacant land and buildings to Henry Stevenson Hurst for approximately £200.[9] Just months later, when a site was being sought to which Tasmanian Aboriginal people at Wybalenna might be relocated, the government settled on Oyster Cove. The buildings, which La Trobe had described as 'small … and very slight', remained intact. Aside from the superintendent's quarters, which were constructed of brick, the built environment was fashioned from sawn timber or slabs and comprised of two mess rooms (one of which also served as a chapel), some huts, a cooking and bake house, hospital and a dozen wooden cells formerly used for solitary confinement.[10] Hurst had the upper hand in the negotiations over Oyster Cove, making a handsome profit when, just months after the government had sold him the site, Hurst sold it back for £400.[11]

In the same public notice in which the government formally announced the return of 45 'Aboriginal inhabitants of Van Diemen's Land to their native country', it reassured readers that only 13 adult men were among the group; of these, two had been brought up by Europeans from early childhood, three had been educated at the Queen's Orphan Schools, one was a farm servant who had been reared by a European and two were incapacitated. The remaining five adult males included four older men who worked with a 'steadiness which would have been praiseworthy in a man bred to labour'. Further, the governor reminded colonists that all of the Aboriginal people had 'lived about fifteen years in civilised habits', and that the women had been living 'in the practices of civilised life for a period even longer than the men'.[12] This strong emphasis on the exposure of the adults to civilising influences is consistent with colonial discourses that equated savagery with irrational violence and civilisation with measured responses to provocation. The transition from Indigenous mobility to more 'settled' lives was seen as an essential precursor to Aboriginal people becoming 'civilised'.

8   La Trobe to Grey, 31 May 1847, cited in Brand 1990: 190–91.
9   Plomley 1987: 171.
10   La Trobe to Grey, 31 May 1847, cited in Brand 1990: 190–91.
11   Plomley 1987: 171.
12   *Colonial Times*, 12 November 1847: 4; 'Editorial', *Examiner*, 17 November 1847: 3.

Prior to their arrival, Denison informed the colonial secretary that he 'approved' of a plan that involved 'parading them [the repatriated Aboriginal people] before the inhabitants of Hobart Town'.[13] This planned appearance echoed the way in which Robinson had triumphantly paraded the remnants of the Big River and Oyster Bay tribes through the streets of Hobart in January 1832, after arranging their removal to Wybalenna.[14] When the survivors returned, a street parade was orchestrated by government officials to visually underline the fact that the numbers of Tasmanian Aboriginal people (particularly men) had greatly diminished, meaning they now lacked any real capacity to re-engage in warfare with the colonists. How such parades were experienced by those subjected to the colonists' 'lively curiosity' remains a matter of conjecture.[15] Such events highlight the ways in which Tasmanian Aboriginal mobility could be coerced by government to fulfil its agenda of appeasing and/or entertaining its colonial populace.

By the time colonists were reading about the repatriation of the exiles, the 45 Aboriginal people had already been relocated to the Oyster Cove Aboriginal Station where they arrived in mid-October 1847.[16] As had been the case at Wybalenna, white protectors were the cornerstone of the colonial policy of containment that sought to constrain Aboriginal mobility and to refashion Tasmania's Indigenous people (particularly the children) in the image of the British colonisers. Dr Joseph Milligan was putatively in charge of the station at Oyster Cove, yet he opted to live in Hobart. Daily responsibility for overseeing the station's residents fell to the catechist, Robert Clark, who, like Milligan, had accompanied the Aboriginal group from Wybalenna. The government also appointed a visiting magistrate to the station.[17] Conforming to a pattern established across other British settler colonies, and at Flinders Island, Aboriginal children were separated from their parents and inculcated with 'those habits of obedience and industry which will ensure their becoming at all events quiet and orderly members of the community'.[18] Of the 10 children, three boys and four girls were sent to the Orphan School. The eldest boy, Charlie, was apprenticed out (off the station) to learn a trade, while the

13   Denison to Colonial Secretary 23 October 1847, CSO 24/32/922, Tasmanian Archive and Heritage Office (hereafter TAHO): 87–88.
14   *Hobart Town Courier*, 14 January 1832: 2.
15   *Hobart Town Courier*, 14 January 1832: 2.
16   Plomley 1987: 150–63.
17   Plomley 1987: 172.
18   See Armitage 1995; *Colonial Times*, 28 January 1848: 3.

youngest, George, and the eldest girl, Fanny Cochrane, were boarded with Fanny's half-sister, Mary Ann, and her husband, Walter George Arthur, at the Oyster Cove Aboriginal Station.[19]

By dint of their mixed descent, Christian marriage and previous occupation as teachers at Wybalenna, the Arthurs were considered by the colonial authorities to be of sufficient standing to act as guardians to these children. The government's willingness to release Tasmanian Aboriginal people into the care of mixed-descent relatives whose living arrangements conformed to white expectations was not without precedent. For example, in 1841, Dalrymple Briggs, the daughter of sealer George Briggs and Woretemoyeteryenner, successfully petitioned for her mother to be released from Wybalenna into her care.[20] Such arrangements were sometimes entered into by the state depending on its public servants' perceptions of the applicants. As Clare Anderson has explained in relation to another part of the British Empire, in the first half of the nineteenth century race was 'a category forged at least partially through broader cultural distinctions, most especially of religion, class and education'.[21] The relative fluidity of racial thinking saw people less bounded by this category than later in the century, and those Aboriginal people whom the colonists perceived to be conforming to their social expectations were granted some concessions.

When the remaining children were transferred to the Orphan School in December 1847, they were accompanied on their one-way journey by their parents. They were packed uncomfortably into two carriages; however, they stopped en route to join the vice-regal couple at New Norfolk (beyond Hobart) for their Christmas festivities. Lady Denison empathised with her husband's plans to 'bring parties of them [the Aboriginal people] up to Hobart Town and the neighbourhood, in order to let people see how perfectly inoffensive they are' and expressed her hopes for the children to be 'trained into civilised and Christian beings'. The Aboriginal group, which was hosted in a separate tent from the Denison's servants, was given food and baubles. They later played games that were seen to provide a visual display of their physical dexterity. Lady Denison described how 'the black tent was evidently the great attraction', as their white visitors and other townsfolk flocked to see the Aboriginal people for themselves.

---

19   Plomley 1987: 173.
20   CO 280/133, 171–171a, TAHO.
21   Anderson 2012: 82.

Despite having become colonial curiosities, coerced into a form of mobility that would see them separated from their children and gazed upon by colonists, the Aboriginal people apparently enjoyed themselves.[22]

A further opportunity to parade the Aboriginal adults before the Hobart citizenry presented itself on the evening of 26 December when they occupied the vice-regal box at the theatre with Milligan and the artist, John Skinner Prout. The antics of the clown 'surprised' them; the Aboriginal group reportedly thought him akin to a supernatural being.[23] Their animation and enthralment stood in marked contrast to their behaviour at Oyster Cover Station. When Lady Denison visited them the following year, she described their 'usual conduct' as 'apathetic'. They only became energetic after they were asked to demonstrate their traditional skills in tree climbing.[24] The burden of continued captivity appeared to be weighing heavily on the repatriated Aboriginal people.

Consistent with the Wybalenna experience, the white staff overseeing the Aboriginal people continued to attract controversy, particularly the catechist Robert Clark who managed the station on a daily basis. Clark had difficulty containing the residents within the boundaries of the station at Oyster Cove. This aspect of colonial oversight was considered fundamental to the 'civilising' process. Early on, tensions arose over Aboriginal mobility (and the unrestrained movements of their dogs). Within two months of their arrival, altercations arose over station dogs attacking neighbouring sheep and goats, and Aboriginal people fraternising with workers in the district.[25] The workers, being from the lower class, were considered to be a bad influence. Aboriginal people's mobility contradicted Denison's 'guarantee for their future good behaviour', which was based on Aboriginal people 'having acquired a taste for settled habits and industrial pursuits, and in their appreciation of the comforts and advantages of domestic life'.[26] Unrestrained mobility not only threatened the governor's credibility and the colonists' peaceful existence (by posing a psychological, rather than a physical, threat), but was also believed to negatively affect Aboriginal morality and wellbeing.

---

22 Davis and Petrow 2004: 72–78.
23 'The Theatre', *Courier*, 29 December 1847: 2.
24 Davis and Petrow 2004: 102–03.
25 CSO24/39/1197 (January–June 1848), TAHO.
26 'The Natives', 4 November 1847, Government Notice No. 109, Colonial Secretary's Office, 4 November 1847; *Colonial Times*, 12 November 1847: 4; 'Editorial', *Examiner*, 17 November 1847: 3.

To assuage colonists' concerns about the repatriation, Denison offered assurances that 'they [Aboriginal people] are almost all addicted to gardening. They raised at Flinders' Island, in gardens fenced by themselves, peas, beans, turnips, cabbages, ear rots, onions, parsnips, and pumpkins, besides cultivating fruit trees'.[27] The increasingly controversial Clark endeavoured to turn Aboriginal attention to domestic tasks. In doing so, he redeemed himself (up to a point), as their proposed activities accorded with Denison's vision for the captives. Despite the reported infertility of the soil, Clark encouraged Aboriginal men and women to grow vegetables with a view to marketing the crops in Hobart.[28] Such activities conformed with the notion of Aboriginal people being contained within the confines of the station. Rather than hunting and foraging (and the mobility implicit in these activities), the idea was that they would become tied to the land and their crops, caught up in a cycle of reaping and sowing. Marketing their crops had the potential not only to draw Aboriginal people further into an engagement with the colonial economy in a productive and 'civilising' way, but also to reduce the costs involved with maintaining the Oyster Cove Aboriginal Station.

Clark also encouraged the women to take up needlework and the men to engage in making baskets and mauls (large hammers used to split wood).[29] Unlike many white overseers in charge of Aboriginal people, Clark was familiar with the languages spoken by Tasmanian Aboriginal people. This was important, as a large number of station residents spoke little or no English. Being able to converse with them, he was well placed to understand and appreciate their concerns and to encourage them to adopt the attributes and attitudes consistent with 'civilised' life. However, by 29 March 1850, Clark was dead and a new overseer was required for the remaining 35 residents. Nearly a quarter of the Aboriginal residents died during the station's first three years of operation.[30]

---

27 'The Natives', 4 November 1847, Government Notice No. 109, Colonial Secretary's Office, 4 November 1847; *Colonial Times*, 12 November 1847: 4; 'Editorial', *Examiner*, 17 November 1847: 3.
28 Clark to Colonial Secretary, 3 May 1848, CSO 24/85/1684, TAHO: 84–107.
29 Clark to Manley, 23 April 1848, CSO 24/47/1637: 412–15; Colonial Secretary to Clark, CSO 24/47/1637: 416; Clark to Colonial Secretary, 8 May 1848, CSO24/47/1637: 417–20; Clark to Milligan, 16 June 1848, CSO 24/85/1684, TAHO: 154–56.
30 Milligan to Colonial Secretary, 30 March 1850, CSO 24/132/4445, TAHO: 329–32, TAHO; Plomley 1987: 178.

Over the following half decade, Milligan ran the station from Hobart with several white staff living on site. The surrounding neighbourhood was changing. More white settlers were taking up land, living alongside a burgeoning population of sawyers and wood splitters. The encroachment of settlers curtailed Aboriginal mobility, yet it also offered opportunities for (sometimes illicit) interactions with settlers. Aboriginal lives were changing considerably over this period too. While Aboriginal people had enjoyed line fishing at Wybalenna, at Oyster Cove they discovered the joys of being at sea and commenced fishing from rowboats provided by the station.[31] Some of the Aboriginal station residents began to travel much farther afield, spending lengthy periods at sea. As Lynette Russell has shown in *Roving Mariners* and in her chapter in this collection, several of the Aboriginal men and boys from Oyster Cover crewed on whaling and sealing vessels. This followed a government order in 1855 that all able-bodied residents should work away from the station. The purpose of the order was to reduce running costs and to encourage station residents to assimilate into wider colonial society. Russell has suggested that for those such as Walter George Arthur, 'life at sea … provided an escape from oppression on land'. William Lanné, who became the last surviving Aboriginal man from Oyster Cove, also went to sea and is thought to have sailed on the *Aladdin*, the *June*, the *Runneymede* and the *Sapphire*. The latter travelled extensively across the Southern, Pacific and into the Indian oceans. As Russell has observed, 'this must have seemed a world away from the disease and despair, rations and regulations of the Oyster Cove settlement, where his kin were confined'.[32] According to the visiting magistrate, James Woodhouse Kirwan, in January 1857, Lanné was on board the whaling vessel the *Jane* with another youth from the station, Adam, and Jack Allen, an adult station resident. Perhaps travelling together in a small group smoothed the transition from land to sea, particularly for the younger men who were presumably under Allen's guidance.[33]

Going to sea of their own volition was not an option for the Aboriginal women and girls at the station; although, as Russell shows in this volume, some Tasmanian Aboriginal women did travel. Even in situations of

---

31   Milligan to Colonial Secretary, 30 March 1850, CSO 24/132/4445: 329–32; Milligan to Colonial Secretary, 17 February 1854, CSO 24/241/9498, TAHO.

32   Russell, 2012: 73–78.

33   Kirwan, 31 January 1857, 'Aboriginal Establishment, Oyster Cove, Reports made by Visiting Magistrate, Surgeon and Chaplain when making calls to the Establishment' (hereafter 'Visitors' Book'), CSO 89/1/1, TAHO: 18.

coerced mobility, we can see their agency in the way they managed the situations in which they found themselves. Together with some of the men left behind, several Aboriginal women at Oyster Cove women adopted behaviour that was viewed by some colonists as inappropriate. In 1850, Milligan raised concerns about Aboriginal women and men obtaining alcohol from their white neighbours and from a nearby public house. Milligan's moralising tone notwithstanding, his writings attest to women travelling beyond the bounds of the station and utilising their bodies as they pleased.[34] By April 1855, the number of Aboriginal residents at Oyster Cove had fallen to five men and 11 women. Kirwan reported to the governor that they were living in 'filthy' conditions and that their onsite overseer was unfit for his role. According to Kirwan:

> For a long time past the natives have appeared to me to be under no control or superintendence whatever, being allowed to wander about the country by themselves wherever they pleased.

Kirwan complained that this had led to a small group frequenting a public house some miles away in Kingston, where 'scenes of disgusting immorality' had been taking place.[35] Such revelries reportedly culminated in the death by drowning of (an allegedly inebriated) Mathinna. Mathinna, a young woman kept at Government House in Hobart 'as a sort of pet' by Lady Jane Franklin, was left at the Orphan School when the Franklins returned to England.[36] Kirwan's paternalistic concern was consistent with nineteenth-century views of Indigenous peoples across the British Empire; they were seen as childlike and in need of protection and instruction, as demonstrated by an offer made a fortnight later by Reverend Edward Freeman to visit the station regularly to teach Christian morals to its Aboriginal residents.[37]

Adverse reports about the lives and living conditions of Oyster Cove residents resulted in the governor appointing a new superintendent, John Strange Dandridge. Dandridge took up residence in July 1855 and spent the rest of his life there. His wife, Maria, was the daughter of renowned colonial artist Prout, whose watercolour landscapes of Wybalenna,

---

34 Milligan to Colonial Secretary, 30 March 1850, CSO 24/132/4445: 329–32; Milligan to Colonial Secretary, 17 February 1854, CSO 24/241/9498, TAHO.
35 Kirwan to Colonial Secretary, 17 April 1855, CSD 1/18/703, TAHO.
36 'The Aborigines', *Mercury*, 20 February 1857: 2.
37 E. Freeman to Governor Henry Young, 1 May 1855, CSD 1/18/703, TAHO.

the Orphan School and Oyster Cove are particularly evocative.[38] Nearly eight years earlier, when Denison had first announced the repatriation of the exiles, he had stated that 'respectable persons may visit the establishment; and, on doing so, they will be required to write their names in a Visitors' Book kept there'. This highlighted both the government's segregationist agenda and that Aboriginal lives were on show for 'respectable' colonists.[39] The only surviving visitors' book dates from when the Dandridges took over; it sheds light on a number of aspects of life there, including ongoing issues over the rations and built environment that were meant to contain the Aboriginal residents.[40]

According to Tim Rowse, rationing was 'an institution of the colonial order' that colonists engaged in for various reasons. It involved 'providing food, clothing, and other goods (such as blankets and tobacco)' to Aboriginal people. The process of rationing was such that 'Indigenous recipients could preserve their own understandings of why they were rationed, of what their entitlements were, and of what were the proper uses of the received goods'.[41] At Wybalenna, Aboriginal people 'performed little labour', as they firmly 'believed it was their right to be kept well supplied with food'. This expectation was conceived in their negotiations with Robinson prior to going into exile. Henry Reynolds has explained how 'such expectations militated against the European desire to encourage the Aborigines to learn labour, which was seen as a vital step in their progress towards "civilization"'.[42] The issuing of rations to the repatriated Aboriginal residents was underpinned by a much more straightforward agenda, that of containment. Denison instructed the colonial secretary that 'they may as well be given as much as they can gorge to keep them at home ... let Mr Clark be warned that his main object should be to keep them at home by any inducement he can hold out to them'.[43]

The government followed the same tender process to source beef and mutton for the station as it did with its other institutions. Contractors were also asked to tender for transporting all necessary supplies to Oyster

---

38   'Marriage', *Courier*, 31 March 1847: 2.
39   'The Natives', 4 November 1847, Government Notice No. 109, Colonial Secretary's Office, 4 November 1847; *Colonial Times*, 12 November 1847: 4; 'Editorial', *Examiner* 17 November 1847: 3.
40   Visitors' Book, CSO 89/1/1, TAHO.
41   Rowse 1998: 3, 5.
42   Reynolds 1995: 160–61.
43   Denison to Colonial Secretary, 23 October 1847, CSO 24/32/922, TAHO: 87–88.

Cove by sea from Hobart.[44] The meat rations that formed the basis of the Aboriginal diet were of variable quality. The mutton observed by visiting magistrate Kirwan in January 1856 was of 'good quality'; however, in June of the same year, Reverend Freeman found that the 'beef & mutton supplied to Est … was exceedingly bad' and speculated that this was attributable to the low costs involved. Early the following year, when Aboriginal residents complained of the poor quality of the meat, Freeman found their complaints to be 'well founded'. He thought that 'in future, provisions should be supplied at market price'. The issue persisted to the point that, in April 1857, Freeman sought the governor's intervention. If this transpired, it did not result in the issue being satisfactorily addressed. In January 1858, Dandridge returned 80 pounds of poor-quality beef to its supplier. The difficulties inherent in sourcing quality meat for the station were such that, by mid-winter, none had arrived, leaving Dandridge little option but to issue extra flour to the residents.[45] The poor-quality rations coincided with a marked increase in respiratory disease, the colonial cure for which was mercury containing calomel. No one at the time was aware of the severe health risks posed by mercury. As Peter Dowling has suggested, it seems probable that the Aboriginal patients were unintentionally hastened to their deaths by the doctor who was trying to assist them.[46]

The inability of the colonial administration to provide adequate care and sustenance for the station residents gave rise to the view that allowing them to resume their traditional hunting practices 'would probably do more to renovate and re-establish their health than almost any other plan that could be devised'.[47] Accordingly, various groups of Aboriginal residents sought permission to go into the bush for days, or even weeks, at a time. Richie Woolley has suggested that such trips may have had their inception with the positive response from Aboriginal people to a trip to Flinders Island in 1850 that was organised by Milligan to obtain 'Killiecrankie diamonds' (topaz) and other Tasmanian minerals to be displayed at the 1851 Great Exhibition in London.[48] Aboriginal residents' mobility was constrained by the need to receive permission for travel from

---

44 See, for example, 'Office of Stores', *Mercury,* 7 November 1862: 4. See also 'Colonial Annual Contracts', *Mercury*, 21 November 1865: 2.
45 Visitors' Book, CSO 89/1/1, TAHO: 9, 13, 19, 20, 27, 29.
46 Dowling, 2006: 59–68.
47 Milligan to Denison July 1851, CSO24/864/6314, TAHO.
48 Woolley n.d.: 335; Oyster Cove Correspondence File, TAHO.

the governor or the overseer. However, it seems they complied, for as Dandridge explained, 'they always ask leave to go upon these excursions, and take with them their bedding, pots and pans, etc., and as many rations as they can carry'.[49] In addition to these frequent hunting excursions of several days or weeks in the vicinity of the station, and numerous visits to the adjacent Huon Valley, in mid-winter 1860, a group of six residents (Augustus, Flora, Emma, Tippo, Patty and Sophia) undertook a two-month excursion to Port Davey in the island's far south-west.[50] A short newspaper article printed in November 1856 revealed that 'four of the natives' were on board the *Cobra*, a vessel conveying missionaries and a large number of residents of Hobart to Oyster Cove to visit the Aboriginal station. The unnamed Aboriginal expeditioners 'had been … according to their customs, to Victoria to hold a corrobory [sic]'.[51] It is possible that they were renewing acquaintances made with Victorian Aboriginal people, whom they had met when they accompanied Robinson to the Port Phillip District in 1839, following his appointment as Chief Protector of Aborigines. In this way, we see that Oyster Cove residents were allowed, even encouraged, to resume some degree of former mobility to mitigate the effects of their treatment by colonial authorities.

The Aboriginal residents at Oyster Cove experienced a severe population decline in the 1860s. During this time, the Tasmanian Government regularly displayed them in Hobart. This was consistent with its earlier practice of allowing controlled Aboriginal mobility to show colonists that Aboriginal Tasmanians were not a threat, while also providing a spectacle. However, the ways in which such visits were orchestrated by the authorities and represented in the media changed. In 1860, Dandridge's complaint about the station residents trading their clothing and blankets for alcohol gave rise to a suggestion that 'clothing made particularly for the blacks' ought to be issued to them, and their 'blankets be branded before issue'; in other words, that Aboriginal people's clothing and blankets ought to be similar to, and as distinctive as, those formerly issued to convicts.[52] Dandridge's claims about Aboriginal people's propensity to dispose of goods to obtain alcohol were later supported by Joseph Russell of

---

49 'Tasmania in 1882, Aborigines', *Mercury*, 11 April 1882: 2.
50 CSD 1/121/4338, TAHO. Unfortunately, those who remained at the station contracted influenza in their absence, an illness that was later contracted by, and killed, three of the expeditioners shortly after their return.
51 'Local News', *The Hobarton*, 28 November 1856: 2.
52 Visitors' Book, TAHO: 45.

Geeveston in his reminiscences of life at the Oyster Cove. Russell, a child of one of the government employees working there, recalled in his old age how 'the natives were addicted to drink' and, 'besides spending the money they raised from the sale of fish and shell necklaces' on alcohol, also 'disposed of the blankets from their bunks to buy rum'.[53] It is evident that station residents had established a substantial trade network that relied not only on their traditional practices of shell necklace making and fishing, but also on colonial-issued supplies to procure alcohol. This illicit trade disturbed colonial authorities, both in terms of its outcome (i.e. more alcohol for Aboriginal people) and Dandridge's lack of oversight. However, such exercises of agency went beyond the bounds of station propriety as imagined by Dandridge and his wife.

In 1866, just a few short years after Dandridge's proposal to brand the station residents' blankets, new ball gowns were being sewn for 'Mary Anne, and her countrywomen', as the names of Mary Ann Arthur and four of her Aboriginal companions appeared on an invitation to Government House. Accompanied by Dandridge and greeted by the governor's wife, Mrs Gore Brown, the Aboriginal guests—who excited the interest of other attendees at the ball—were reportedly 'pleased with the attention paid to them'.[54] In 1858, Walter and Mary Ann Arthur had attempted to remove themselves from the constraints of Oyster Cove and establish a farm, but had not been successful. However, their former ward, Fanny, achieved a degree of independence they may well have envied. Given permission to marry, she eventually relocated with her husband to nearby Nicholls Rivulet. According to a newspaper report, Fanny Cochrane Smith ought to have been invited to Government House along with 'the others showed off their white kid gloves and enjoyed the sherry and tarts'. Yet, according to the newspaper, 'having married a gentleman following the lucrative industrial employment of a sawyer, she is out of the pale of the haut ton [people of high fashion] of the city'.[55] Apparently Fanny's marriage to an emancipated convict precluded her from being on the guest list alongside her kin who, towards the end of their lives, were represented as royalty (of sorts).

---

53   'Old-Timer's Memories, Taught to Smoke by Truganini, Life with Natives', *Mercury*, 25 July 1939: 8.
54   'The Birthday Ball', *Mercury*, 25 May 1866: 4.
55   'Tasmania in 1882, Aborigines', *Mercury*, 11 April 1882: 2.

Jakelin Troy has explained how, as the nineteenth century progressed and Aboriginal populations (and the perceived threat they posed to settlers) dwindled, 'nostalgia developed among the colonial population for Aboriginal traditions'.[56] The way in which the few surviving Aboriginal residents from Oyster Cove were paraded and feted in Hobart during their final years is consistent with a pattern of nostalgia for those considered to be the 'last' of an apparently 'dying race'. Nowhere is this repositioning of Aboriginal people more apparent, in Tasmanian history at least, than in the way in which William Lanné—tellingly also known as 'King Billy'—was dressed in 'a blue suit, with gold lace band around his cap' to be introduced to Prince Alfred, the Duke of Edinburgh, in 1868. According to a later report, 'the two of them strolled on the Hobart Town regatta ground, conscious that they alone were in possession of Royal blood'.[57] Despite not being included among Tasmanian Aboriginal 'royalty', Fanny may have lived content in the knowledge that she had regained sufficient freedom to traverse the lands of her ancestors, and to pass down some of their cultural knowledge and language to her descendants.

In colonial Tasmania, the potentially unrestrained mobility of Aboriginal people incited fear and unrest among the predominantly white settler population. Such fears were not altogether misplaced, and stand as testament to the effectiveness of the campaigns waged by Aboriginal warriors following the incursion onto their ancestral lands of white settlers and their sheep. Such fears mirrored concerns about the mobility of the burgeoning society's underclasses of convicts (particularly those being transferred from Norfolk Island—known as a place of ill repute). The repatriation of less than 50 of the Aboriginal exiles from Flinders Island to Oyster Cove Aboriginal Station saw a continuation of the government's policy of segregating Aboriginal people, with a view to training them in preparation for their eventual integration into the lower rungs of colonial society. The cornerstone of this policy involved severe restrictions on Aboriginal mobility, while allowing particular, highly controlled forms of coerced mobility that were designed to allay settlers' fears; for example, by parading visibly non-threatening Aboriginal people through the streets of Hobart.

---

56   Troy 1993: 35.
57   *The World's News*, 19 June 1954: 21. Note that Trucanini, wrongly understood by her contemporaries to have been 'the last of the original inhabitants of Tasmania', was likewise known as Queen Trucanini in her final years. *Mercury*, 12 May 1876: 2.

After the removal of most of the Aboriginal children to the Orphan School, the increasingly ageing and unwell adult population at Oyster Cove experienced mixed success in subverting colonial attempts to contain them. Attempts at containment included appointing an onsite overseer to manage the station and its residents, rationing and instituting a system of official visitors to instruct the Aboriginal people in Christianity; such visitors also attended to matters of health and material comfort. Over time, and in response to the colonial system's failure to secure residents' health and wellbeing, restrictions on the station's adult residents' mobility were eased; although, in most instances, residents still required permission to travel beyond the confines of the station. Those who achieved the greatest success in loosening the constraints over their mobility were, perhaps, the men and boys who crewed on sealing and whaling vessels and who enjoyed the relative freedom of being at sea for months at a time. On land, groups of adults ventured into the bush on hunting expeditions and possibly to conduct ceremonies; indeed, some travelled as far as Victoria to engage in ceremony with their Aboriginal counterparts. By conforming to colonial ideals through contracting a Christian marriage, Fanny Cochrane Smith managed to negotiate a life for herself beyond the boundaries of the Aboriginal station. Born in captivity on Flinders Island, Fanny, through marriage, gained access to the mobility that had been the right of her forebears. As the Aboriginal population at Oyster Cove aged and diminished in number, colonial fears faded and were replaced with nostalgia. This involved romanticising the few (known) remaining Tasmanian Aboriginal people who, while they continued to be physically contained within the boundaries of the Oyster Cove Aboriginal Station, were once again paraded through Hobart. These people may have experienced social mobility of sorts when titles such as 'King' and 'Queen' were bestowed upon them. Further, they may have viewed such titles as a somewhat belated acknowledgement of their significance as leaders within the Oyster Cove community; however, such a conclusion must remain speculative.[58]

58   Troy 1993: 41.

References

Anderson, Clare 2012, *Subaltern Lives: Biographies of Colonialism in the Indian Ocean World, 1790–1920*, Cambridge University Press, Cambridge.

Armitage, Andrew 1995, *Comparing the Policy of Aboriginal Assimilation: Australia, Canada, and New Zealand*, University of British Columbia Press, Vancouver.

Brand, Ian 1990, *The Convict Probation System: Van Diemen's Land 1839–1854*, Blubber Head Press, Hobart.

Brodie, Nicholas 2015, '"He had been a faithful servant": Henry Melville's lost manuscripts, Black Tom, and Aboriginal negotiations in Van Diemen's Land', *Journal of Australian Colonial History* 17: 45–64.

Brodie, Nick 2017, *The Vandemonian War*, Hardie Grant Books, Melbourne.

Clements, Nicholas 2014, *The Black War: Fear, Sex, and Resistance in Tasmania*, University of Queensland Press, St Lucia.

Davis, Richard and Stefan Petrow (eds) 2004, *Varieties of Vice-Regal Life (Van Diemen's Land Section) by Sir William and Lady Denison*, Tasmanian Historical Research Association, Hobart.

Dowling, Peter 2006, 'Mercury poisoning at Oyster Cove? Suspected cases of unintentional poisoning of Tasmanian Aboriginal internees', *Tasmanian Historical Studies* 11: 59–68.

Foucault. Michel 1991 [1977], *Discipline and Punish: The Birth of the Prison*, Alan Sheridan (trans.), Penguin Books, London.

Harman, Kristyn 2009, 'Send in the Sydney natives! Deploying mainlanders against Tasmanian Aborigines', *Tasmanian Historical Studies* 14: 5–24.

Johnson, Murray and Ian McFarlane 2015, *Van Diemen's Land: An Aboriginal History*, UNSW Press, Sydney.

Lawson, Tom 2014, *The Last Man: A British Genocide in Tasmania*, I.B. Tauris, London.

Plomley, N.J.B. 1987, *Weep in Silence: A History of the Flinders Island Aboriginal Settlement*, Blubber Head Press, Hobart.

Reynolds, Henry 1995, *Fate of a Free People*, Penguin, Ringwood.

Rowse, Tim 1998, *White Flour, White Power: From Rations to Citizenship in Central Australia*, Cambridge University Press, Cambridge.

Russell, Lynette 2012, *Roving Mariners: Australian Aboriginal Whalers and Sealers in the Southern Oceans, 1790–1870*, SUNY Press, Albany.

Ryan, Lyndall 2012, *Tasmanian Aborigines: A History Since 1803*, Allen & Unwin, Crows Nest.

Said, Edward 2002, *Reflections on Exile and Other Essays*, Harvard University Press, Cambridge, MA.

Troy, Jakelin 1993, *King Plates: A History of Aboriginal Gorgets*, Aboriginal Studies Press, Canberra.

Woolley, Richie n.d., *The Oyster Cove Aborigines and the Huon*.

7

Looking Out to Sea: Indigenous Mobility and Engagement in Australia's Coastal Industries

Lynette Russell

Aboriginal mobility is—and always has been—highly political, drawing on a history in which mobility was key to racial discourse; that is, Aboriginal people were seen as inappropriately mobile. Consciously or unconsciously, implicitly or explicitly, the concept of mobility has been a key component of historical and contemporary views of Aboriginal people. The much maligned and erroneous legal fiction of terra nullius was not built on the belief that the land was empty, but rather on an idea that the occupants wandered without structure or planning and had no notion of land ownership. Without identifiable social and political hierarchies or laws, they could be dispossessed and their land acquired as part of the imperial project. 'Wanderer', 'nomad' and 'walkabout' are all terms that abound with the idea of movement, fluidity and mobility. Mobility discourse has framed conceptions of Aboriginal authenticity and has been linked to racist themes like 'walkabout' and to the perception of the aimless, wandering (starving) nomad. Almost counterintuitively, these concepts have limited our ability to imagine the past and have been both contentious and restrictive for contemporary race-relations debates. Ironically, Aboriginal movements were also seen as extremely local—that is, mobility within a relatively small area. Containing Indigenous people and managing Indigenous mobility was key to the 'civilising' mission.

It is obvious, with over 220 years of perspective, that this containment was really about access to land. As Martin Thomas revealed in his study of surveyor-turned-ethnographer R.H. Matthews, the notebooks and journals of those measuring and carving up the land make for interesting reading. As they measured, pegged, claimed and opened up land for colonisation, they also observed and recorded.[1] With containment, be it via missions or stations, came the (attempted) erasure of authenticity. As Maximilian Christian Forte pointed out, the authenticity of indigenous peoples continues to be connected to the idea that they were and are rooted to place and disconnected from the mobility associated with modernity.[2] Such a view is, of course, completely at odds with anthropological and archaeological understandings of indigenous settlement and mobility patterns. Therefore, today we have a conundrum that is almost an inversion of the system that was established in the nineteenth century. Popular contemporary views of Aboriginal people that suggest they are highly mobile are juxtaposed against the image of Aboriginal culture and Aboriginal people as fixed and local. Where once being contained reduced authenticity, now it is mobility that undermines it.

Inspired by Daniel Richter's *Facing East from Indian Country*, my aim is to examine case studies as stories of coastal Australia during European colonisation, rather than as aspects of the European colonisation of coastal Australia.[3] As inhabitants of an island continent, those Indigenous people living along the coastline encountered new arrivals, for the most part, by sea. As these newcomers made their way to the shores of what came to be known as Australia, numerous sea-based industries were developed. These included bêche-de-mer (sea cucumber) and pearl shell in northern Australia and the Torres Strait, and pearling in Broome and Western Australia. Sealing was contained to the southern coastlines and whaling was ubiquitous. Indigenous men and women who engaged with these industries were often highly mobile, travelling significant distances. Given that Aboriginal people and Islanders have always taken advantage of new economic niches, this engagement might be read as a simple extension of the traditional range of activities. I argue that Aboriginal people looked out to sea for economic reasons, to gain freedom from colonial restriction and, ultimately, as a way for culture to be maintained away from the strictures of life on government stations, missions and camps.

---

1   Thomas 2011: 21.
2   Forte 2010: 2.
3   Richter 2003: 9.

Two case studies form the basis of my argument. First, I argue that Henry Whalley, as a whaler, found freedom from racially based restrictions in an environment of relative equality. In the second case study, I discuss a group of Aboriginal women who travelled across the Indian Ocean and back again, maintaining their freedom away from colonial officials and continuing to work as sealers while bringing up their families.

Indigenous Mobility

Recent historians, including many in this volume, have begun to consider the conceptual framework of a nineteenth-century indigenous diaspora and cosmopolitanism. Within Australian historiography, groundbreaking foundational works have documented exchanges of pre-colonial sea-based contact in northern Australia; these have undermined views of Aboriginal culture as fixed and local, and have challenged colonially informed historical views of Aboriginal people as mobile but aimless. Work in this field looks at the extension of relationships into Macassar and South-East Asia, showing evidence of sustained and reciprocal mobility.[4]

The uncontested relationship between Aboriginal people and country or place has led to an emphasis on Aboriginal culture, perceived as spatially fixed or rooted. However, as historians Heather Goodall and Allison Cadzow note, 'mobility was and is as much a defining characteristic of Aboriginal cultures as affiliations with meaningful bounded places'.[5] Mobility was an essential component of Aboriginal life ways. Over the course of millennia, the Australian landscape's environmental and climatic zones shifted and changed; as Libby Robin puts it, in the post–Ice Age period 'mobility, more than rooted dwelling, may be a survival skill for an increasingly arid and unpredictable world'.[6] This travelling through and across territory creates country.[7]

Elsewhere, I have discussed at length how Australian Aboriginal culture has been historically and popularly perceived as nestled within a discourse of homogeneity.[8] This operates at both a spatial and chronological level, in which Indigenous cultures with a history of over 40,000 years are

---

4   Marika-Mununggiritj 1999. See also Thomas 2012.
5   Goodall and Cadzow 2009: 21.
6   Robin 2012: 288.
7   Robin 2012: 290.
8   Russell 2001: Chapter 2.

compressed into a single phase or unit: an 'unchanging people in an unchanging landscape', as the earlier observers put it.[9] Contemporary Aboriginal people have been multiply disadvantaged by these models, chiefly because change or adaptation—or, indeed, the adoption of modernity—is seen to challenge the authenticity of Aboriginal people. Today, there is a commonly held view that the contemporary Indigenous Australian population is highly mobile, even transient. According to the Australian Bureau of Statistics and the 2011 census, Indigenous people were both more likely to be away from their place of usual residence on census night and to have changed their living arrangements in the previous five years than non-Indigenous people. However, as demographers Biddle and Markham have noted, there is 'as much variation within the Indigenous population as there is between Indigenous and non-Indigenous Australians'.[10]

Recently, historians have begun to examine what we might think of as a nineteenth-century Indigenous diaspora. Both Aboriginal and Māori mobility have been mapped and analysed in a growing body of literature. This work (my own included) has shown that, for the greater part of the last 200 years, Antipodean indigenous people have been moving, settling and resettling throughout the region. The groundbreaking work of Judith Binney,[11] which examines Māori on Norfolk Island, and the doyenne Ann Salmond's *Between Worlds*,[12] now sit alongside the more recent scholarship of Tony Ballantyne, Rachel Standfield, Kristyn Harman and Cassandra Pybus in demonstrating that mobility, travel and journeying were normative for many people throughout the nineteenth and early twentieth centuries.[13] As Cahir and Clark have observed, the movement of 'Māori and Australian Aboriginal people was far more complex than histories that imagine indigenous peoples as fundamentally local and place-bound allow'.[14]

Most of these analyses have focused on Southern Ocean traffic. While I barely scratch the surface of northern Australian ocean traffic, it is worthwhile contemplating whether there is a broader model that we might consider that supposes coastal-based Indigenous people were

---

9   Pulleine 1929: 310.
10   Biddle and Markham 2011: 2.
11   Binney 2004.
12   Salmond 1997.
13   Ballantyne 2014; Ballantyne 2011: 64; Standfield 2012; Harman 2012.
14   Cahir and Clark 2014.

highly mobile and adaptive and sought out the opportunities that contact and later empire brought. Crucially, these movements and engagements should not be seen as contradicting the importance of place, country or connections to specific rivers, mountains and other features.[15] Fred Cahir has documented how the Australian goldfields attracted significant numbers of Aboriginal people from both the mainland and Tasmania.[16] John Maynard's work on the transcultural connections of the early twentieth century resulted from a study of the movements of Aboriginal people in the maritime and wharf industries.[17] These travels brought them into contact with black and civil rights activists in America and the inspired writings of Marcus Garvey. Maynard has suggested that these twentieth-century connections were an extension of early movements that can be traced back to the whaling and sealing industries. Intriguingly, Maynard suggests the possibility that Māori and Aboriginal people may have travelled to the Californian goldfields via the American Civil War.[18]

This mobility and movement was two way, with visitors arriving in Australia from Macassar and, later, from elsewhere in South-East Asia. For hundreds of years in the north of continental Australia, the bêche-de-mer industry flourished and trade and exchange was a feature of relations between local Indigenous people and the visiting Macassan fishers. Cultural traits that tell of these relationships include oral tradition, songs, folklore and rock art. Yolngu, Yanyuwa and many other groups talk of their kin over the seas and there are familial ties between Northern Australian Aboriginal people and the inhabitants of Sulawesi and other islands.[19] Similarly, I have been told in Indonesia by people born in Macassar of their 'Australian families'.[20] Linguist Paul Thomas has shown that the similarity of language terms between these two groups is clear evidence for not merely occasional visits but rather sustained and bi-directional exchanges.[21] Colonial policies to curtail mobility outlawed Macassan connections; however, Regina Ganter, in this volume, explores not only the possibility that this contact extended over greater areas of the Australian mainland than has previously been recognised, but also how this bi-directional exchange is being re-established.

15 Cahir and Clark 2014.
16 Cahir 2012: 5–6, 27, 68.
17 Maynard 2007; Maynard 2005a.
18 Maynard 2005b.
19 Yanyuwa Families, Bradley and Cameron 2003.
20 Basoeki Koesasi, pers. comm. 2012.
21 Thomas 2012: 131.

Anthropologist John Bradley has documented Aboriginal people who travelled to Macassar, settled there and never returned.[22] The pioneering research of Campbell Macknight supported a strong case for regarding the northern coast of Australia as the westernmost extremity of South-East Asia.[23] Macknight's comments are certainly a chastening reminder that 'Australia was never terra nullius (a timeless land without history), nor its seas mare nullius, and [that] the idea of the island nation as separate, isolated, quarantined was a myth'.[24] As Ganter has demonstrated, pearling in Broome and Western Australia, and the more recent pearl shell trade in the Torres Strait, caused an influx of travellers to the region and facilitated the movement of local people.[25]

Maritime Worlds

The mobility of a life at sea, or at least employment within the maritime industries, provided economic potential, freedom of movement and adventure. These and possibly other factors attracted Aboriginal people (predominately men) to the maritime worlds. Within the American maritime and fur trades, some of the work I have found to be critical to my own has included that by Susan Sleeper-Smith, Sylvia Van Kirk, Carolyn Podruchny and, more recently, Brian Rouleau.[26] In terms of whaling and sealing, there are parallels with what Rouleau has noted as the transcultural nature of the American industry and the mobility this enabled. He argues that 'African Americans long favored waterborne work for its more egalitarian character, as did Native Americans and Pacific Islanders'.[27] The Australian maritime industry, like those of Europe and the Americas, was built on multiracial and multinational crews and has its origins in the transnational (and transcultural) mobility of the early contact period when Aboriginal people (and, in Aotearoa/New Zealand, Māori people) travelled, worked and looked out to sea.

In what follows, I want to consider two (out of many) examples of Indigenous travels. While these case studies are very specific, the biographical approach allows for extrapolation and theorising. The first is Henry Whalley. Born on Kangaroo Island to his European father and

---

22 Yanyuwa Families, Bradley and Cameron 2003.
23 Macknight 1972; Macknight 1976: 2.
24 Balint 2012: 546.
25 Ganter 1994.
26 Sleeper-Smith 2001: 6; Van Kirk 1983; Podruchny 2006; Rouleau 2014.
27 See Rouleau 2010: 394.

Tasmanian Aboriginal mother, Whalley became a colonial success story through travel and mobility. My second example is focused on the travels of a group of Tasmanian women who sailed across the Indian Ocean to Mauritius and home again.

The whaling industry of Hobart in the early to mid-nineteenth century was a thriving industry that provided a much-needed economic base for the colonial outpost. The ships that sailed within these fleets were crewed by Aboriginal and Māori men, as well as Polynesians, Europeans and, on occasion, Native Americans and Africans.[28] The crews were subject to frequent changes when crewmen left the ships and, in this dangerous world, the replenishment of crew was often necessary as 'death was an ever present shipmate'.[29] Life on a ship was extreme; cramped quarters and communal sleeping arrangements prohibited privacy, and work conditions ensured that no one escaped observation. For their chequerboard crews, a whaleship acted as a microcosm of wider society, yet mobility and life at sea offered a kind of freedom that was difficult to achieve on land. Ian McNiven has described the ocean and the sea as a transitive or inverted place where the beach/shoreline provides a portal into its liminality.[30]

Since the early colonial period in Tasmania, Aboriginal people had been rounded up and confined to the government station. Harman's chapter in this volume sets out the conditions for the Aboriginal people at the Oyster Cove settlement, where they had been sent in 1847 after their initial exile to Flinders Island in the Bass Strait, and she examines the mobility that was possible around the settlement for those people who were confined to the land. For Whalley and his compatriots, the transitive space of the ship and their time at sea offered the opportunity to be assessed on the basis of their skills and expertise, rather than their ethnicity. Whaling, in particular, offered social and economic opportunities not usually available to Indigenous people in the early colonial period. For these men, life at sea occasioned different sets of race relations to those on land. There was a much greater sense of equality among sailors and whalemen than might be anticipated in the colonial ports they visited. Survival at sea and success in pursuit of whales was dependent on each member of the crew operating in synthesis. Since everyone had a role to fulfil, a level of egalitarianism was necessary.[31] Life on land could stand in stark contrast to this world.

---

28 See Morrell 1832.
29 Lawrence 1966: xvii.
30 McNiven 2001.
31 Russell 2012: 67.

Whaler John Philp worked in the twilight years of the Tasmanian industry and, decades later, as an old man, he recorded his and some of his colleagues' memories, some of which dated back to the 1870s. He reflected on the difficulties of whaling, which he acknowledged 'was a hard school'; however, he also added: 'The native youth took to whaling like a duck to water, and in the years that followed were recognized as able to hold there [sic] own in any company of whatever nationality'.[32]

Whaling was an industry where a seaman's skill and expertise ensured his economic and even physical survival. Although by no means a utopian or idyllic existence devoid of race-related problems, the whaling industry nonetheless required men of all races and nationalities to get along together: safety and profit depended on it. It is not surprising, then, that for some Aboriginal men, life at sea was appealing. The version of freedom it offered, especially in contrast to indentured or convict labour, was something on which whalers prided themselves. For the Aboriginal whalers, this freedom enabled them to exert autonomy in ways that were not possible on land.

It is known that at least six (and probably many more) Tasmanian Aboriginal men went whaling in the nineteenth century. There is indirect evidence that across Australia the whaling industry attracted the attention of many Aboriginal people. In 1829, George Augustus Robinson wrote several journal entries documenting attempts to 'rescue' Aboriginal people from Kelly's whaling station south of Hobart.[33] Elsewhere in the country, Aboriginal whalers were much sought after. At Eden and Twofold Bay in New South Wales, entire crews of Aboriginal whalers worked,[34] and in Western Australia some of the whale boats were manned entirely by Aboriginal crews.[35] The excellent skill Aboriginal men showed in spear throwing translated well onto the boats—they tended to be excellent harpooners.[36] Aboriginal and mixed-race men became actively involved in the Hobart based industry and one whaleboat in 1839 had an entirely Aboriginal crew.[37]

---

32 Philp 1936: 27.
33 Russell 2012: 68.
34 Russell 2012: 37.
35 Russell 2012: 32.
36 Wesson 2000: 30–31.
37 Nash 2003: 91.

When Whalley died in 1877, the *Tasmanian Mail* recorded this simple death notice: 'WHALLEY—In August last, at Macquarie Islands from the effects of a severe accident, Henry Whalley, mariner, 58 years of age'.[38] Obituaries for Aboriginal people in colonial times were unusual. Whalley, whose mother was a traditional tribal Aboriginal woman from Tasmania, was a rare example of a 'half-caste' success story. Whalley was born on Kangaroo Island sometime towards the end of the second decade of the nineteenth century. He was the son of Henry Senior (known as Robert), the self-proclaimed unofficial 'governor' of Kangaroo Island.[39] The name of his Tasmanian Aboriginal mother is unknown; however, it is likely that she was known as Bet or Betty.[40] It is clear that she was a Tasmanian Aboriginal woman who had been taken to Kangaroo Island by sealers or whalers. She may have been a sister of Truganini or a relative of William Lanné. Elsewhere, I have suggested that Whalley's close relationship with Lanné was possibly on account of this existing kinship.

Whalley sealed with British Captain John Inches Thomson in the sub-Antarctic sealing grounds, including Campbell and Macquarie Islands, on board the ship *Bencleugh*.[41] During a storm near Macquarie Island in August 1877, with waves that 'seemed to reach the heavens', 58-year-old Henry Whalley, first mate, whaler and harpooner, was badly injured.[42] As the ocean tossed his ship to and fro, he was flung across the deck and, as a result, either dislocated his leg at the hip or broke it; he may even have broken his spine. His crewmates were unable to determine exactly what his injuries were. The next day, a concerted effort was made to get the now paralysed Whalley ashore and to tend to his injuries. As he was quite incapacitated, they constructed a hoist and pulled him aloft with ropes and pullies. That evening, one of the crewmen who had taken it upon himself to stay with Whalley gave him some coffee. After he finished it, Whalley is reputed to have said: 'That is good; now I will have a long sleep'.[43] These were his last words, as he never woke.

---

38 *Tasmanian Mail*, 9 March 1878: 11, col. 4.
39 Taylor 2002: 25. According to Taylor, Whalley's father is sometimes referred to as 'Robert' and sometimes 'Henry', 'Whallen', 'Wharley', 'Wallon' and 'Wally'. For convenience, the spelling Whalley is adopted and, to avoid confusion, Whalley senior will be designated Robert, while the son is named Henry. See also Copland 2002: 135.
40 Taylor 2002: 33–34.
41 Taylor 2002: 66. Taylor also notes that Whalley whaled in sub-Antarctic seas. The importance of these sealing grounds and the Macquarie Island Elephant seal population is shown in Cumpston 1958. See also Jones 1971.
42 Thomson 1913: 142.
43 Thomson 1913: 142.

After a solemn, short funeral, Whalley's shipmates set about digging his grave. His epitaph was inscribed into the folding-slate ship's log of the *Bencleugh* with the words:

> There, calmly let him sleep.
> Not all the winds that blow
> Can shake his bed, and he shall keep
> A quiet watch below.[44]

Thomson's journal has a heartfelt poignancy. This British captain, himself translocated thousands of miles from his homeland, recollected the loss of a valued friend and crewmate. From my perspective, it is particularly pertinent to note that here there is no mention of Whalley's ethnicity, unlike the earlier ship's log references to him as a 'half-caste'. Instead, the story is told of Whalley, mariner. Whalley had transcended his racial category. This is also how he was described in the Hobart marriage register 15 years earlier in 1862 when he married Margaret Elizabeth Cole; she was described as a spinster and he, simply, as a mariner.[45] Travel, particularly the mobility afforded by the maritime industries, enabled Whalley to move not just across the oceans, but also, I argue, across race and class divides.

Incidents of Aboriginal people travelling to Europe and even the Americas were not common, but they did occur.[46] Usually travel was enabled by their roles as domestic servants to European families. On a number of occasions, this involved travelling with these families when they returned to Europe. An Aboriginal woman from Hobart known as Kitty left Port Jackson with Mr Hogan and his wife in the ship the *Minerva* in 1818.[47] The family were relocating to Batavia (Jakarta). Two years later, Catherine Knopwood, a young Aboriginal Tasmanian woman who was a servant to Mrs Briggs, the wife of the captain of the *Admiral Cockburn*, immigrated with the family to London.[48] That same year, an Aboriginal man from Hobart, William Thomas Derwent, left for England onboard the *Medway*.[49] Unfortunately, most of those who travelled disappear from the historical records. Perhaps they perished in the harsh European

---

44   Thomson 1913: 15.
45   Registry of Marriages in the District of Hobart, 1862, R6037/1/21, Archives Office of Tasmania, Hobart.
46   In her meticulously researched study of a troupe of Aboriginal performers, Roslyn Poignant has documented their travels across eastern and western Europe and North America. Poignant 2004.
47   Mollison and Everitt [1976]: entry for 1818.
48   Knopwood 1977.
49   Mollison and Everitt [1976]: entry for 1818.

winters, or succumbed to diseases such as cholera or consumption. However, maybe some lived on, forging new lives in unfamiliar places. Perhaps among these we might one day find those who travelled to the Californian goldfields and the American Civil War.

Aboriginal men from Western Australia were also employed on whaling expeditions and were known to sail on American and French ships.[50] The acquisition of new languages and cultural knowledge was one of the many side effects of travel. In 1832, Quaker missionaries Backhouse and Walker met a group of Aboriginal women who had spent time sealing in the Bass Strait. The missionaries were surprised to discover that, as well as speaking English, several of them could speak a 'passable' French.[51] These women were among the five who had travelled from Tasmania, along with their children and their dogs, to Mauritius, Rodriguez, Amsterdam and St Paul Island in the southern Indian Ocean. This level of mobility suggests a degree of (admittedly attenuated) agency and autonomy. Although they may have been compelled, coerced or forced to undertake the travel, their later actions belie the status of victim. As Angela Wanhalla's contribution to this volume sets out, scholars are yet to fully explore Indigenous women as mobile subjects and find ways to recognise and account for their agency, including in situations where mobility may not have been a freely made choice.

I have argued that these women used their expertise as sealers to negotiate their way to the Indian Ocean and, perhaps more importantly, back to their Tasmanian homelands. While the archive is rich with their travels and travails, unfortunately, the women's own voices are silent; the archive is only ever about them and not from them. The women first appear as the subjects of a contractual agreement; it is noted that they were taken on King Island, Van Diemen's Land, on 3 August 1825.[52] The archivally anonymous women had sexual and possibly domestic relationships with some (perhaps all) of these men. The agreement notes:

---

50   Gibbs 2003: 6. See also Gibbs 2000: 17–18; Gibbs 1998.
51   Robinson 2008: 685. See also Backhouse 1843; Plomley and Henley 1990.
52   All the material relating to this incident was copied from the Colonial Office and is housed in the Tasmanian State Archives. CSO 1/121/3067, Hobart. See Letter from CSO to Commander of ship Admiral Cockburn, 22 May 1827; CSO1/121/3067; Letter from EA Abbott, Launceston, re death of one of the women, 25 August 1827; CSO1/121/3067; Statutory Declaration of A Delabye, Thomas Taylor and Twelyer, 12 December 1826; CSO1/121/3067.

> This is to certify that Thos Taylor, John Seweler and five women natives of Van Diemen's Land are left on Rodriguez Island to remain until the vessel returns from the Isle of France to convey them to the Island of St Pauls and Van Diemen's Land.
>
> Signed G.W. Robinson,
> lodged with John Finniss
> [the Acting Chief of Court Police, based in St Louis] in Mauritius.

Tyack did not remain on Rodriguez Island for long before he travelled to Mauritius, where he found employment. For those that remained on Rodriguez Island, almost a year passed and the Mauritian authorities (and possibly the women and men sealers themselves) believed that they had been abandoned. However, on 15 December 1826, John Finniss wrote to A.W. Blane, acting chief secretary to the Mauritius Government, informing 'his Excellency the Governor' that the group had been rescued by the schooner *Les Deux Charles* and relocated to Mauritius. In reply, Blane requested advice on 'how these persons are to be disposed of until an opportunity offers of conveying them back to New Holland'. Taylor, an Englishman, possessed documentation proving that he was not indentured; he requested that 'he might be employed in some vessel sailing from this Port, if it should be his Excellency's pleasure'.

Finniss was concerned about the situation and he continued his documentation with a statement taken from the sailors. He did not record whether the women were present when the statement was made or whether they made statements of their own. He noted that the sailors had a written agreement with the captain of the '*Hunter*, with five women and a child who [also] joined the vessel'; they were to proceed to 'St Paul's Island to process seal skins' and they were entitled to 'remain … if they chose' on this or any other island.

According to the official, this was at least the second time they had been stranded (previously the captain had left the group at King George's Sound, Western Australia, for several months). When the captain returned, they continued into the Indian Ocean towards St Paul's Island. Again the captain was ill-prepared; within a very short time their provisions were limited and they encountered difficult weather. After further delays and hardships associated with a lack of provisions, Taylor (whose voice is the only one evident in the records) and the group relocated to Rodriguez Island in the Indian Ocean, where 'they [the male sealers] put ashore with those five women and three children with provisions for seven weeks at the rate of forty pounds of bread flour [each]'. They remained there for many months. When another ship arrived they were informed that their vessel had shipped out of Mauritius twice since leaving them on Rodriguez Island and the group assumed they had been abandoned. Once again, they were returned to Mauritius. When interviewed the male sailors:

> Declare[d] that the Capt[ain] ... told them that the reason he sent those women on shore was for fear of meeting a Kings vessel between Rodriguez and this island, that the Capt[ain] of the Man-O-War would not believe that those women were free people and would seize the *Hunter*.

It is unclear what happened to the group over the next five months. I think we can assume that they lived within the township of Port Louis in Mauritius, which, since 1810, had been a British colony (prior to this it had been administered by the French). The town was made up of white and 'coloured' settlers, Indians and around 60,000 slaves. The women most likely lived among those who were described as the 'free coloureds', who numbered over 7,000.[53] Port Louis was a bustling trade port, filled with ships and sailors from all around the globe. Vessels were stocked with sugar, textiles, spices and, of course, seal skins. Perhaps—even though the culture and language were different—the similarities to the port town of Hobart enabled them to negotiate their time there with relative ease.

The authorities permitted one of the children to remain in Mauritius with his father, Tyack, provided 'his mother voluntarily allowed him to stay'. Finniss witnessed this in his own office and he allowed the boy to stay. By this stage, Tyack had secured employment in the Office of the Registry of the Admiralty. On the same day, 3 March 1827, he recorded that 'one woman died'. Unfortunately he did not enter her name in his journal; although, on the death certificate, he recorded her as Wateripitau. She entered the government hospital on 24 December and died on 4 January of dysentery.

The Mauritian colonial office arranged for the group to be transported to Sydney. On 12 May 1827, Alex McLeay of the Colonial Secretary's Office in Sydney noted that they had arrived 'on board the *Orpheus* at the NSW government's expense the women, their two children and several dogs'. The Sydney officials were keen to have the women relocated and McLeay requested 'that an endeavour to ascertain the wishes [of the women be made,] that direction may be given for their disposal. Perhaps they may

---

53   Norvill and Bell 1864: 82. Compare with Toussaint 1954.

wish to join the natives in this neighbourhood'. Two days later, on 14 May 1827, the Master of Attendants Office of Thomas Nicholson wrote to the colonial secretary, having determined the women's wishes. He noted that:

> They are desirous of returning to their native place, consequently I should recommend that they be forwarded in the *Admiral Cockburn* which sails for Van Diemen's Land tomorrow, or on the next vessel that may be destined for that Island.

The group was transported on the *Admiral Cockburn* to Van Diemen's Land for the sum of five pounds. Disputes arose around payment for their passage between the various colonial governments, New South Wales and Van Diemen's Land, and, by 1829, the government of Mauritius still had not finalised the bill for their transferral from the Indian Ocean to Sydney and then on to Tasmania.

These women, who travelled across the Indian Ocean and returned home, engaged with colonial society at both an economic and personal level. They made personal choices within the confines and impositions of the British Empire. As Aboriginal women, they were restricted in what they could and could not do, but there were some freedoms they both sought and achieved. It seems an irony that, in order to maintain their sense of themselves culturally, they chose to travel away from their home. The idea that Aboriginal people are fixed to place would seem to fall apart when we take a closer look at these mobility patterns.

Conclusion

Aboriginal people travelled. It seems such a simple concept and yet the historical literature and popular accounts of history are so often mute on this. By the time of Federation, the presence of 'coloured labour' was the subject of dispute. In an extension of the White Australia Policy, in 1904 the Australian Government passed into law the 'White Ocean Policy', which stated that no shipping company employing black labour would be permitted to carry Australian mail. Designed to protect the employment of white Australian sailors, it was assumed to rest:

On one argument only—the maintenance of the purity of the whole race on this continent. There must be no intermarriage of blacks and whites … the white ocean policy was on a different footing, inasmuch as the colored seamen did not settle on the land—they took the white man's place at sea.[54]

For the best part of a century, Australian ships had been transnational; they had employed black and white, native and settler, and immigrant and sojourner. As the newly formed nation became increasingly anxious about its place in the world, ships' crews became whiter and the ships decks were not so much a liminal zone.[55]

References

Backhouse, James 1843, *A Narrative of a Visit to the Australian Colonies*, Hamilton, Adams, London.

Balint, Ruth 2012, 'Aboriginal women and Asian men: a maritime history of color in white Australia', *Signs* 37(3): 544–54.

Ballantyne, Tony 2011, 'On place, space and mobility in nineteenth-century New Zealand', *New Zealand Journal of History* 45(1): 50–70.

Ballantyne, Tony 2014, *Webs of Empire: Locating New Zealand's Colonial Past*, UBC Press, Vancouver.

Biddle, Nicholas and Francis Markham 2011, *Mobility*, Census Papers: Indigenous Population Project: Paper No. 9, The Australian National University, Centre for Aboriginal Economic Policy Research, Canberra.

Binney, Judith 2004, 'Tuki's universe', *New Zealand Journal of History* 38(2): 215–32.

Cahir, Fred 2012, *Black Gold: Aboriginal People on the Goldfields of Victoria, 1850–1870*, ANU E Press, Canberra.

Cahir, F. and I. Clark 2014, 'Aboriginal and Māori interactions in Victoria, Australia, 1830–1900: A preliminary analysis', *New Zealand Journal of History* 48(1): 109–26.

---

54 *The Advertiser*, 8 March 1905.
55 At this point, many of the sailors chose to 'pass as white' for the purposes of their maritime career.

Copland, George 2002, 'The mysteries of Karta: Creation, colonisers and Crusoes', in *Alas, for the Pelicans: Flinders, Baudin & Beyond: Essays and Poems*, A. Chittleborough (ed.), Wakefield Press, Adelaide: 129–40.

Cumpston, J.S. 1958, *Macquarie Island: A Bibliography*, The Stone Copying Company, Cremorne.

Forte, Maximilian C. 2010, 'Introduction: Indigeneities and cosmopolitanisms', in *Indigenous Cosmopolitans: Transnational and Transcultural Indigeneity in the Twenty-First Century*, M.C. Forte (ed.), Peter Lang, New York: 1–16.

Ganter, Regina 1994, *The Pearl-Shellers of Torres Strait: Resource Use, Development and Decline 1860s–1960s*, Melbourne University Press, Carlton.

Gibbs, Martin 1998, 'Colonial boats and foreign ships: the history and archaeology of nineteenth century whaling in Western Australia', in *The Archaeology of Whaling in Southern Australia and New Zealand*, S. Lawrence and M. Staniforth (eds), Brolga Press for the Australasian Society for Historical Archaeology and the Australian Institute for Maritime Archaeology, Gundaroo: 36–47.

Gibbs, Martin 2000, 'Conflict and commerce: American whalers and the Western Australian colonies 1826–1888', *Great Circle* 22(2): 3–23.

Gibbs, Martin 2003, 'Nebinyan's songs: an Aboriginal whaler of Western Australia', *Aboriginal History* 27: 1–15.

Goodall, Heather and Allison Cadzow 2009, *Rivers and Resilience: Aboriginal People on Sydney's Georges River*, UNSW Press, Sydney.

Harman, Kristyn 2012, *Aboriginal Convicts: Australian, Khoisan and Māori Exiles*, UNSW Press, Sydney.

Jones, A.G.E. 1971, 'Island of desolation', *Antarctic* 6(1): 22–26.

Knopwood, Robert 1977, *The Diary of the Reverend Robert Knopwood, 1803–1838: First Chaplain of Van Diemen's Land*, M. Nicholls (ed.), Tasmanian Historical Research Association, Sandy Bay.

Lawrence, Mary Chipman 1966, *The Captain's Best Mate: The Journal of Mary Chipman Lawrence on the Whaler Addison, 1856–1860*, S. Garner (ed.), Brown University Press, Rhode Island.

Macknight, C.C. 1972, 'Macassans and Aborigines', *Oceania* 42(4): 283–321.

Macknight, C.C. 1976, *The Voyage to Marege: Macassan Trepangers in Northern Australia*, Melbourne University Press, Carlton.

Marika-Mununggiritj, Raymattja 1999, 'The 1998 Wentworth lecture', *Australian Aboriginal Studies* 1: 3–9.

Maynard, John 2005a, '"In the interests of our people": The influence of Garveyism on the rise of Australian Aboriginal political activism', *Aboriginal History* 29: 1–22.

Maynard, John 2005b, 'Transcultural/transnational interaction and influences on Aboriginal Australia', in *Connected Worlds: History in Transnational Perspective*, A. Curthoys and M. Lake (eds), ANU E Press, Canberra: 195–208.

Maynard, John 2007, *Fight for Liberty and Freedom: The Origins of Australian Aboriginal Activism*, Aboriginal Studies Press, Canberra.

McNiven, Ian J. 2001, 'Torres Strait Islanders and the maritime frontier in early colonial Australia', in *Colonial Frontiers: Indigenous–European Encounters in Settler Societies*, L Russell (ed.), Manchester University Press, Manchester: 175–97.

Mollison, Bill and Coral Everitt [c. 1976], *A Chronology of Events Affecting Tasmanian Aboriginal People Since Contact by Whites (1772–1976)*, Psychology Department, University of Tasmania, Hobart.

Morrell, Benjamin 1832, *A Narrative of Four Voyages to the South Sea, North and South Pacific Ocean, Chinese Sea, Ethiopia and Southern Atlantic Ocean, from the Year 1822 to 1832*, Harper, New York.

Nash, Michael 2003, *The Bay Whalers: Tasmania's Shore-Based Whaling Industry*, Navarine Publishing, Woden.

Norvill, G. and R. Bell 1864, *Geography of Mauritius: To Which Is Appended an Abstract of Its History*, Council of Education, Mauritius.

Philp, J.E. 1936, *Whaling Ways of Hobart Town*, Walch, Hobart.

Plomley, N.J.B. and Kristen Anne Henley 1990, *The Sealers of Bass Strait and the Cape Barren Island Community*, Blubber Head Press, Hobart.

Podruchny, Carolyn 2006, *Making the Voyageur World: Travelers and Traders in the North American Fur Trade*, University of Toronto Press, Toronto.

Poignant, Roslyn 2004, *Professional Savages: Captive Lives and Western Spectacle*, Yale University Press, New Haven.

Pulleine, R.H. 1929, 'The Tasmanians and their stone culture', in *Report of the Nineteenth Meeting of the Australasian Association for the Advancement of Science (Australia and New Zealand)*, C.E. Lord (ed.), Government Printer, Hobart: 294–314.

Richter, Daniel 2003, *Facing East from Indian Country: A Native History of Early America*, Harvard University Press, Cambridge.

Robin, Libby 2012, 'Seasons and nomads: Reflections on bioregionalism in Australia', in *The Bioregional Imagination: Literature, Ecology, and Place*, T. Lynch, C. Glotfelty, K. Armbruster and E.J. Zeitler (eds), University of Georgia Press, Athens: 278–94.

Robinson, George Augustus 2008, *Friendly Mission: The Tasmanian Journals and Papers of George Augustus Robinson, 1829–1834*, N.J.B. Plomley (ed.), Quintus Publishing, Hobart.

Rouleau, Brian 2010, 'Maritime destiny as manifest destiny: American commercial expansionism and the idea of the Indian', *Journal of the Early Republic* 30(3): 377–411.

Rouleau, Brian 2014, *With Sails Whitening Every Sea: Mariners and the Making of an American Maritime Empire*, Cornell University Press, Ithaca.

Russell, Lynette 2001, *Savage Imaginings: Historical and Contemporary Constructions of Australian Aboriginalities*, Australian Scholarly Press, Melbourne.

Russell, Lynette 2012, *Roving Mariners: Australian Aboriginal Whalers and Sealers in the Southern Oceans, 1790–1870*, SUNY Press, New York.

Salmond, Anne 1997, *Between Worlds: Early Exchanges between Māori and Europeans, 1773–1815*, Viking, Auckland.

Sleeper-Smith, Susan 2001, *Indian Women and French Men: Rethinking Cultural Encounter in the Western Great Lakes*, University of Massachusetts Press, Amherst.

Standfield, Rachel 2012, *Race and Identity in the Tasman World, 1769–1840*, Pickering & Chatto, London.

Taylor, Rebe 2002, *Unearthed: The Aboriginal Tasmanians of Kangaroo Island*, Wakefield Press, Adelaide.

Thomas, Martin 2011, *The Many Worlds of R.H. Mathews: In Search of an Australian Anthropologist*, Allen & Unwin, Crows Nest.

Thomas, Paul 2012, 'Oodeen, a Malay interpreter on Australia's frontier lands', *Indonesia and the Malay World* 40(117): 122–42.

Thomson, J. Inches 1913, *Voyages and Wanderings in Far-Off Seas and Lands*, Headley Brothers, London.

Toussaint, Auguste (ed.) 1954, *Early American Trade with Mauritius*, Esclapon, Port Louis.

Van Kirk, Sylvia 1983, *Many Tender Ties: Women in Fur-Trade Society, 1670–1870*, University of Oklahoma Press, Norman.

Wesson, Sue 2000, *A History of Aboriginal Involvement in Whaling at Twofold Bay*, New South Wales National Parks and Wildlife Service and Bega, Eden and Merrimans Aboriginal Forests Management Committee, Sydney.

Yanyuwa families, John Bradley and Nona Cameron 2003, *Forget About Flinders: A Yanyuwa Atlas of the South West Gulf of Carpentaria*, Yanyuwa families, John Bradley and Nona Cameron, Brisbane.

8

Miago and the 'Great Northern Men': Indigenous Histories from In-Between

Tiffany Shellam

The history of Australian exploration is one that is richly contextualised by the Aboriginal individuals who travelled—on foot, horse or by ship—over vast distances, across language groups and within Aboriginal domains. This movement was primarily enabled by Aboriginal people's attachment to European exploring parties as intermediaries. Acting as guides or 'native aides' brought Aboriginal travellers into contact with previously established networks of kin, as well as with Aboriginal strangers and feared enemies. Until recently, Australian exploration histories have privileged encounters between European explorers and Aboriginal people in a dyadic, hierarchical relationship. This has strengthened the assumption that cross-cultural encounters only occurred, or were most meaningful, when they were in a dichotomous relationship between Aboriginal people and Europeans. By framing exploration encounters in a triangular relationship—between Europeans, Aboriginal intermediaries and Aboriginal people met along the way—we can perceive the mobility of intermediaries and assess the ways in which they had the ability to shift the dimensions of power in European encounters with Aboriginal strangers. According to Alida Metcalf, the triangular position of an intermediary was 'rarely neutral', as their very presence influenced the 'power dynamics at play'.[1] They occupied a place of 'multiple interactions, negotiations, mediations and translations', as Miles Ogborn has noted.[2] An Aboriginal guide or intermediary was often attached to an expedition in the crew's expectation of his (rarely her) Aboriginal cultural universalism and ability to effectively communicate with all Aboriginal people met along the way. Yet, exploration archives indicate that explorers quickly became aware of the extra dynamic that the presence of an Aboriginal aid brought to these meetings, stressing their unfamiliarity, their incompatible languages and the misunderstandings between them. In considering such encounters as histories in-between, rather than 'top down' or 'from below', as David Phillip Miller has suggested, the fluidity, mobility and affect of Aboriginal intermediaries will be explored in this chapter, bringing meetings across Aboriginal language groups to the fore.[3]

I will discuss this mobility through Miago, a Nyungar man from the south-west of Western Australia, who was an intermediary on board HMS *Beagle*'s north-west Australian hydrographic expedition in 1837–38.[4] This expedition was instructed by the admiralty to determine whether Dampier Land (near Roebuck Bay on Australia's north-west coast) was an island; the great tides and configuration of the coast as described by earlier explorers had led to this supposition. Like most Indigenous intermediaries, Miago's experience of this expedition was chronicled by the European explorers who kept the logbooks and published their journals. However, as will be discussed, Miago catalogued his experience in particular ways, such as through song and story, and these were preserved by some of the explorers in their archives. In studying the expedition texts and Miago's stories, we can perceive his challenge in navigating between the familiar and the strange, both during meetings with Aboriginal strangers over the course of the expedition, and on his closely scrutinised return to country at the end of the expedition.

***

Miago's history and the context of the rapidly shifting political ground of the Swan River settlement in the mid-1830s is important to understanding Miago's mobility during the *Beagle* voyage. Miago was a Beeloo Nyungar

---

1   Metcalf 2005: 2–3.
2   Ogborn 2013: 167.
3   Miller 2011: 610–13.
4   Miago's name was also written as 'Migo' and 'Migeo' in colonial records.

man from Wurerup country, located around the upper reaches of the Swan River to the north of the Perth township. He had family and kin networks across the Swan and Canning river systems, which made it difficult for settlers to restrict him to a particular tribal group in their census reports and observations. By 1833, Miago was well known to settlers in the Swan River colony. He was represented in the local newspapers as a mediator between the Aboriginal groups living around Perth and was described by colonial observers as a 'messenger of peace' and an 'ambassador'.[5]

Miago was not just mobile himself; he was also effective at mobilising others. At a meeting with Governor Stirling in September 1833, at a time when the relationship between settlers and Nyungar people was particularly hostile, Miago and Munday (a Beeloo elder) advised that 16 Swan River Aboriginal people had been killed by settlers since the arrival of Europeans in 1829. They described the growing strength of the more distant Aboriginal groups who retained access to regenerating and exchangeable resources, which the rapidly dispossessed Swan River groups now lacked. As Mark Finnane and Heather Douglas have observed, at this meeting Miago and Munday described the 'uneven impact of the settlement on Aboriginal life' and effectively laid claim to special treatment by settlers; they suggested the settlers align themselves with the Swan River groups and shoot the more distant ones.[6] In March 1835, Miago brokered a meeting in Perth between the Bindjareb people from the Murray River near Pinjarra in the south, the Swan River Aboriginal groups and Stirling. Again, this was an attempt by Miago to facilitate a new order; in this instance, it followed a violent massacre at Pinjarra in 1834 that involved settlers, mounted police and government agents in a retributive attack against the Bindjareb people.[7] As well as his mediating skills, Miago was considered a useful tracker and guide, having assisted survey parties and tracking lost settlers in the bush.[8] He was employed as a guide in 1835 on Government Surveyor John Septimus Roe's overland expedition from Swan River to what was then known as King George's Sound.[9]

---

5   *Perth Gazette*, 7 September 1833.
6   *Perth Gazette*, 7 September 1833; Finnane and Douglas 2012: 21.
7   *Perth Gazette*, 3 January1835; CSR 37/178, 230 State Records Office of Western Australia (hereafter SROWA); Perth Gazette, 29 March 1835.
8   CSR 29/157-9, SROWA.
9   Roe 2005 [c. 1835].

In planning for the *Beagle*'s Australian survey, the admiralty encouraged the captain, John Wickham, to 'hire, at a low rate, some person acquainted with the dialects of the natives, which you are subsequently to visit, and with whom it will be essential to be on friendly terms'.[10] John Septimus Roe advised Wickham to hire Miago. Roe had knowledge of the diversity of Aboriginal languages and had previously worked with Aboriginal intermediaries and guides. As midshipman on Phillip Parker King's 1817–22 Australian hydrographic survey (jointly funded by the admiralty and the colonial office), which had travelled on several occasions to the north-west coast, Roe had noted that Aboriginal 'languages can change within 50 or 60 miles' along the coast.[11] Boongaree, a Garigal man from Broken Bay to the north of Port Jackson, had been the intermediary on King's survey in 1818 and Roe had noted how Boongaree's physical presence—his Aboriginal body—served as an effective conduit to communication with Aboriginal people onshore. Boongaree relied on his body, particularly when both his Garigal language and broken English were not understood by Aboriginal strangers.[12] When Roe travelled overland with Miago to King George's Sound from Swan River in 1835, he observed the foreignness between Miago and Aboriginal people only a few hundred kilometres from Swan River. During an encounter with an Aboriginal man and boy near 'the Williams', Miago could not translate their conversation, and the strangers' 'mode of talking, afforded [Miago], for many days afterwards abundant opportunity for the display of his own powers of mimickry [sic]'.[13] Roe knew that Miago would not be acquainted with the Aboriginal languages in the north. However, he valued Miago's assistance as a guide and broker, mentioning him frequently in his journal and even bestowing an island near Torbay with Miago's name:

> Our friend Migo having very narrowly escaped drowning while swimming to this Island, I distinguished it by the name Isle Migo, in remembrance of him and his many sterling good qualities.[14]

---

10 Beaufort, 8 June 1837, Hydrographer's Instructions to Captain J C Wickham, cited in Stokes vol. 1 1969 [c. 1846]: 20. Captain James Cook's 1770 voyage had set a precedent for Indigenous aides to be attached to maritime expeditions.
11 Roe 1821.
12 For a larger discussion about Boongaree's technique of brokering on that survey see Shellam 2015.
13 Roe 2005 [c. 1835].
14 Roe 2005 [c. 1835].

Despite his linguistic limitations, Roe advised Captain Wickham that Miago was indeed a valued intermediary who would suit the *Beagle*'s planned voyage to the north-west in 1837.[15]

Lieutenant John Lort Stokes, assistant surveyor on the *Beagle* and chronicler of the 1837–43 voyage, wrote that:

> Among the many useful hints, for which we were indebted to Mr Roe, was that of taking a native with us to the northward … named Miago; he proved in some respects, exceedingly useful, and made an excellent gun-room waiter.[16]

The servant in the gun room was the lowest possible position on board and was typically held by boys younger than 12. Like Boongaree on the earlier 1817 hydrographic survey, Miago's Aboriginal body would become the object of much observation on the *Beagle*'s voyage, both by the crew and Aboriginal strangers.

While Miago had not travelled to the north-west coast before, he had stories and deep knowledge of the northern Aboriginal groups, and this, I suggest, significantly shaped his experiences of travel and encounter. Like many Nyungar people in this period, Miago had a great fear of his northern neighbours, the Waylo, Weel or Will people, who were not only considered to be physically large and violent, but in possession of supernatural powers. Rather than the name of a particular group, Waylo was a generic term used by Aboriginal people throughout the south-west to refer to their northern neighbours.[17] This is demonstrated in Swan River settler George Fletcher Moore's observation that 'some of the northern tribes … appear to be indiscriminately referred to under the name Waylo or Weel men'.[18] Miago's fear of Waylo people was deeply imbedded in his psyche. Stokes recorded that Miago 'evidently holds these north men in great dread'. Indeed, Miago had needed some coaxing before he agreed to join the expedition: 'after some trouble', Stokes wrote, 'we shipped an intelligent man, named Miago'.[19] Stories about the north-west coast being inhabited by 'giants' or 'big men' were not specific to southern Aboriginal groups, but were also noted by European explorers. As Shino Konishi has observed, François Péron, the naturalist on board Nicholas

---

15 Stokes vol. 1 1969 [c. 1846]: 58.
16 Stokes vol. 1 1969 [c. 1846]: 58 (emphasis added).
17 Shellam 2009: 42.
18 George Fletcher Moore, cited in Shellam 2009: 42.
19 Stokes vol. 1 1969 [c. 1846]: 58.

Baudin's scientific expedition in 1803, wrote about 'extraordinarily big, strong men' who were 'like giants'.[20] Miago's fear of the northern men was recorded by crew members in every encounter with Aboriginal people on shore during the expedition.

Rather than embracing his role as Aboriginal mediator, Miago used his in-between position in interesting ways. For one, he attempted to place the crew at the centre of meetings with the northern groups to protect himself. As Stokes recorded:

> The northern men are, according to Miago's account, 'Bad men—eat men—Perth men tell me so: Perth men say, Miago, you go on shore very little, plenty Quibra men [men of the ship] go, you go'.[21]

This suggests that Miago used the explorers as his mediators upon encountering the northern men—a position he was advised to take by his own countrymen prior to the expedition.[22] These instructions to stay close to the ship and the crew, Stokes further noted, were 'very carefully pressed upon him by his associates' and 'succeeded in inspiring him with the utmost dread of this division of his fellow countrymen'.[23] Miago had previously utilised this technique of showing alliance to the Europeans when he and Munday met with Governor Stirling in 1833.

Miago was not the only Aboriginal guide to use Europeans to mediate relations with other Aboriginal communities. There were many instances of Europeans on the frontier being enlisted by Aboriginal mediators to settle disputes or inter-group grievances. For example, at King George's Sound in the early 1830s, Mineng Nyungar frequently propositioned soldiers at the garrison settlement to form a coalition with them and to use their flintlocks against the feared Waylo. As I have argued, such alliances were not necessarily a post-contact phenomenon but, rather, were part of an ongoing or traditional strategy of gaining political strength and self-protection.[24] While the soldiers refused to become involved in Nyungar regional politics, Nyungar people used them and the garrison 'as a safe haven for protection against their traditional enemies'.[25] Likewise, as Philip Jones has noted, when the explorer and anthropologist Alfred Howitt was in Diyari country at Lake Hope in 1861 there was a senior

20   Konishi 2008: 12.
21   Stokes vol. 1 1969 [c. 1846]: 75.
22   Stokes vol. 1 1969 [c. 1846]: 75.
23   Stokes vol. 1 1969 [c. 1846]: 75.
24   Shellam 2009: 114.
25   Shellam 2009: 114.

Diyari man, Jalina-piramurana, who requested that Howitt 'go with him and kill all the "Kunabura-kana", that is, the men of kunabura, who were "Malingki kana", that is, bad men'.[26] It is worth considering here the affect that a go-between or intermediary, such as Miago, had in such encounters. Alida Metcalf has observed in her work on the colonisation of Brazil that 'go-betweens may exploit their positions for their own benefit' because they are indifferent to the outcome desired by Europeans.[27] Miago certainly used the crew to his own advantage, placing them in a mediating position between himself and the feared northern strangers.

One of the ways that Miago hoped to exploit his participation in the journey was to collect 'evidence' of his travels to display to his kin. At the first sighting of Aboriginal people from the deck of the *Beagle*, Miago was, according to Stokes, 'delighted that these blackfellows, as he calls them, have no throwing sticks', as he wished to kill one of the men and carry off one of their wives.[28] Miago frequently expressed his desire to kidnap an Aboriginal woman from the north-west to take back to Swan River. Stokes concluded that a woman would be tangible proof of the extent of Miago's travelling. This theme of evidence—this desire by Aboriginal travellers to validate their new knowledge and experience of travel to their countrymen—is present in other exploration accounts in Western Australia. For instance, in 1833, when Manyat, a Nyungar man from King George's Sound, travelled well beyond his known geographic domain with colonial surgeon and naturalist Alexander Collie, he brought back bark from trees he had never seen before to show his countrymen how far he had travelled in foreign Aboriginal country.[29]

Miago's desire for evidence (in the form of a woman) of his travel also reveals that he had the expedition's aftermath in mind. Evidently, he was thinking about his return home and, perhaps, even the reception he would receive from his countrymen and women. However, Miago's fear of encountering northern coastal people was too great to carry out his plan of taking a woman: 'all his boasting', Stokes wrote, 'about killing some of them and taking one of their women as proof of his prowess, back to Perth, failed to concern'.[30] This failure was clearly distressing for Miago, as Stokes recorded:

---

26 Jones 2014: 98.
27 Metcalf 2005: 3.
28 Stokes vol. 1 1969 [c. 1846]: 223.
29 Shellam 2010: 121–32.
30 Stokes vol. 1 1969 [c. 1846]: 75.

His countenance and figure became at once instinct with animation and energy, and no doubt he was then influenced by feelings of baffled hatred and revenge, from having failed in his much-vaunted determination to carry off in triumph one of their gins. I would sometimes amuse myself by asking him how he was to excuse himself to his friends for having failed in the premised exploit, but the subject was evidently a very unpleasant one, and he was always anxious to escape from it.[31]

Adding to the difficulties of northern travel, Miago was frequently described as homesick and unsettled at sea and onshore. Near Cape Villaret, Stokes recorded that Miago accompanied a small party onshore:

Though he evidently showed no great devotion to the deed. They said he watched everything, aye, every bush, with the most scrutinizing gaze: his head appeared to turn upon a pivot, so constantly was it in motion.[32]

On the *Beagle*'s return journey, Miago was increasingly impatient for Swan River and would stand by the gangway singing songs. Stokes suggested that Miago's songs were mournful and that he was homesick for his country. Some of his songs were also intended for the northern men he had met with:

Miago … was as anxious as any one on board for the sight of his native land. He would stand gazing steadily and in silence over the sea, and then sometimes, perceiving that I watched him, say to me 'Miago sing, by and by northern men wind jump up': then would he station himself for hours at the lee-gangway, and chant to some imaginary deity an incantation or prayer to change the opposing wind … there was a mournful and pathetic air running through the strain, that rendered it by no means unpleasing; though doubtless it owed much of its effect to the concomitant circumstances.[33]

The explorer Sir George Grey also commented on Miago's songs. Prior to departing England, Wickham had been instructed by the admiralty to take Lieutenant Grey and Lieutenant Lushington aboard the *Beagle* as they were to undertake a separate, overland expedition from the north-west of Australia. At the Cape of Good Hope in South Africa, Grey purchased a schooner called the *Lyhner* and sailed directly to Hanover Bay on the north-west coast. Meanwhile, the *Beagle* sailed directly to Swan River where Wickham and Stokes would learn about the north-west from

---

31   Stokes vol. 1 1969 [c. 1846]: 221–23.
32   Stokes vol. 1 1969 [c. 1846]: 78.
33   Stokes vol. 1 1969 [c. 1846]: 221–22.

the Swan River settlers and recruit an intermediary before sailing up the coast. In April 1838, the *Beagle* met up with Grey in Hanover Bay. Since Grey's arrival on the north-west coast, he had experienced a difficult land-based expedition that included hostile meetings with Aboriginal people and being wounded in the hip by a spear. On meeting up with Wickham's expedition in Hanover Bay, Grey spent the night on board the *Beagle* and 'as all had much to hear and much to communicate, the evening wore rapidly away'.[34] Miago served Grey that evening in the gun room mess; it was their first meeting. Grey then sailed to Swan River, arriving in September 1838, to retrieve a new schooner before returning to the north-west. However, he was delayed there and spent several months undertaking local expeditions to the south of Perth and north to the Gascoyne River with the local Nyungar guides.

In 1838, at Swan River, Grey again met up with Miago. They spent time together at Grey's residence and Miago offered him descriptions of Nyungar culture.[35] Grey recorded these in his journal alongside details gathered from other cultural experts and events he had observed around the Swan River area. Nyungar songs were of particular interest to him. He wrote that 'if a native [is] afraid, he sings himself full of courage; in fact under all circumstances he finds aid and comfort from a song'.[36] Miago's singing on board the *Beagle* may have been a way of dealing with his homesickness, but it could also have been a means of protecting himself from potential sorcery from the Waylo, or attempting some kind of sorcery on them. Grey recorded a Nyungar woman's song that was sung to encourage Nyungar men to avenge the death of a young man, which she attributed to 'witchcraft and sorcery' from the north. The song begins: 'The blear-eyed sorcerers of the north/ Their vile enchantments sung and wove/ And in the night they issued forth/ A direful people-eating drove'.[37] Clint Bracknell has recently highlighted the gendered nature of Nyungar songs. For example, in this era, women's songs had particular functions, which included encouraging their countrymen to fight.[38] Other women's songs expressed maternal instincts of concern for their children who were travelling in foreign country.[39]

---

34 Grey vol. 1 2006 [c. 1841]: 129.
35 Grey vol. 2 2006 [c. 1841]: passim.
36 Grey vol. 2 2006 [c. 1841]: 404.
37 Grey vol. 2 2006 [c. 1841]: 414.
38 Bracknell 2014: 6.
39 Grey vol. 2 2006 [c. 1841]: 266–67.

Grey recorded the song that Miago's mother sang constantly during his absence at sea: 'ship bal win-jal bat-tar-dal gool-an-een', which he translated as 'whither is that lone ship wandering, my young son I shall never see again'.[40] Grey wrote that this song 'made a great impression on the natives'. Nyungar guide, Kaiber, who travelled with Grey to the Gascoyne River in February 1839, sang Miago's mother's song when Grey's expedition was desperately low on supplies. Worried about their survival, Kaiber also crafted his own song to reassure his mother—'Thither, mother oh, I return again, Thither oh, I return again'—and sang the two songs together as he sat with Grey by the fire.[41]

Miago ordered and remembered an account of the *Beagle*'s expedition in his mind. Stokes questioned him about 'the account he intended to give his friends of the scenes he had witnessed [while at sea]', writing that:

> He seemed to have carried the ship's track in his memory with the most careful accuracy. His description of the ship's sailing and anchoring were most amusing: he used to say, 'Ship walk—walk—all night—hard walk—then by and by, anchor tumble down'.[42]

This form of Aboriginal expedition chronicling was similar to Manyat's mind map of 1830. It also shares the structure of an account from another Nyungar guide, Warrup, of his journey with Roe in search of George Grey in 1839, suggesting that there was a particular genre of Aboriginal remembrance of travel.[43] On Miago's safe return to Swan River in May 1838, another song was composed by a Nyungar man after hearing the stories that Miago relayed about his adventures at sea.[44] The lyrics, 'Kan-de maar-o, kan-de maar-a-lo, Tsail-o mar-ra, tsail-o mar-ra', translate as, 'Unsteadily shifts the wind-o, unsteadily shifts the wind-o, The sails-o handle, the sails-o handle-ho'. These songs remained in Nyungar repertoire as a continuing chronicle of notable events; recorded to be recited, recited to be remembered.

Martin Gibbs has written about the Nyungar songman and whaler Nebinyan, revealing how 'the novel experience of whaling' provided Nebinyan with 'material to translate into song and dance, and consequently

---

40   Grey vol. 2 2006 [c. 1841]: 409–10.
41   Grey vol. 2 2006 [c. 1841]: 266–67.
42   Stokes vol. 1 1969 [c. 1846]: 223.
43   See Manyat's account in Shellam 2010. Warrup's account is published in Grey vol. 2 2006 [c. 1841]: 434–36. See also Jacky's testimony in Nugent 2015.
44   Grey vol. 2 2006 [c. 1841]: 410.

further facilitated his rise in standing within ... Nyungar society'.[45] Likewise, Bracknell has revealed how Western Australian colonial archives point to 'the existence of an Indigenous culture in which song is central to communication in everyday life'.[46] The shipboard experience gave Miago material for a story-song too. The development of song by Aboriginal people as a process for recording events occurred around Australia. For example, as Rachel Standfield has documented, William Thomas, Aboriginal Protector in the Port Phillip District, observed an Aboriginal man singing about 'the coming of the white fellow, the first appearance of the horse, bullock, wheelbarrow (cart), dog, sheep [and] flour'.[47]

While songs were constructed about travel experiences, Australian exploration archives reveal that singing (and talking) was an improvised and unpractised, or unrehearsed, technique required of intermediaries in the context of their brokering too, and utilised in many cross-cultural encounters with Aboriginal strangers; singing was part of the repertoire of an intermediary. For example, Boongaree utilised his songs during his expeditions with Matthew Flinders and, later, with Phillip Parker King's Australian hydrographic survey. In this context, his songs were not a tool to recount his adventures but a mediating technique. This method was also used by explorers. As Vanessa Agnew has traced for earlier maritime expeditions, 'failing other measures, such as proffering trade goods, music may have been seen [by explorers] as an alternative means of recourse in an attempt to initiate exchange'. Agnew used the term 'encounter music' for 'the cross-cultural exchange of music' during exploration encounters that often enabled the opening up of communication between Aboriginal people and explorers.[48] Bracknell discussed Nyungar cross-cultural dexterity in their incorporation of English and Scottish songs with their own music at King George's Sound.[49]

Miago also improvised using his catalogue of acquired languages. According to Stokes, at Beagle Bay he 'very sagaciously addressed' the Nyul Nyul people:

45   Gibbs 2003: 12.

46   Bracknell 2014: 5.

47   William Thomas, undated notebook within the Robert Brough Smyth papers, State Library of Victoria, MS 8781, Box 1176/6: 105, cited Standfield 2015: 56.

48   Agnew 2001: 6. See also Fornasiero and West-Sooby 2014: 17–35.

49   Bracknell 2014: 5.

In English; shaking hands and saying, 'How do you do?' and then began to imitate their various actions, and mimic their language, and so perfectly did he succeed that one of our party could not be persuaded that he really understood them; though for this suspicion I am convinced there was in truth no foundation.[50]

Miago's use of English rather than Nyungar reveals, as David Turnbull suggested, 'the improvised resort of a go-between trying to create an auditory common ground, but relying on the language he had acquired during an earlier boundary crossing'.[51] Yet, it was precisely these acquisitions that expedition leaders sometimes wished their intermediaries to downplay. While explorers were often well aware of the strangeness between their guides and the Aboriginal locals, they also frequently attempted to render these people more familiar to each other by encouraging them to forget their broken English and remove their clothes to be an 'authentic Aborigine', rather than the 'civilised native' they had become.

While travelling vast distances from country was something to be admired in the Aboriginal community, for the travellers the experience could be sad, stressful and frightening. In 1839, Tommy (whose Nyungar name was Yee-lal-nar-nap) replaced Miago on the *Beagle*'s voyage for an expedition to the north-west. He was a young man who joined the expedition with his 'mother's consent'. While it is difficult to know what was meant by Tommy obtaining his mother's approval to travel, it is a reminder that individual Aboriginal travellers were not always freely independent; instead, they were mobile within the ongoing constraints of community responsibilities and obligations, as Standfield's chapter in this volume also demonstrates. Other Nyungar travellers in this era— such as Mineng Nyungar men Manyat and Gyalliput who travelled with newcomers from King George's Sound to Swan River in the early 1830s— had to receive 'full consent from their tribe' before departing. According to the Lieutenant Governor Frederick Chidley Irwin, their safe return was hailed 'by their Tribe with great satisfaction, and increased confidence in our good faith and friendship'.[52] Crawford Pasco, the master's mate, wrote that:

---

50 Stokes vol. 1 1969 1 [c. 1846]: 92.
51 Turnbull 2009: 422.
52 Irwin to Lord Viscount Goderich, *Perth Gazette* 19 January 1833: 10.

Poor Tommy soon felt homesick or mammy-sick, for I noticed [him] one evening under the lee of the spanker crying. 'What are you crying about, Tommy?' I inquired. 'Cos my mudder cry now, I know, so I cry'.[53]

This example, together with the song of Miago's mother and Kaiber's song to his mother, suggests community concern for the welfare of these mobile Aboriginal men, particularly on travels to the north-west where the Waylo people lived. Grey further noted that songs were created to alleviate concern for travellers. For example, a song by Nyungar people living near the Murray River, south of Perth, was sung 'in the event of the absence of any of their relatives or friends upon a hunting or war excursion', and included the lyrics 'Return hither'.[54]

Like Miago, Tommy also dreaded the northern men, and his encounters were also shaped by his history and knowledge of the Waylo. Lewis Fitzmaurice, one of the mates, had been surveying the coast ahead of the expedition in a whaler. When Fitzmaurice had chosen to retreat rather than use his guns after being confronted by Aboriginal people onshore, Stokes made note of Tommy's reaction:

> It was of much the same complexion as that of Miago; and he threatened magnanimously to inflict the most condign punishment on the fellows who opposed Mr Fitzmaurice's landing. He had a strong impression that these northern people were of gigantic stature; and in the midst of the silent and gaping interest with which he listened to Mr Fitzmaurice's account of his adventure, the words 'big fella' often escaped from his lips; and he appeared quite satisfied when assured that his opinion was correct.[55]

This record suggests that Miago's and Tommy's encounters with these 'big fellas' in the north affirmed the often-told stories and songs about them throughout the Nyungar world in the south. These confrontations, while terrifying, worked to further cement Miago's and Tommy's Aboriginal domain.[56]

---

53 Pasco 1897: 112.
54 Grey vol. 2 2006 [c. 1841]: 407.
55 Stokes vol. 2 1969 [c. 1846]: 174.
56 It is worth noting here that Tommy also sailed with the *Beagle* to Coepang, Timor, where he was immediately identified as a 'Marege' by the locals—connecting him with Aboriginal people from northern Australia who have a long history of mobility.

Moving In-Between

Miago's physical body was both an important vehicle and a site for connection during meetings with Aboriginal strangers. At Beagle Bay, Stokes recorded an encounter with a group of Nyul Nyul people, and their reaction to Miago:

> They seemed astonished to find one apparently of their 'own clime, complexion, and degree' in company with the white strangers, who must have seemed to them a distant race of beings; nor was their wonder at all abated when Miago threw open his shirt, and showed them his breast curiously scarred after their fashion … as a convincing evidence that he, though now the associate of a white man, belonged to the same country as themselves.[57]

At Beagle Bay, a group of Nyul Nyul men very closely examined Miago's body. Stokes wrote that Miago:

> Submitted to be handled by them with a very rueful countenance, and afterwards construed the way in which one of them had gently stroked his beard, into an attempt to take him by the throat and strangle him![58]

To Miago, this was:

> An injury and indignity which, when safe on board, he resented by repeated threats, uttered in a sort of wild chant, of spearing their thighs, backs, loins, and indeed, each individual portion of the frame.[59]

One might question whether Miago was, in fact, attempting to enact sorcery against these feared enemies.

During Phillip Parker King's hydrographic survey in 1821, the Port Jackson Aboriginal intermediary Bundle (who had taken over when Boongaree retired) also stripped off his clothes when meeting with the Worrorra people at Hanover Bay. However, Bundle was from Dharawal country and so did not share Miago's and Tommy's fear of the Waylo. At Hanover Bay, Bundle had the confidence to initiate the meeting himself, calling out to the Worora, placing his open hands on his heart and opening up his arms as a gesture of peace as he approached them.[60]

---

57 Stokes vol. 1 1969 [c. 1846]: 92.
58 Stokes vol. 1 1969 [c.1846]: 92.
59 Stokes vol. 1 1969 [c. 1846]: 99.
60 Shellam 2018.

Bodies were also a site for comment and concern by the crew of the *Beagle*, as they closely scrutinised Miago's mobility. Some explorers utilised the suspended space of the expedition (i.e. being on board a ship) to quiz, observe and test the mobility of their Aboriginal companions. Stokes described how he questioned Miago about particular aspects of Aboriginal culture. 'The rude savage—separated from all his former companions', Stokes wrote:

> Made at once an intimate and familiar witness of some of the wonders of civilization, carried by his new comrades to their very country, and brought face to face with his traditionary foes, the dreaded 'northern men', and now returning to recount to his yet ruder brethren the wonders he had witnessed—could not fail to interest the least imaginative.[61]

In the contained 'laboratory' of the expedition space, the intermediary became the archetype or axis upon which all other Aboriginal people were compared or contrasted.[62] Other experiments tested the intermediary's resolve to remain in the 'civilised space' that the expedition encouraged. Such close scrutiny and concern by explorers eager for the transformation of their intermediaries as a result of an expedition is a common theme in exploration archives. Edmund Kennedy reflected on the positive, civilising effect that his 1847 expedition into Central Australia had on his Aboriginal intermediary, Harry:

> He has picked up so much English on the journey that he can make himself understood whatever he wishes to say; and in addition to this, he has acquired an activity and obedience that would be no discredit to a white boy older than himself. His appearance has greatly improved. No longer a poor child, he has become a tall well-set lad, with a kind but bold expression of countenance.[63]

Don Baker commented on Thomas Mitchell's similar judgements of his guide, Piper, after their return to Sydney at the end of their overland expedition:

---

61   Stokes vol. 1 1969 [c. 1846]: 221–22.
62   Bronwen Douglas discusses how intermediaries could be a mobile representation of Port Jackson. See Douglas 2014: 120–21.
63   Edmund Kennedy, 'Journal of an Expedition into Central Australia', entries for April 22, November 17 and December 26, 1847, JMS 13/58, Royal Geographic Society, cited in Kennedy 2013: 176.

> To Mitchell's great pleasure, Piper abstained from intoxication and looked with contempt on those wretched, drunken Aboriginal people who led an abandoned, sordid existence around Sydney. But Piper soon tired of city life and became impatient to return to his own country, near Bathurst.[64]

Just as Australian explorers sometimes commented on how their travels positively transformed Aboriginal intermediaries, Dane Kennedy has discussed a comparable sensibility among British explorers in Africa. Some explorers wrote in a humanitarian language of how they freed young boys from slavery, employing them on their expeditions as mediators and guides. At the close of the expedition, these boys were sometimes sent to missionary schools or found other expeditions to be attached to.[65] David Livingstone was one of many explorers of Africa who collected 'stray boys displaced by the slave trade'.[66] However, the freedom granted to such 'stray boys' was a relative term, as the children, having been displaced from their own communities, were far from 'free'.

Sailors, like the crew of the *Beagle*, were certainly not foreign to conceiving shipboard space as liminal or transformative. Indeed, they were members of a culture that had a long history of viewing the space of a ship as a site for ritualised initiations. When ships sailed across the equatorial line, a rite of passage was enacted to initiate a sailor's first equatorial crossing. This performance was a test by seasoned sailors to ensure their new shipmates were capable of handling long and rough sea voyages. Like other initiations, it was a moment of transformation in which an inexperienced sailor transitioned to an advanced stage.[67] Upon crossing the equatorial line, ceremonies centred on the transformation of initiates through a contrived physical improvement; their faces were slopped with dirty tar, before being washed and shaved clean, their appearances altered.

Closely tied to the failure of Miago's shipboard initiation, Miago's physical appearance and the way he dressed (or undressed) himself was the topic of considerable commentary by crew members on board the *Beagle*. Stokes described the crew's attempts to transform Miago while on board the ship:

---

64 Baker 1997: 130.
65 Baker 1997: 130.
66 Baker 1997: 130.
67 Griffiths 2007: 108.

During the time that Miago was on board we took great pains to wean him from his natural propensity for the savage life by instilling such information as his untutored mind was capable of receiving, and from his often expressed resolutions we were led to hope a cure had been effected.[68]

However, Miago was diffident on his return home, as Stokes observed:

We were considerably amused with the consequential air Miago assumed towards his countrymen on our arrival, which afforded us a not uninstructive instance of the prevalence of the ordinary infirmities of our common human nature, whether of pride or vanity, universally to be met with both in the civilized man and the uncultivated savage. He declared that he would not land until they first came off to wait on him.[69]

Other crew members represented Miago's much anticipated return to Swan River as a crisis of identity. The master's mate, Benjamin Francis Helpman, found this crisis amusing, representing it in the following way:

A great piece of fun! Miago the New Hollander, went ashore. He had one of the Captain's old dress coats; a gold-laced cap with feathers in it; my old sword and belt, with a pair of new trowsers [sic]. He looked more like a stuffed monkey. On landing he was distant with his old friends and brothers. He would not allow them to kiss him, because he said they were not 'wilgayed'. And the cream of the joke is, he would not speak his own language, but would persist in speaking English, although they did not understand a word of what he said.[70]

It is difficult to know what Miago's actions meant to him and his community. Was he acting out his own feelings of superiority? Was his differentiation due to metaphysical or spiritual causes? Was he still affected by the 'pollution' of having met with the dreaded Waylo? Stokes presented Miago's return in a negative frame, commenting on the rapidity with which Miago went back to his 'uncivilised' ways at the end of the expedition, and his failure to remain a transformed man:

Great was our disappointment on finding that in less than a fortnight after our arrival, he had resumed his original wildness, and was again to be numbered amongst the native inhabitants of the bush.[71]

68 Stokes vol.1 1969 [c. 1846]: 228.
69 Stokes vol.1 1969 [c. 1846]: 226–27.
70 Helpman cited in Christie 1943–44: 13 (wilgayed means washed).
71 Stokes vol. 1 1969 [c. 1846]: 226–29.

When asked to rejoin the expedition, Miago decided to remain at home with his wife. It is worth reflecting on what might have occurred in the Aboriginal world in the fortnight between embarkation at Swan River and Miago's return to his community. Did the Nyungar mulgarrdocks (doctors) enact ceremonies to normalise Miago and ward off possible sorcery from the Waylo that he encountered?[72] Recall his songs at sea that were meant for these enemies: did the Nyungar have to sing songs of their own for their protection and for Miago's on his return?

A few years later, George Grey commented on the tension for Miago between the imperial space of the expedition and Nyungar life. He compared the 'apparently perfectly civilised' native he had first met on board the *Beagle* in April 1838 who 'waited at the gun room mess, was temperate (never tasting spirits), attentive, cheerful, and remarkably clean' with the 'savage, almost naked' man he encountered at Swan River in September 1838.[73] Yet, Grey also sympathised with Miago's decision to return to his community, viewing it as a strategic move to reject the role of servant to the white man, as this was inevitable had he remained living among the settlers:

> He never could have been either a husband or a father, if he had lived apart from his own people; where among the whites was he to find one who would have filled for him the place of his black mother, who he is much attached.[74]

Grey understood that Miago would never be accepted in colonial society—that his initiation into that world could never be complete—and also recognised Miago's attachment to his family. While the ship was a space of transformation for uninitiated seamen upon crossing the equatorial line, for Aboriginal intermediaries like Miago, the transformation could neither be permanent on board nor onshore due to insurmountable racial differences. As Stokes recorded, Miago's role on the *Beagle* included being an 'excellent gun room waiter': a servant to the explorers.

Historians have helped to continue this expedition-as-civilising–experiment narrative. Marsden Hordern described Stokes' failed attempt to induce Miago from his Aboriginal life as a process of 'weaning':

---

72 I am grateful to Lachy Paterson for his suggestions here.
73 Grey vol. 2 2006 [c. 1841]: 370–71.
74 Grey vol. 2 2006 [c. 1841]: 370–71.

Torn between the attractions of the new life and the forces of the old, [Miago] struggled for several days, trying to reconcile the two. In the end, discarding his clothes and with them his recently acquired white man's habits, he re-joined the tribe.[75]

However, experience and culture were not so easily shed. As Grace Karskens reminds us, Aboriginal people's particular use of clothes and style of dressing (often in the scraps of military uniforms) has been framed by settlers and historians as a sign of cultural degradation. Yet, according to Karskens, Aboriginal people wore and removed clothes in meaningful ways, signifying strategic mobility between domains.[76] Discussing examples of intermediaries' autonomy in Australian exploration, Dane Kennedy gave these men the identity of 'deracinated' figures, or 'marginal men' who had been ripped from their communities and 'forced by the circumstances of their estrangement to forge a new niche for themselves at the intersection of cultures'.[77] However, this generalisation was not the experience of all Aboriginal intermediaries involved in exploration. Karskens has also written about Eora motivation for sea travel in the early decades of the colony at Port Jackson, noting that 'what attracted these young men to sailing' was not necessarily cultural, but the possibility of 'talk with sailors, the lure of adventure, the realisation that people could go beyond the horizon'.[78] I further suggest that for some Aboriginal single men, exploring in foreign Aboriginal country gave them an elevated status in their own community on their return. For example, for Mineng Nyungar at King George's Sound, travel enabled by exploration with the Europeans had the possibility of 'extending kin networks and enhancing geographic knowledge and perspectives of country'.[79] Thus, for Aboriginal intermediaries, being part of the team of an expedition, while it could be transformative, could also be as much about strengthening Aboriginal identity as about severing ties with community.

By closely analysing the *Beagle*'s texts, we can read how Miago's mobility and the strength of his expanding Aboriginal world were reduced to a failed experiment by the crew. However, we can also view Miago's vast travels across Aboriginal and settler domains as enabling an increased mobility in both worlds. His experience of voyaging to the north-west coast can be

---

75   Hordern 1989: 88.
76   Karskens 2011.
77   Kennedy 2013: 166.
78   Karskens 2009: 428.
79   Shellam 2009: 177.

understood as reinforcing his Nyungar world: meeting the dreaded north men gave further weight to Miago's ongoing stories about them. As the *Beagle* approached Swan River, Stokes questioned Miago about his return and the stories he would tell 'of the scenes he had witnessed'. Stokes wrote: 'I was quite astonished at the accuracy with which he remembered the various places we had visited during the voyage … His manner of describing his interviews with the "wicked northern men", was most graphic'.[80] Miago's mobility enabled him to meet the dreaded Waylo; they caressed his beard and studied his ritual scarifications; he mimicked their language and brought home 'graphic' stories to add to a growing southern anthology about the north. Miago's fluidity between the Aboriginal and colonial worlds, like other go-betweens, reminds us that the Aboriginal domain was dominant and strong. It is not accurate to read Miago as a 'deracinated figure', for Nyungar society remained a priority for him, despite the strengthening presence and influence of newcomers.

References

Agnew, Vanessa 2001, 'A "Scots Orpheous" in the South Seas, or, the use of music on Cook's second voyage', *Journal of Maritime Research* 3(1): 1–27. doi.org/10.1080/21533369.2001.9668310

Baker, D.W.A. 1997, *The Civilised Surveyor: Thomas Mitchell and the Australian Aborigines*, Melbourne University Press, Carlton.

Bracknell, Clint 2014, 'Kooral Dwonk-katitjiny (listening to the past): Aboriginal language, songs and history in south-western Australia', *Aboriginal History* 38: 1–18.

Christie, E.M. 1943–44, *Being Extracts and Comments on the Manuscript Journals of Benjamin Francis Helpman of H.M. Sloop 'Beagle' 1837–38–39–40*, Extract from Proceedings 1943–1944, Royal Geographical Society of Australasia South Australian Branch Incorporated, Adelaide: 1–59.

Douglas, Bronwen 2014, *Science, Voyages and Encounters in Oceania: 1511–1850*, Palgrave Macmillan, New York.

---

80   Stokes vol. 1 1969 [c. 1846]: 223.

Finnane, Mark and Heather Douglas 2012, *Indigenous Crime and Settler Law: White Sovereignty After Empire,* Palgrave Macmillan, New York.

Fornasiero, J. and J. West-Sooby 2014, 'Cross cultural inquiry in 1802: Musical performance on the Baudin Expedition to Australia', in *Conciliation on Colonial Frontiers: Conflict, Performance and Commemoration in Australia and the Pacific Rim,* Kate Darian-Smith and Penelope Edmonds (eds), Routledge, New York: 17–35.

Gibbs, Martin 2003, 'Nebinyan's songs: An Aboriginal whaler of south-west Western Australia', *Aboriginal History* 27: 1–15.

Grey, George 2006 [c. 1841], *Journals of Two Expeditions of Discovery in North-West and Western Australia, During the Years 1837, 1838 and 39, in Two Volumes,* vol. 1 and vol. 2, The Echo Library, Middlesex.

Griffiths, Tom 2007, *Slicing the Silence: Voyaging to Antarctica,* University of New South Wales Press, Sydney.

Hordern, Marsdern 1989, *Mariners be Warned: John Lort Stokes and HMS Beagle in Australia, 1837–1843,* Melbourne University Press, Carlton.

Jones, Philip 2014, 'The theatre of contact: Aborigines and exploring expeditions', in *Expedition into Empire: Exploratory Journeys and the Making of the Modern World,* Martin Thomas (ed.), Routledge, New York: 88–107.

Karskens, Grace 2009, *The Colony: A History of Early Sydney,* Allen & Unwin, Crows Nest.

Karskens, Grace 2011, 'Red coat, blue jacket, black skin: Aboriginal men and clothing in early New South Wales', *Aboriginal History* 35: 1–36.

Kennedy, Dane 2013, *The Last Blank Spaces: Exploring Africa and Australia,* Harvard University Press, Cambridge. doi.org/10.4159/harvard.9780674074972

Konishi, Shino 2008 (March), '"Inhabited by a race of formidable giants": French explorers, Aborigines and the endurance of the fantastic in the great south land, 1803', *Australian Humanities Review* 44: 7–22.

Metcalf, Alida 2005, *Go-Betweens and the Colonization of Brazil: 1500–1600,* University of Texas Press, Texas.

Miller, David Philip 2011, 'Histories from between', *Technology and Culture* 52(3), July: 610–13 doi.org/10.1353/tech.2011.0109

Nugent, Maria 2015, 'Jacky Jacky and the politics of Aboriginal testimony', in *Indigenous Intermediaries: New Perspectives on Exploration Archives,* Shino Konishi, Maria Nugent and Tiffany Shellam (eds), ANU Press, Canberra: 67–84. doi.org/10.22459/II.09.2015

Ogborn, Miles 2013 (April), '"It's not what you know…": Encounters, go-betweens and the geography of knowledge', *Modern Intellectual History* 10(1): 163–75. doi.org/10.1017/S147924431200039X

Pasco, Crawford 1897, *A Roving Commission: Naval reminiscences*, George Robertson, Melbourne.

Roe, John Septimus 1821, Letter to William Roe, 6 June 1821, Mitchell Library: MLMSS 7964 / vol. 5 (Safe 1 / 468).

Roe, John Septimus 2005 [c. 1835], 'Journal of an expedition from Swan River overland to King George's Sound, by J.S. Roe esq, Surveyor General, 19 October to 21 November 1835', in *Western Australian Exploration volume 1: 1826–1835,* Peter Bridge and Kim Epton (eds), Hesperian Press, Victoria Park.

Shellam, Tiffany 2009, *Shaking Hands on the Fringe: Negotiating the Aboriginal World at King George's Sound,* University of Western Australian Press, Crawley.

Shellam, Tiffany 2010, '"Manyat's sole delight: Travelling knowledge in Western Australia's south west, 1830s', in *Transnational Lives: Biographies of Global Modernity, 1700–Present*, Desley Deacon, Penny Russell and Angela Woollacott (eds), Palgrave Macmillan, Basingstoke: 121–32. doi.org/10.1057/9780230277472_10

Shellam, Tiffany 2015, 'Mediating encounters through bodies and talk', in *Indigenous Intermediaries: New Perspectives on Exploration Archives,* Shino Konishi, Maria Nugent and Tiffany Shellam (eds), ANU Press, Canberra: 85–102. doi.org/10.22459/II.09.2015

Shellam, Tiffany 2018, 'Ethnographic inquiry on Phillip Parker King's hydrographic survey', in *Expeditionary Anthropology: Teamwork, Travel and the 'Science of Men'*, Martin Thomas and Amanda Harris (eds), Berghan Books, New York.

Standfield, Rachel 2015, '"Thus have been preserved numerous interesting facts that would otherwise have been lost": Colonisation, protection and William Thomas's contribution to *The Aborigines of Victoria*', in *Settler Colonial Governance in Nineteenth Century Victoria*, Lynette Russell and Leigh Boucher (eds), ANU Press, Canberra: 47–62. doi.org/10.22459/SCGNCV.04.2015

Stokes, John Lort 1969 [c. 1846], *Discoveries in Australia; Wth an Account of the Coasts and Rivers Explored and Surveyed During the Voyage of the Beagle in the Years 1837–38–39–40–41–42–43*, T. and W. Boone, London (Libraries Board of South Australia, Adelaide, South Australia).

Turnbull, David 2009, 'Boundary-crossings, cultural encounters and knowledge spaces in early Australia', in *The Brokered World: Go-Betweens and Global Intelligence 1770–1820*, Simon Scaffer, Lissa Roberts, Kapil Raj and James Delbourgo (eds), Science History Publications USA, Sagmore Beach: 387–428.

9

Indigenous Women, Marriage and Colonial Mobility

Angela Wanhalla

Imperial events, transport routes and communication networks created out of exploration, trade and colonisation opened up new possibilities for global Indigenous mobility during the eighteenth and nineteenth centuries.[1] In recent decades, patterns of Indigenous mobility across these imperial routes and pathways have begun to be traced in an effort to challenge the assumption that 'networks are associated only with colonisers' and that 'indigenous societies are exclusively local'.[2] As the editors of a special issue of *American Quarterly* on alternative contact histories argued, to interpret Indigenous peoples as 'invested only in concerns of their lands' ignores instances of 'Indigenous peoples in the role of active, mobile, and even cosmopolitan actors on the world stage' that 'complicate static or incomplete definitions of Indigenous identity'.[3]

---

1   My thanks to Sherry Farrell Racette and Krista Barclay, as well as Frank Tough and his research team at the Métis Archival Project at the University of Alberta, for sharing their knowledge of fur trade families and métis history with me, and for sourcing archival material for this article. I am also grateful to Sarah Carter and Adele Perry for enabling my visit to the University of Alberta and the University of Manitoba as a Distinguished Visitor at both universities in early 2015, which allowed me to conduct research on the Grieve and Harrold families at local archives. I would like to particularly acknowledge participants at the Indigenous Mobilities workshop for their critical feedback on a draft version of this chapter, and Rachel Standfield for her thoughtful and considered advice. Finally, I gratefully acknowledge the support of a Royal Society of New Zealand Rutherford Discovery Fellowship, which supported the research for this chapter. Paterson 2013; Burton 2012.
2   Lester 2014: 2.
3   Lai and Smith 2010: 408, 409.

In this scholarship though, Indigenous women's mobility within and across imperial and colonial spaces is not as coherently described or examined as that of Indigenous men who are firmly located in intellectual, religious, political, trade and print culture networks.[4] As chapters in this volume indicate, Indigenous men's motivations and experiences of global travel are increasingly gaining scholarly attention; however, Indigenous women's mobility is rarely recognised.[5] Although some recent work has demonstrated that Indigenous women *were* involved in networks of Indigenous activism, *were* writers and critics of imperialism and colonialism, authored petitions and engaged in humanitarian debates,[6] scholars have yet to fully explore Indigenous women's participation in imperial networks or elaborate the variety of ways in which they were active mobile subjects.

As historical subjects, Indigenous women tend to be associated with forms of involuntary movement; their mobility across imperial and colonial space is often equated with violence, coercion and abandonment. A well-known example from early New Zealand is Atahoe (1790–1810), the daughter of Ngāpuhi chief Te Pahi, who accompanied her English husband, the ex-convict George Bruce, to Malacca, was then kidnapped and taken to Calcutta, before eventually being abandoned by Bruce in Sydney, where she died.[7] In Hawai'i, Indigenous women were among the earliest travellers to the Pacific Northwest Coast of modern-day Oregon, Washington state and British Columbia, sometimes by choice, but more often facilitated by engagement in domestic service for European families or, under duress, as captives.[8] The link between involuntary mobility and Indigenous women's labour is also prevalent in relation to their involvement in early colonial maritime resource economies, especially sealing.[9] In an important intervention into this history, Lynette Russell queried whether the method of their mobility—that is, whether they 'were captured or traded, were forced or voluntarily arrived at their location'— should 'be the framework through which we see the rest of their lives?'[10] Russell's chapter in this volume applies this conceptual approach to

---

4   For instance, O'Brien 2014; Warrior 2005; Carey and Lydon 2014; Lester 2014; Laidlaw 2014; Elbourne 2005.
5   O'Malley 2015; Weaver 2014.
6   For instance, Banivanua Mar 2013; Hoxie 2014.
7   Legge 1991. See also, O'Brien 2006; Banivanua Mar 2015.
8   Barman and McIntyre Watson 2006.
9   Russell 2012.
10   Russell 2012: 18.

analyse Aboriginal Tasmanian women's travel in the nineteenth century. In this chapter, I utilise the 'life geographies'[11] of two women whose paths crossed momentarily in southern New Zealand to argue that marriage and kinship networks are an important, but overlooked, pathway to track the specificities of Indigenous women's mobility. Agnes Grieve (1830–1903), of Swampy Cree ancestry, was born in Canada, and her travel across vast distances followed imperial pathways, bringing her to New Zealand in 1848. Agnes lived near Jane Palmer (1830–98), whose localised pattern of seasonal mobility was enabled by Indigenous geographies and kinship networks. These women's lives overlapped between 1849 and 1861 when, during that period, they shared space in colonial Otago, where their respective kinship networks energised their ties to place.

Agnes Grieve and Jane Palmer lived near each other at the small river settlements of Taieri Ferry and Maitapapa. Both villages are on the Taieri Plain, which is dominated by a tidal river that was a main communication and transport route for colonists and travellers, carrying them, their goods and stock inland from the coastal port of Taieri Mouth on a route that took them through a narrow gorge before opening out onto the plain itself. Here, travellers disembarked at the settlement of Taieri Ferry, where Agnes Grieve managed an accommodation house on the tribal lands of local Kāi Tahu, directly across the river from the Indigenous people who had been dispossessed, including my three-times great-grandmother, Jane Palmer. In this region, waterways were an essential conduit of people and goods, connecting inland regions to the coast and the sea. More importantly, the river, inland lakes and wetlands were compelling sites of coexisting, overlapping and, at times, competing colonial and Indigenous geographies and kinship networks.

Indigenous women participated in imperial networks; however, the unevenness of the archival record limits the possibility of making any broad assessment of the patterns of their mobility or its scale. Agnes Grieve and Jane Palmer, like many Indigenous women, left a light imprint on the textual archive. Neither woman left behind a cache of letters or correspondence and Agnes has no direct descendants in New Zealand to maintain her memory. Yet, a paucity of documentary material is not necessarily an impediment to reconstituting subaltern or Indigenous lives, as Clare Anderson and Adele Perry's work has demonstrated.[12] Instead,

---

11   Daniels and Nash 2004: 450.
12   Anderson 2012; Perry 2015. See also Ballantyne 2012: 105–22; Anderson 2011.

as contended by Turtle Mountain Chippewa scholar Danika Medak-Saltzman, a wider array of sources ought to be utilised to illustrate the 'many ways that Indigenous peoples have always been active actors on the global stage'; to 'do otherwise would be to perpetuate historical silences'.[13] Medak-Saltzman examined encounters between Indigenous women at the 1904 St Louis Exposition as depicted in photographs, focusing on how such:

> Moments of colonial celebrations of empire may have inadvertently served anticolonial purposes by presenting the Indigenous participants with opportunities to interact across larger distances than had been practical or possible in the past.[14]

According to Medak-Saltzman, to relate Indigenous–Indigenous moments of contact and engagement at international exhibitions and world's fairs solely within an analytical framework of imperial ethnographic display practices was a 'rationale for leaving questions about Native experiences unexamined'.[15] Opening her mind to alternative interpretations that arise from photographs of two Indigenous women conversing with each other *outside the exhibition space*, she argued that such photographs were evidence of Indigenous experiences on the world's stage that had been sidelined in favour of the more abundant visual source material that depicted Indigenous people on display. This alternative visual evidence of Indigenous–Indigenous encounter serves as a reminder that imperial and colonial exhibitions were forums through which Indigenous peoples could connect with each other and create spaces for themselves.

While noting the increased attention paid to uncovering modes of Indigenous participation in imperial networks in the context of settler colonialism and dispossession in recent decades, Alan Lester and Zoe Laidlaw have pointed out that 'where and how Indigenous people connect with trans-global networks [remains] ill-defined'.[16] One important pathway yet to be integrated into the analysis of imperial networks and mobility is intermarriage: a social, political and economic practice utilised by Indigenous peoples in many colonial contexts to manage the impacts of contact and colonisation. In this chapter, I depart from the standard view of intermarriage as a process deployed by Indigenous communities

13   Medak-Saltzman 2010: 592–93.
14   Medak-Saltzman 2010: 593.
15   Medak-Saltzman 2010: 593.
16   Lester and Laidlaw 2015: 7.

to tie an outsider, usually a white man, to a particular place and family, towards an interpretation that regards intermarriage as one pathway for the global mobility of Indigenous and mixed-descent women. Through intermarriage, as the lives of Agnes and Jane reveal, Indigenous women's lives intersected with the processes of global economic expansion and settler colonialism in ways that were different from the experience of their male relatives. To map the terrain of Agnes' and Jane's mobility through their marriage and kinship networks, I draw upon archival fragments from several colonial sites (Canada, the Orkney Islands and New Zealand) produced by several bodies (the Hudson's Bay Company, colonial provincial governments and the colonial state) that inadvertently reveal Indigenous women's circulation across and within colonial spaces.[17]

Life Geographies and Kinship Networks

Imperial and colonial pathways of mobility enacted through the fur trade relied upon technologies and infrastructure, such as global communication and transport networks.[18] Agnes was born into a Cree world that coexisted and engaged with an expanding fur-trade economy and infrastructure in western Canada that drew upon a mobile population of employees. The land-based fur trade grew up around posts and stations located near lakes and rivers, which were vitally important for conveying goods, pelts and letters across country; it founded its success, in part, upon the processing skills of Indigenous women, many of whom were drawn into the trade through marriage.[19]

While the trade had a significant impact upon Indigenous societies in western Canada, tying places and peoples together through capital and kinship connections, it also created work for the largely impoverished male population of the Orkney Islands, near the Scottish mainland. Agnes' father, James Grieve, was one of these Orcadians. He entered into a five-year contract with the Hudson's Bay Company (HBC) at Stromness on 1 June 1816, aged 19. Like many Orcadians in the trade, Grieve joined up at a time when the company was expanding both territorially

---

17　On the convergence of local and global mobility, settler colonialism and indigeneity, see Lester and Laidlaw 2015: 1–23.
18　See Ballantyne 2011.
19　Van Kirk 1980: 4. On mobility in Métis culture and history, see St-Onge, Podruchny and Macdougall 2012.

and in terms of labour requirements.[20] Orkneymen sought employment with the HBC, as they had few other options—outside of the merchant navy or northern whaling expeditions to Greenland and the Davis Strait. A contract with the company promised stable employment, far better wages than they could get elsewhere and the chance to accrue some savings. Noted for their fishing and boatbuilding skills, as well as their reputation for reliability, Orcadians were sought by the HBC too, leading them to dominate the western Canadian fur trade. By the last decade of the eighteenth century, 416 out of 530 overseas HBC servants—a category that included labourers, canoemen, fishermen, carpenters, boat builders, sailors, blacksmiths and tailors—were from the Orkney Islands.[21]

Fur-trade employees were peripatetic. Grieve, for instance, was employed in the northern department at York Factory, the first HBC trading post, which was regarded as company headquarters. He also worked as a bowsman at Island Lake, but spent the majority of his life, from 1824 until his death in 1876, at Oxford House in northern Manitoba.[22] Initial contracts with the company were for five years, and many men served their time and returned to the islands with their savings. Others, like James Grieve, lived out their life in Canada, especially after establishing kinship ties in the country. Marriage to an Indigenous woman, whether by the 'custom of the country' or Christian rite, increased the likelihood of a trader settling in the region; this was the case with Grieve, who married a Swampy Cree woman, known in HBC records as 'Mary'. James and Mary had six children: John, James, Thomas, William, George and Agnes.[23] Agnes' future husband, James Harrold, hailed from Rousay, in the northern Orkney Islands; he signed up as a labourer for the HBC in 1836.[24] Harrold initially worked in the Mackenzie River District, but, by the early 1840s, was at York Factory. He probably encountered Agnes while employed as a labourer and fisherman at Island Lake, near Oxford

---

20 Van Kirk 1980: 21. For further discussion of the predominance of Orkney Islanders in the Canadian fur trade, see Burley 1997.
21 Van Kirk 1980: 4; Burley 1997: 66–71; Stephen 2006: 6, 30.
22 Beaumont 1984: 2. For a Cree perspective, see Beardy and Coutts 1996. Oxford House was established as an HBC fur-trading post in 1798. Today, it is the home of a First Nations Cree community. Located near the mouth of Hayes River, Oxford House is situated on the fur-trade route between Norway House, to the south, and York Factory, to the north. Traders used Hayes River to move between these sites.
23 Whyte 1995: 114.
24 Transcript of Census Returns—Rousay, Egilsay and Wyre 1841, Orkney Library and Archive, Orkney Islands.

House. They married at York Factory on 16 September 1847.[25] Agnes was 16 years old. Barely a week later, the newly married couple took passage on the HBC ship *Prince Rupert* for London, and then to the Orkney Islands.[26]

Fur traders utilised the HBC's global transportation routes to enable the mobility of their families. For instance, it was not uncommon for children of fur traders and Indigenous women to be sent to the Orkney Islands for schooling, although this opportunity was largely restricted to the sons of men from the upper echelon of fur-trade society.[27] Children born to men of means and some wealth may have gained access to an education, and lived transcolonial lives, but their mothers rarely journeyed to the birthplace of their fur-trader partner.[28] There is evidence that some women moved to Britain with their husbands in the post-1821 era, when the HBC's London Committee 'lifted its ban on employees taking their native wives to Britain provided they had adequate means to support their families'.[29] However, as Sylvia Van Kirk noted, this was a rare event; in the cases she cited, it was limited to the officer class who had the means, connections and opportunity to do so.[30] Agnes and James married at a time when fur-trade marriage patterns were undergoing a transition; as the HBC expanded and employed greater numbers of men, intermarriage expanded beyond the confines of the officer class to servants and labourers, giving them access to rights and privileges previously enjoyed by officers alone.[31] As intermarriage became more common within all ranks of the company, a hierarchy of marriage partners emerged that correlated with the HBC rankings; officers were encouraged to marry European women, while those of medium rank were encouraged to marry women of mixed ancestry.[32] In this way, marriage facilitated opportunities for mobility: it registered social and economic mobility within fur-trade society and, for some, such as Agnes, generated the opportunity for international travel.

---

25   Whyte 1995: 120. Grieve Family Search File, Hudson's Bay Company Archives (HBCA), Archives of Manitoba, Winnipeg. The couple 'were married according to form of the Church of England' by the chief trader. Extracts from York Factory Journal, Autumn 1847, B.239/a/167, HBCA, Archives of Manitoba, Winnipeg.
26   Marriage certificate, York Factory Marriage Certificates and certified promises of marriage, 1829–1853, HBCA, Archives of Manitoba, Winnipeg. Ships' Logs 1847.
27   Van Kirk 1980: 83.
28   Van Kirk 1980: 45. On the transcolonial lives of some of these mixed-race children, see Morgan 2014; McCormack 2011; Thorson 2000.
29   Van Kirk 1980: 125.
30   Van Kirk 1980: 126. From the mid-eighteenth century, a number of HBC officers took their wives and children to England, see Stephen 2006: 284–85.
31   Rollason Driscoll 2001: 93.
32   Rollason Driscoll 2001: 99–100.

As the wife of a servant of the HBC, Agnes' brief relocation to London and the Orkney Islands marks her as unusual within fur-trade society; yet, it also usefully points to how, at times, Indigenous women's mobility was tied to the agency of mobile white men whose movement relied upon the global networks created out of resource economies such as the fur trade. While scholars of colonialism tend to agree that newcomers were commonly integrated into Indigenous communities through sex, marriage and kinship obligations, they tend to overlook the fact that Indigenous women's relationships with such men knitted them into global-trade networks, facilitating their movement across several colonial sites.[33] The early New Zealand resource economy networks based around the timber trade, sealing and shore whaling operated in the same way, providing opportunities for Māori mobility, inclusive of the wives and daughters of Māori men or male newcomers. For instance, Irihāpeti Pātahi, a Kāi Tahu woman married by custom to the Australian-born and Otago-based shore whaler Edwin Palmer, travelled to Port Jackson (Sydney) with him in the 1830s, and thus into the economic heart of the trans-Tasman whaling trade.[34]

While marriage was at the centre of fur-trade society, Orcadians also drew families together into economic and social alliances through the bonds of marriage.[35] Agnes, far removed from her own family, built familial ties that would sustain her for the remainder of her life. Upon her arrival in the Orkney Islands, she was brought into a tight kinship network; many of the families there were linked through marriage, and this pattern was replicated in New Zealand. The Harrolds arrived at Port Chalmers on the *Bernicia* in December 1848, one of the first group of colonists to the newly created colony of Otago. Also on board was James' mother, Margaret, his stepfather, Hugh Craigie, his brother Sinclair Harrold and half-brother Richard Craigie. Economics were the catalyst for the family's migration to southern New Zealand; previously tenants of a large estate, they had been pushed off the land by the owner who wished to consolidate the property into one large sheep farm.[36]

---

33   Ballantyne and Burton 2009.
34   See West 2009: 205–65.
35   See Harland 2013.
36   Stuart 1973: unpaginated.

As the first Orkney family at the Taieri, the Harrolds actively sought to replicate Orkney social patterns and family life, for such practices invested place with meaning, activating important social and economic support networks. Not long after James and Agnes settled at Taieri, James' siblings followed them. The brothers set up a shipbuilding business and engaged in the coastal and river trade.[37] The Harrold and Craigie families would eventually be joined by wider kin, including cousins, aunts and uncles, in a process of chain migration to Dunedin. Their cousin, William Harrold, migrated in 1861 from Victoria (Australia) on the advice of his relatives. James advertised in Orkney newspapers, encouraging islanders, especially young women of marriageable age, to seek out opportunities in Otago.[38] In 1859, the Yorston family arrived. Having originally intended to migrate to Red River in modern-day Manitoba, they changed their mind on receiving a letter from the Harrolds.[39] In New Zealand, marriage tied the Orkney families together into a tight-knit community: Richard Craigie married into the Marwick family, who had arrived in Otago in 1857;[40] James Knarston married Ann Marwick; and Julia Yorston married Walter Sinclair.[41] These Orkney families were valuable employees, working as carpenters in the boatbuilding business and as labourers; they added value to the Harrold's ferry business by building stables and fences, as well as a 'two-storey residence, which … was considered both stylish and large', in addition to an accommodation house.[42] In 1857, the Otago Provincial Council assumed control of the building complex, leasing the tavern to Agnes and James.[43]

Orcadians were a reliable workforce and a vital economic support for the Harrolds. Their presence built the foundations of a small Orkney community at the lower Taieri, one tightly linked to the Presbyterian Church.[44] Agnes and James lent support to the church, to local families and to the community. Charitable and generous, they cared for orphaned children without hesitation, notably the Harrison children, whose

---

37   Harper 1980: 94.
38   Harrold 1850.
39   Stuart 1981: 43, 51.
40   Stuart 1973: unpaginated; *Otago Daily Times*, 5 May 1978: 10.
41   Stuart 1981: 44, 46.
42   Obituary, *Otago Witness*, 2 June 1898: 55. James Harrold's bankruptcy file demonstrates the importance of his Orkney connections, his chief creditor being a relation, Hugh Marwick. Harrold 1864.
43   Parkes and Hislop 1980: 25.
44   *Otago Witness*, 21 August 1858: 1.

parents died on the journey to Otago.[45] When they moved to Stewart Island in search of new economic opportunities in 1861, these familial relationships drew them back to the Taieri regularly—to mark important social occasions, attend funerals of family members and friends and to visit their son, James Joseph (1864–1911), who lived with relatives and attended the local school.[46] Taieri remained an important touchstone and ongoing site of familial connection for the remainder of their lives—a place invested with deep social connections.

Agnes was an Indigenous woman; however, once she stepped ashore at Port Chalmers, she became a colonist. She benefited from the processes that facilitated the dispossession of Kāi Tahu, the local tribe. Between 1849 and 1861, Agnes bore witness to the flow of colonial goods, peoples and produce along the Taieri River, and profited from this mobility. She entered Kāi Tahu space, a location abundant with food that sustained Kāi Tahu communities who utilised long-established routes to access the riches of the Taieri Plain. Kāi Tahu knew Taieri Ferry as Takāihitau, one of many seasonal settlements conveniently located near the inland lakes and wetland that was utilised during the summer months as a base for resource gathering. Prior to systematic colonisation of the region in 1848, Kāi Tahu occupation at lower Taieri was concentrated along the banks of the river, underlining its significance as a travel route, economic and food resource, and site of seasonal and permanent settlement.[47] While there is very little known about the history of these sites, their existence testifies to the mobile and seasonal nature of Kāi Tahu settlement, providing a map of Kāi Tahu mahika kai (resource gathering) trails and sites, as well as being indicators of use, occupation and the exercise of rights.[48] Taieri was a dynamic space of seasonal mobility and settlement, and this pattern continued after formal British colonisation began.

Agnes' mobility contrasts with that practised by Jane Palmer. Jane lived at Maitapapa, the main settlement of the Taieri Native Reserve, situated at the point where the Taieri and Waipori rivers meet. The daughter of Irihāpeti Pātahi and Edwin Palmer, Jane and her older sister, Betsy, were born into the shore whaling industry that was prominent in southern regions during the 1830s and 1840s. These connections are

45   *Otago Witness*, 27 December 1856: 3.
46   Anon. 1905: 894.
47   Taylor 1952: 181; Bray, Thomas and MacGill 1998: 8; Sutherland 1962: 9.
48   See Anderson 1998.

most obviously reflected in the social and economic ties generated by that industry, especially through marriage. Betsy, for instance, married Richard Sizemore, a cooper at the Waikouaiti whaling station, who was the brother-in-law of the whaling magnate, Johnny Jones, who was owner of the station that Jane and Betsy's father was employed to manage.[49] Like the Canadian fur trade, shore whaling stations had their own particular social hierarchies and marriage patterns, with Betsy's marriage to Sizemore marking Palmer as a man of rank and status in the shore whaling world. Jane, in contrast, married Robert Brown, also of mixed ancestry, and lived her entire married life at the reserve, where she and Robert raised eight children. Jane's kinship ties at Taieri were extensive, for Robert's sister lived at Maitapapa, as did Robert's mother, Mata Te Wharerimu, who was the senior woman there. Jane's father lived two kilometres away at the farming settlement of Otokia, but regularly stayed at her home. Jane's paternal uncle, William McLeur Palmer, lived at Maitapapa with his third wife, Ann Holmes, also a Kāi Tahu woman, and their growing family.[50]

Having grown up in a culturally diverse world, Agnes may have recognised many of the economic and social patterns in place at the reserve. From across the river, and in her role as hotel manager, she may have observed the mixed population in residence, which comprised Kāi Tahu and ex-whalers who had worked at several shore whaling stations along the Otago coastline. Among the residents were Australian-born brothers Edwin, William and Ned Palmer; uncle and nephew Robert and William Sherburd, also from Australia; William Low from Antigua; and John MacKenzie, a 'man of colour' from Jamaica. These men all married Kāi Tahu or mixed-descent women, and their residence on the reserve testifies to the importance of shore whaling stations in southern New Zealand as central sites for cross-cultural exchange. Intermarriage was an essential ingredient of the shore whaling industry; alliances were entered into by newcomers with the strong encouragement of Māori leaders, often with women of high status so as to gain the patronage of the local chief and access to land on which to establish a whaling operation. Interracial relationships were mutually beneficial. Newcomers were welcomed because the whaling industry fostered new economic conditions and trade relationships, bringing wealth to communities as well as to chiefly families. At the same time, marriage drew whalers into a network of

---

49   See Wanhalla 2005; Wanhalla 2008a.
50   The lives of these families are detailed in Wanhalla 2009.

economic, political and social obligations. Like the Canadian fur trade, the relationships formed out of shore whaling were more than economic in nature. While they may have been contracted within the context of new trade conditions, what emerged out of the shore whaling era were permanent (rather than temporary) relationships, and the production of a mixed-descent population. Decades of intermarriage meant that cross-cultural couples were not an unusual sight at Taieri, while the proximity of the river communities meant that colonists, Kāi Tahu and cross-cultural couples encountered each other on a regular basis. Agnes and James would not have looked unlike their close neighbours across the river, although their ties to the church and to local industry no doubt gave them a social respectability rarely accorded to ex-whalers in Otago's nascent colonial society.

Surrounded by kin, both Kāi Tahu and Pākehā (European), Jane's life was strongly tied to the lower Taieri, a native space she understood and no doubt experienced as 'a vast web of familial, political, and geographic relationships', constantly energised, animated and dynamically remade through a 'network of rivers and relations'.[51] Jane lived on a native reserve, an archetypal 'native space' generated by settler colonialism. Taieri's creation derived from the Otago Purchase of 1844, negotiated by the New Zealand Company, a private colonisation company. It was one of three areas excepted from purchase at the request of 21 Kāi Tahu chiefs; they chose to retain Taieri because it was a vital route to the inland lakes and the wetland, rich in essential foods, including ducks, eels, weka and flounder.[52] Added to this, the Taieri Plain contained the only large swamps south of the Waitaki River (the boundary of north Otago) that grew both harakeke (flax) and raupō (bulrush), the raw materials needed to make kete (baskets), apparel, rope, mats and fishing nets.[53] Kāi Tahu also sought to retain access to their food cultivations and gardens located on the banks of the river.[54] Apart from maintaining control over mahika kai (resource gathering sites), the area was of broader cultural significance, for it was the site of a traditional urupā (burial-place).[55]

---

51   Brooks 2008: xli.
52   Wilson 2002: 1.
53   Davis 1974: 58.
54   7 June 1844, Barnicoat Journal, MS-0440/01, Hocken Collections, Dunedin.
55   Clarke 1880.

These resource sites marked out Kāi Tahu pathways of mobility; however, this Indigenous geography would, over time, be disrupted by the creation of a native reserve on the northern bank of the river. Created out of the uneven power structures of colonialism and designed to fix people in one place, constraining, regulating and controlling their economic, social and cultural lives, native reserves altered Indigenous geographies. Although, as Canadian geographer Cole Harris noted, initially 'life came to be lived in, around, and well beyond these reserves', as settler colonialism expanded its reach, Indigenous movement became increasingly constrained, even in circumstances where mobility was not directly restricted by colonial authorities.[56]

Although they were residents of a native reserve, the Taieri Kāi Tahu families were free to come and go, which they did for purposes of employment, hunting and fishing, and to partake in social, cultural and political events. There was no pass system. Unlike other colonial sites in which oversight on reservations and mission stations was a common part of the colonial experience, no resident missionary or colonial official closely managed the lives of Taieri's residents. Nevertheless, Jane and her kin lived in an environment in which the land was largely uneconomic, forcing them to rely on seasonal employment and to turn to the river and wetland as an essential source of sustenance. This reliance on the waterway system became increasingly fraught and difficult in the decades between the 1870s and 1920s, as local councils, river boards and central government sought to turn what they considered 'waste' land into productive farms.[57] Eventually, the erosion of resources and the constraints of settler colonialism instituted new forms and patterns of Kāi Tahu mobility, leading to the abandonment of the reserve as a site of permanent residence by the 1940s.

***

Just like their male counterparts, Indigenous women's mobility followed imperial and colonial pathways that were not necessarily satisfying or productive of new relationships, connections or ties. Mobility could be an isolating experience, involving compulsion, violence and abandonment. Indigenous women's mobility could encompass great distances for reasons

---

56   Harris 2002: xxi.
57   See Wanhalla 2015. On the impact of swamp drainage on Indigenous communities in New Zealand, see Park 2013.

ranging from the personal to the political, or follow much smaller and confined patterns along the routes and pathways of seasonal resource gathering, such as at the lower Taieri, where the river, lakes and wetland helped to sustain family life and cultural practices in the face of increasing pressures from local settlers, councils, river boards and central governments that sought to erode and erase Kāi Tahu resource rights. Jane Palmer's mobility was structured around this pattern of resource gathering for the purposes of maintaining connections to important cultural practices and, more pragmatically, to simply survive.[58] New colonial conditions, namely life upon a native reserve, posed new challenges. At Taieri, systematic colonisation and the creation of a reserve space disrupted access to traditional seasonal settlements, which saw some localities abandoned and others activated as permanent sites of residence centred on agriculture.[59] Rather than eradicating patterns of hunting or fishing, the reserve became one of a number of Indigenous geographies moved through and utilised by Kāi Tahu across the lower Taieri.

Jane's life, lived within the Taieri Native Reserve and its immediate vicinity, reinforces Alan Lester's claim that the 'majority of indigenous peoples tried to stay "grounded" in the midst of colonisation'. As Lester stressed, these were not static places, nor were their residents immobile; rather, the localities that 'indigenous people sought to cling onto simply became dynamic in new ways'.[60] As places, Taieri Ferry and the native reserve were constantly being moved through. In the mid-nineteenth century, they were busy with people, boats and goods, and were places where a lively, richly textured social life developed around work, harvesting, the church, picnics and weddings. Both communities participated in these events and practices.[61] In its dynamic mixing of people, goods, accents and social practices, the lower Taieri was, to use Lester's phrase, 'a crossroads' constituted by a range of ongoing and ever-evolving connections and relationships.[62] Tracing networks of kinship underscores the spatial dynamics of these localities. In general, the story of Taieri and its people is deeply tied to histories of dispossession, poverty and social marginalisation; however, by drawing attention to the coexisting

58 For further details about Kāi Tahu patterns of mobility as it was shaped by colonial conditions, see Waitangi Tribunal 1991.
59 For a discussion of the native reserve's geographies, and the impact of imposed colonial boundaries on mobility, see Wanhalla 2007.
60 Lester 2014: 53.
61 These shared geographies are outlined in Wanhalla 2015.
62 Lester 2013: 130.

and overlapping colonial and Indigenous mobilities existing there, a more nuanced set of experiences are revealed. Taieri becomes a bustling and lively community of mobile men engaged in seasonal work; local and global networks of commerce and trade; and men, women and families who hunted and fished. When they gave evidence before commissions of inquiry, received the government gazette or Māori newspapers, wrote petitions and donated what little money they had to Te Kerēme (the Ngāi Tahu Claim Fund), these men, women and families were plugged into Kāi Tahu political networks and were active participants in colonial political discourse.[63] Jane Palmer put her name to a petition: she sought to articulate her land and resource rights, and attended and participated in Kāi Tahu political meetings.[64] Negating Caroline Daley's contention that Māori women's 'concerns [during the nineteenth century] were not national, let alone imperial', she was one of many Kāi Tahu women to engage in such practices.[65] Indigenous women, including non-elites such as Jane, participated in empire, sometimes as its victims, but also as active and engaged participants who sought to make use of global networks and connections for their personal advantage, and on behalf of their family and community. Although, as Lester and Laidlaw noted, there were many Indigenous peoples who did not or could not engage with these imperial networks, their 'experience was no less shaped' by them and 'they were no less active participants in the new social assemblages attending colonization'.[66] These dynamic histories and intersections are brought to life when mobility is integrated into the analysis of place.

For Jane, like many Indigenous women and their families, mobility was intimate and localised rather than expansive and transcolonial. For other Indigenous women, like Agnes, imperial pathways of mobility opened up different possibilities. In the first instance, imperial networks created opportunities for Indigenous–Indigenous encounters that could include profiting from the dispossession of others.[67] Indigenous–Indigenous encounters, fashioned out of the pathways of imperial and colonial

---

63   Te Kerēme was a fighting fund established by Kāi Tahu leaders in the 1870s to gain restitution for historic injustices relating to Crown land purchases.

64   Although exposed to the English language from a young age, the documentary record associated with Jane and Robert demonstrates a preference for communicating with colonial officials in te reo Māori. While te reo was deployed for formal occasions, inclusive of hui (meetings) and official correspondence, the necessity of bartering with local colonists and employment on local farms meant the lingua franca of everyday communication was a mixture of English and Māori.

65   Daley 2009: xxvi.

66   Lester and Laidlaw 2015: 8.

67   See Aikau 2010.

networks, did not necessarily lead to natural alliances based on shared histories of injustice. In the case of Agnes and Jane, there is little evidence of any connection between them, even though their lives overlapped; there is no mention of Agnes in Kāi Tahu sources, and there is nothing in the remaining documentary record associated with Agnes to suggest that she built any sustained relationships with the Taieri Kāi Tahu families. It appears that her ties to the Orcadian community sustained her subsequent relationship with Taieri, rather than any meaningful relationship with Maitapapa and its residents.

Mobility was important for Agnes, but in different ways; it presented her with economic, social and political opportunities that would have been unavailable to her in Canada. In 1893, when universal women's suffrage was achieved in New Zealand, Agnes gained political citizenship; she was also a landowner.[68] In New Zealand, she was identified as Canadian.[69] This identity and political status would not have been available to her had she remained in her birthplace; in Canada, her everyday life would have been structured and shaped by federal legislation—namely, the *Indian Act 1876* that established patriarchal systems of descent, legal and political status, and property rights.[70] Under the Act, male descent was entrenched as the primary mode of membership in a band, and an Indian was defined as any man of Indian blood, a child of an Indian man and any woman married to an Indian man.[71] Any woman who married a non-status man—that is, someone not recognised under the Indian Act—or who engaged in intermarriage, was excluded from band membership and all the rights that came with having status, including living with her family and relations on a reserve. In short, marrying 'out' had serious material implications, including enforced mobility and disconnection from kinship networks.[72]

As decades of feminist scholarship have demonstrated, intermarriage meant that Indigenous women were integrated into and experienced imperialism and colonialism differently to their fathers, brothers and uncles. Intermarriage also shaped how some Indigenous women experienced mobility, as illustrated by the two women in this chapter whose lives momentarily overlapped,

---

68   Probate and Will of Agnes Harrold 1908, DAFG/D328/9066 Box 21/1790, Archives New Zealand.
69   The national census identifies only one Canadian woman living on Stewart Island in 1896, which I assume was Agnes Harrold. New Zealand Government 1896: 137.
70   Peters 1998: 672.
71   See Lawrence 2003.
72   See Wanhalla 2008b.

before taking very different paths over the remainder of the nineteenth century. In New Zealand, intermarriage did not limit Agnes from achieving political freedom or prevent her from assuming a Canadian identity, nor did it restrict her from gaining a measure of economic independence, symbolised by her wide-ranging mobility. However, intermarriage did disconnect Agnes from her family in Canada, forcing her to build new kinship ties with Taieri's Orcadian community, far from Manitoba. In contrast, intermarriage gave Jane a wide network of relations that stretched into southern New Zealand and across to Sydney. As she entered adulthood and raised a family, Jane's cultural, economic and social world was increasingly constrained by colonial development and 'progress' in which Kāi Tahu patterns of seasonal mobility were neither valued, nor acknowledged; yet, she remained highly mobile. Kin-based geographies, which could stretch across a vast terrain, are crucial methodological tools for making visible the various ways in which Indigenous women's mobilities were activated and shaped by imperial and colonial power relations, including how colonisation facilitated opportunities for women to be mobile in new ways.[73]

References

Aikau, Hokulani K. 2010, 'Indigeneity in the diaspora: The case of native Hawaiians at Iosepha, Utah', *American Quarterly* 62(3): 477–500. doi.org/10.1353/aq.2010.0014

Anderson, Atholl 1998, *The Welcome of Strangers: An Ethnohistory of Southern Maori, AD 1650–1850*, Otago University Press, Dunedin.

Anderson, Clare 2011, 'Writing Indigenous women's lives in the Bay of Bengal: Cultures of empire in the Andaman Islands, 1789–1906', *Journal of Social History* 45(2): 480–96. doi.org/10.1093/jsh/shr054

Anderson, Clare 2012, *Subaltern Lives: Biographies of Colonialism in the Indian Ocean World, 1790–1920*, Cambridge University Press, Cambridge. doi.org/10.1017/CBO9781139057554

Anon. 1905, 'Harrold, James Joseph', in *The Cyclopedia of New Zealand*, volume 4, Otago and Southland Provincial Districts, Cyclopedia Company Ltd, Christchurch.

---

73 On the the opportunities and contraints colonisation offered Indigenous women, see Haskins 2009.

Ballantyne, Tony 2011, 'On place, space and mobility in nineteenth-century New Zealand', *New Zealand Journal of History* 45(1): 50–70.

Ballantyne, Tony 2012, *Webs of Empire: Locating New Zealand's Colonial Past*, Bridget Williams Books, Wellington. doi.org/10.7810/9781927131435

Ballantyne, Tony and Antoinette Burton (eds) 2009, *Moving Subjects: Gender, Mobility and Intimacy in an Age of Global Empire*, University of Illinois Press, Urbana.

Banivanua Mar, Tracey 2013, 'Imperial literacy and Indigenous rights: Tracing transoceanic circuits of a modern discourse', *Aboriginal History* 37: 1–28.

Banivanua Mar, Tracey 2015, 'Shadowing imperial networks: Indigenous mobility and Australia's Pacific past', *Australian Historical Studies* 46(3): 340–55.

Barman, Jean and Bruce McIntyre Watson 2006, *Leaving Paradise: Indigenous Hawaiians in the Pacific Northwest, 1787–1898*, University of Hawai'i Press, Honolulu.

Beardy, Flora and Robert Coutts (eds) 1996, *Voices from Hudson Bay: Cree Stories from York Factory*, McGill-Queens University Press, Montreal.

Beaumont, Raymond M. 1984, 'The Grieves of Oxford House', unpublished manuscript, Hudson's Bay Company Archives (HBCA), Archives of Manitoba, Winnipeg.

Bray, Sharron, Graeme Thomas and Victor MacGill 1998, *Under the Eye of the Saddle Hill Taniwha: Maori Place Names and Legends as Viewed from Saddle Hill, Extending from Green Island South to Taieri Mouth and across to Maungatua, then North to the Silverpeaks,* Ngā Tutukitanga o Taieri, Mosgiel.

Brooks, Lisa 2008, *The Common Pot: The Recovery of Native Space in the Northeast*, University of Minnesota Press, Minneapolis.

Burley, Edith I. 1997, *Servants of the Honourable Company: Work, Discipline, and Conflict in the Hudson's Bay Company, 1770–1879*, Oxford University Press, Oxford.

Burton, Antoinette 2012, 'Travelling criticism? On the dynamic histories of Indigenous mobility', *Cultural and Social History* 9(4): 491–96. doi.org/10.2752/147800412X13434063754409

Carey, Jane and Jane Lydon (eds) 2014, *Indigenous Networks: Mobility, Connections and Exchange*, Routledge, London.

Clarke jnr, George 1880 (7 April), Letter to Commissioner of Land Purchases, Appendix 33 in Minutes of Evidence, Smith-Nairn Commission, MA 67/8, Archives New Zealand (ANZ).

Daley, Caroline (ed.) 2009, *Women and Empire, 1750–1930. Primary Sources of Gender and Anglo-Imperialism*, volume 2, New Zealand, Routledge, London.

Daniels, Stephen and Catherine Nash 2004, 'Lifepaths: Geography and biography', *Historical Geography* 30: 449–58. doi.org/10.1016/S0305-7488(03)00043-4

Davis, G.F. 1974, 'Old identities and new iniquities: The Taieri Plain in Otago Province 1770–1870', MA thesis, University of Otago.

Elbourne, Elizabeth 2005, 'Indigenous peoples and imperial networks in the early nineteenth century: The politics of knowledge', in *Rediscovering the British World*, Philip Buckner and R. Douglas Francis (eds), University of Calgary Press, Calgary: 59–86.

Harland, Jill 2013, 'The Orcadian odyssey: The migration of Orkney Islanders to New Zealand, 1848–1914 with particular reference to the South Island', PhD thesis, University of Otago.

Harper, Barbara 1980, *Petticoat Pioneers: South Island Women of the Colonial Era,* book 3, Reed, Wellington.

Harris, Cole 2002, *Making Native Space: Colonialism, Resistance, and Reserves in British Columbia*, University of British Columbia Press, Vancouver.

Harrold, James 1850 (10 January), Letter to Superintendent, Otago Provincial Council, AAAC/707/D500 Box 132/a/11, ANZ.

Harrold, James 1864, Debtor's File, DAAC/D256/20364 Box 620/181, ANZ.

Haskins, Victoria 2009, 'From the centre to the city: Modernity, mobility and mixed-descent Aboriginal domestic workers from Central Australia', *Women's History Review* 18(1): 155–75. doi.org/10.1080/09612020802608108

Hoxie, Frederick E. 2014, 'Denouncing America's destiny: Sarah Winnemucca's assault on US expansion', in *Critical Perspectives on Colonialism: Writing the Empire from Below*, Fiona Paisley and Kirsty Reid (eds), Routledge, London: 27–45.

Lai, Paul and Lindsey Claire Smith 2010, 'Introduction', *American Quarterly* 62(3): 407–36.

Laidlaw, Zoe 2014, 'Indigenous interlocutors: Networks of imperial protest and humanitarianism in the mid-nineteenth century', in *Indigenous Networks: Mobility, Connections and Exchange*, Jane Carey and Jane Lydon (eds), Routledge, London: 114–39.

Lawrence, Bonita 2003, 'Gender, race, and the regulation of native identity in Canada and the United States: An overview', *Hypatia: A Journal of Feminist Philosophy* 18(2): 3–31.

Legge, Carol 1991, 'Ata-Hoe', in *The Book of New Zealand Women: Ko Kui Ma Te Kaupapa*, Charlotte Macdonald, Merimeri Penfold and Bridget Williams (eds), Bridget Williams Books, Wellington: 23–25.

Lester, Alan 2013, 'Spatial concepts and the historical geographies of British colonialism', in *Writing Imperial Histories*, Andrew S. Thompson (ed.), Manchester University Press, Manchester: 118–42.

Lester, Alan 2014, 'Indigenous engagements with humanitarian governance: The Port Phillip Protectorate of Aborigines and "humanitarian space"', in *Indigenous Networks: Mobility, Connections and Exchange*, Jane Carey and Jane Lydon (eds), Routledge, London: 50–74.

Lester, Alan and Zoe Laidlaw 2015, 'Indigenous sites and mobilities: Connected struggles in the long nineteenth century', in *Indigenous Communities and Settler Colonialism: Land Holding, Loss and Survival in an Interconnected World*, Alan Lester and Zoe Laidlaw (eds), Palgrave Macmillan, London: 1–23.

McCormack, Patricia A. 2011, 'Lost women: Natives wives in Orkney and Lewis', in *Recollecting: Lives of Aboriginal Women of the Canadian Northwest and Borderlands*, Sarah Carter and Patricia A. McCormack (eds), Athabasca University Press, Edmonton: 61–88.

Medak-Saltzman, Danika 2010, 'Transnational Indigenous exchange: Rethinking global interactions of Indigenous peoples at the 1904 St. Louis exposition', *American Quarterly* 62(3): 591–615.

Morgan, Cecilia 2014, '"Write me. Write me": Native and metis letter-writing across the British Empire, 1800–1870', in *Critical Perspectives on Colonialism: Writing the Empire from Below*, Fiona Paisley and Kirsty Reid (eds), Routledge, London: 141–56.

New Zealand Government 1896, *Results of a Census of the Colony of New Zealand Taken for the Night of the 12th April 1896*, Government Printer, Wellington.

O'Brien, Patricia 2006, *The Pacific Muse: Exotic Femininity and the Colonial Pacific*, University of Washington Press, Seattle.

O'Brien, Patricia 2014, 'Ta'isi O.F. Nelson and Sir Maui Pomare: Samoans and Maori reunited', *Journal of Pacific History* 49(1): 26–49. doi.org/10.1080/00223344.2013.878288

O'Malley, Vincent 2015, *Haerenga: Early Māori Journeys Across the Globe*, Bridget Williams Books, Wellington.

Park, Geoff 2013, '"Swamps which might doubtless easily be drained": Swamp drainage and its impact on the Indigenous', in *Making a New Land: Environmental Histories of New Zealand*, Eric Pawson and Tom Brooking (eds), Otago University Press, Dunedin: 174–92.

Parkes, Win and Kath Hislop 1980, *Taieri Mouth and its Surrounding Districts*, Otago Heritage Books, Dunedin.

Paterson, Lachy 2013, '"The similarity of hue constituted no special bond of intimacy between them": Close encounters of the Indigenous kind', *Journal of New Zealand Studies* (14): 19–40.

Perry, Adele 2015, *Colonial Relations: The Douglas-Connolly Family and the Nineteenth Century Imperial World*, Cambridge University Press, Cambridge. doi.org/10.1017/CBO9781139794701

Peters, Evelyn J. 1998, 'Subversive spaces: First nations women and the city', *Society and Space* 16(6): 665–85.

Rollason Driscoll, Heather 2001, '"A most important chain of connection": Marriage in the Hudson's Bay Company', in *From Rupert's Land to Canada*, Theodore Binnema, Gerhard J. Ens and R.C. MacLeod (eds), University of Alberta Press, Edmonton: 81–110.

Russell, Lynette 2012, *Roving Mariners: Australian Aboriginal Whalers and Sealers in the Southern Oceans, 1790-1870*, SUNY Press, New York.

Ships' Logs 1847, Prince Rupert (V), C.1/952 and C.1/954, HBCA, Archives of Manitoba, Winnipeg.

St-Onge, Nicole, Carolyn Podruchny and Brenda Macdougall (eds) 2012, *Contours of a People: Metis Family, Mobility, and History*, University of Oklahoma Press, Norman.

Stephen, Scott P. 2006, 'Masters and servants: The Hudson's Bay Company and its personnel, 1668–1782', PhD thesis, University of Manitoba.

Stuart, R.J. 1981, *Henley, Taieri Ferry and Otokia: A Schools and Districts History*, Henley, Taieri Ferry and Otokia School Jubilee Committee, Outram.

Stuart, R.J. 1973, *Craigie-lea: Written for the 125th Anniversary of the Emigration of the Craigies, of Brugh, Rousay, Orkney, to New Zealand*, R. Stuart, Dunedin.

Sutherland, Gwen 1962, *Coast, Road and River: The Story of Taieri Mouth, Taieri Beach, Glenledi and Akatore*, Clutha Leader, Balclutha.

Taylor, W.A. 1952, *Lore and History of the South Island Maori*, Bascands Limited, Christchurch.

Thorson, Bruce 2000 (November/December), 'The bay connection: Orkney Islanders discover their metis heritage', *Canadian Geographic* 120(7): 98–104.

Van Kirk, Sylvia 1980, *Many Tender Ties: Women in Fur-Trade Society, 1670–1870*, University of Oklahoma Press, Norman.

Waitangi Tribunal 1991, *The Ngai Tahu Report*, Waitangi Tribunal, Wellington.

Wanhalla, Angela 2005, 'Transgressing boundaries: The mixed descent families of Maitapapa, Taieri, 1840–1940', PhD thesis, University of Canterbury.

Wanhalla, Angela 2007, '"My piece of land at Taieri": Boundary formation and contestation at the Taieri Native Reserve, 1844–1868', *New Zealand Journal of History* 40(1): 44–60.

Wanhalla, Angela 2008a, '"One white man I like very much": Intermarriage and the cultural encounter in southern New Zealand, 1829–1850', *Journal of Women's History* 20(2): 34–56. doi.org/10.1353/jowh.0.0013

Wanhalla, Angela 2008b, 'Women "living across the line": Intermarriage on the Canadian prairies and southern New Zealand, 1870–1900', *Ethnohistory* 55(1): 29–49. doi.org/10.1215/00141801-2007-045

Wanhalla, Angela 2009, *In/visible Sight: The Mixed Descent Families of Southern New Zealand*, Bridget Williams Books, Wellington. doi.org/10.7810/9781877242434

Wanhalla, Angela 2015, 'Living on the rivers' edge at the Taieri Native Reserve', in *Indigenous Communities and Settler Colonialism: Land Holding, Loss and Survival in an Interconnected World*, Alan Lester and Zoe Laidlaw (eds), Palgrave Macmillan, London: 138–57.

Warrior 2005, *The People and the Word: Reading Native Non-Fiction*, University of Minnesota Press, Minneapolis.

Weaver, Jace 2014, *The Red Atlantic: American Indigenes and the Making of the Modern World, 1000–1927*, University of North Carolina Press, Chapel Hill.

West, Jonathan 2009, 'An environmental history of the Otago peninsula: Dialectics of ecological and cultural change from first settlement to 1900', PhD thesis, University of Otago.

Whyte, Donald 1995, *A Dictionary of Scottish Emigrants to Canada Before Confederation,* volume 2, Ontario Genealogical Society, Toronto.

Wilson, Catherine 2002, 'Tatawai, Kai Tahu and the claim', BA (Hons) long research essay, University of Otago.

10

Pāora Tūhaere's Voyage to Rarotonga

Lachy Paterson

In May 1863, Māori readers of the government's Māori-language newspaper, *Te Karere Māori*, learned that the Ngāti Whātua chief, Pāora Tūhaere, had sailed the *Victoria*, a 56-ton schooner, 3,000 kilometres to Rarotonga to trade with the locals there. This chapter looks at the voyage and the ongoing relationships it fostered and consolidated. Like Regina Ganter's discussion of Aboriginal interactions with Malaccan seafarers in this volume, the chapter examines Tūhaere's voyage from the perspective of Indigenous mobility, which facilitated contact between Indigenous peoples, allowing both Ngāti Whātua and Rarotongans to construct spaces for themselves outside their home bases.

Up to 1863, colonial spaces in New Zealand had been realised through land purchase. Annexation had ushered in Crown colony status in 1840, succeeded by responsible settler government from 1858. However, political power in mid–nineteenth century New Zealand lay in possessing land, and the ability to define it. Despite large-scale purchases in the first two decades of formal colonisation, in many parts of New Zealand, considerable amounts of land still remained in Māori hands, unsold and unconverted to Western systems of land tenure. Although nominally British subjects, Māori who retained land were better placed to maintain their mana (authority) and rangatiratanga (autonomy), something many Māori became increasingly conscious of during the 1850s.

One manifestation of this awareness was the Kīngitanga, a loose coalition of tribes in the central North Island who, choosing not to have their lands re-imagined as colonial spaces, organised themselves under a newly created Māori kingship. In contrast, Rarotonga remained a native space, ruled by ariki (high chiefs), although missionary influence was also powerful.[1] The Cook Islands, of which Rarotonga is a part, became a British protectorate in 1888 with some degree of Indigenous internal authority, until annexed to New Zealand in 1901.[2]

Indigenous spaces are sometimes conceptualised in opposition to colonised spaces. Parts of what were entirely Indigenous lands may be left, or allotted, to the original owners as 'native spaces', while the rest is progressively assimilated by colonisers.[3] As Jacqueline Holler suggested in her discussion of sixteenth-century Mexico, 'reimagining the indigenous spaces as colonial ones was … a process carried out throughout the Americas'.[4] The transformations that such a process implies were not unique to America or to New Zealand and Rarotonga, but pertain to all lands of Indigenous peoples intruded upon by European colonisation. Rather than see 'native spaces' purely as ancestral domains held by, or reserved to, Indigenous peoples—encircled, constricted or being nibbled away at—this chapter examines other kinds of locations that Indigenous peoples might imagine for themselves away from their native land, even if these were temporary constructions.

Seeing land as 'native' or 'colonised' positions it with other 'sanctified binaries' identified by Anne McClintock (e.g. 'colonizer–colonized, self– other, dominance–resistance, metropolis–colony, colonial–postcolonial') that fail to explain all aspects of the colonial experience.[5] The reality was often more complex and messy. Nor does a binary of 'static' native and 'mobile' European fully cover how newcomers and Indigenous peoples lived their lives.[6] Ironically, it was the mobility that colonisation introduced—the imperial or missionary networks, the technology of shipping and the openings that European capitalism provided—that facilitated new and wider opportunities for Indigenous peoples in the

---

1   Crocombe 1983: 24–25.
2   McIntyre 1992: 342.
3   Harris 2002: xviii–xxi.
4   Holler 2007: 107.
5   McClintock 1995: 15.
6   Carey and Lydon 2014: 2–3; Ballantyne and Burton 2009: 5.

Pacific to travel,[7] whether to metropolitan, colonised or other Indigenous places, or even in-between.[8] 'Space', after all, can refer both to physical masses and the gaps that exist or are created between them, as well as more abstract constructions.[9]

Indigenous travellers often came with a different set of assumptions and cultural understandings than those experienced by Europeans, leading to different kinds of relationships with the people they met, as other chapters in this volume show (see chapters by Standfield and Shellam).[10] Both Cook Islanders and New Zealand Māori belong to Eastern Polynesian societies with close linguistic and cultural similarities. The first known modern encounter between these peoples demonstrates that Māori could integrate relatively easily into Rarotongan society. The earliest recorded ship visit to Rarotonga was the ill-fated *Cumberland* from Sydney in 1814, which hoped to secure sandalwood; its crew included two Ngā Puhi men picked up in Northland.[11] Upon arriving at Rarotonga, the Māori men, known locally as Veretini and Tupe, married local women, lived in their communities and may have intended to remain.[12] Unfortunately, both died; one was implicated in shooting a Rarotongan chief and suffered utu (revenge); the other was shot by his European crewmates for supposedly inciting the Rarotongans against them.[13] Notwithstanding their fates, it is clear that these Māori men were able to blend into Rarotongan society. In this way, they were unlike the Europeans, who stole food, molested women, ignored local tapu (spiritual restrictions) and were killed. While several of the slain European crewmen were eaten, 'both Veretini and Tupe were buried in accordance with the tradition and custom of the time by the respective families of their wives'.[14] When Tūhaere arrived in 1863, he was also able to fit into Rarotongan society. Sustained contact with Europeans had engendered significant cultural change in both New Zealand and Rarotonga. Although Britain had annexed New Zealand while Rarotonga still retained its chiefly rule, Māori and Rarotongans had converted to Christianity and begun to engage in commercial activities. The respective societies had changed, but in analogous ways.

---

7   See Mallon 2012: 77–95.
8   See Paterson 2013: 19–40.
9   Lester 2013: 125.
10   An exception, perhaps, is when Ngāti Mutunga and Ngāti Tama chartered a ship to invade Rēkohu (the Chatham Islands), the homeland of the Moriori people in 1835. See King 2000: 57–75.
11   Maude and Crocombe 1962: 35–36.
12   Petrie 2006: 64.
13   Maude and Crocombe 1962: 35–36; Henry 2002: 84, 90–91; Maretu 1983: 44–46.
14   Henry 2002: 92.

Tūhaere's voyage is unique. As with many other Pacific societies, a number of Māori had already made trips to Sydney, and some had travelled to London and other foreign places as crew, guests or paying passengers.[15] Māori-owned ships were active in coastal shipping around New Zealand.[16] Fairly extensive trading already existed between Auckland and Rarotonga, and travel opportunities associated with this trade may have stimulated links between Rarotonga and Ngāti Whātua.[17] However, Tūhaere's *Victoria* was the first and, to my knowledge, the only Māori-owned vessel to undertake such entrepreneurial voyages beyond New Zealand's shores in the nineteenth century.

That the colonial gaze stretched out into the Pacific can be seen in contemporary New Zealand newspapers' coverage of Tūhaere's activities; some articles were even reproduced in Australian papers, such as the *Geelong Advertiser*. However, more recent historiography is patchier. A few scholarly works, such as Hazel Petrie's *Chiefs of Industry*, make brief mention of Tūhaere's venture. While interesting and indicative of early Māori business endeavours, the unique features of Tūhaere's journey make it an outlier to more New Zealand–bound commerce or international Māori travel.[18] Rosemary Anderson briefly discussed Tūhaere and the links that grew from his endeavour in her thesis on Cook Islands migration.[19] Dick Scott, who wrote a history of the Cook Islands, suggested that Tūhaere was in league with Auckland merchants to effect New Zealand's annexation of the island, an assertion this essay addresses below. In 1938, Eric Ramsden published a newspaper account (no. 62 of 'Strange Tales from the South Seas') in Sydney's *The World's News* that borrowed heavily from *Te Karere Maori's* (*The Maori Messenger's*) accounts of Tūhaere's activities.[20] That Tūhaere's entrepreneurial achievements have not projected more prominently into New Zealand historiography is due, in part, to the latter's focus on Māori–Pākehā engagements and clashes. Tūhaere is better known for his more significant and ongoing political work, such as his involvement at the 1860 Kohimarama Conference, his role in convening a Māori parliament at his marae at Ōrākei in 1879 and his subsequent collaboration with the Kīngitanga.[21]

---

15   Chappell 1997.
16   Petrie 2006: 70–71, 121–26.
17   Gilson 1980: 44–45; Salesa 2012: 99.
18   Petrie 2006: 66; Hogan 1994: 263.
19   Anderson 2014: 21–22, 24.
20   Scott 1991: 19; Ramsden 1938: 6, 23. This story, however, does not appear in Ramsden 1944.
21   Oliver 2012.

While the trade perspective is undoubtedly noteworthy, I feel that looking at Tūhaere's journey in terms of place and people is much more productive, especially with regard to the themes of this volume. Imperial power, colonial trade and missionary religion may have been steadily enveloping the Pacific Ocean and its islands, but there was still scope for Indigenous peoples to operate according to their own agency and understandings. This chapter discusses Tūhaere's base in Auckland, his marae at Ōrākei and the New Zealand political context at the time of his voyage. It then explores this journey, how it was projected to Māori by the Māori-language newspapers, why he went (including whether this fitted into Pākehā aspirations for a New Zealand Pacific) and what his presence on their island might have meant to Rarotongans. The relationships Tūhaere built with the Rarotongan people conformed to Polynesian understandings and lasted much longer than his travels might suggest; thus, the chapter explores the Rarotongan context, and how Tūhaere's voyage provided Rarotongan visitors to Ōrākei with their own stopping point in New Zealand—a home away from home in both a conceptual and actual sense, well into the twentieth century. Finally, the essay looks at subsequent Cook Islands migration to New Zealand in the decades following World War II (WWII) and its repercussions for the bonds created a century earlier.

***

Ngāti Whātua 'lands border four harbours—Hokianga, Kaipara, Waitematā and Manukau'.[22] Near the southern margin sits Ōrākei, one of Tūhaere's marae, on the north-eastern edge of the Auckland isthmus. A few kilometres to the west, across Hobson Bay, Governor William Hobson established Auckland, New Zealand's second capital, in 1841. For Ngāti Whātua, a tribe with powerful enemies to the north, their proximity to the small but growing city allowed some protection, as well as excellent opportunities to trade with Pākehā settlers. Yet, Ngāti Whātua bought these benefits at a price; in 1840, the tribe parted with 3,000 acres for £341 in cash and goods to provide space for Pākehā settlement and, within 10 years, had relinquished most of their best land in Auckland.[23] In 1863, their base at Ōkahu Bay at Ōrākei remained secure, and Ngāti Whātua were still able to offer manaakitanga (hospitality) to other tribes visiting the city.[24] However, as Auckland grew and surrounded them, their

---

22 Ministry of Culture and Heritage 2006: 196.
23 Waitangi Tribunal 1987: 23; Ministry of Culture and Heritage 2006: 200.
24 Kawharu 1975: 15.

surviving land holdings diminished; although 700 acres were declared 'inalienable' in 1869, this was whittled down to 39 acres by 1898. By 1928, only 10 acres remained. In the 1940s, Pākehā were complaining of the 'deplorable conditions' at Ōrākei[25] and government took the last of the tribe's ancestral land in 1950.[26] As Penny Edmonds has observed, 'colonial frontiers did not only exist in the bush, backwoods or borderlands', they were also well within city limits.[27] Auckland was no exception.

In its first two decades, the government had little effective control of Māori, relying mainly on persuasion and inducements to chiefs to advance its various frontiers through land purchasing. The pressure to sell land was corrosive to Māori society, often leading to conflicts between and within tribal groups. In response, in the late 1850s, tribes from the central North Island formed the Kīngitanga (Māori King Movement), a pan-tribal movement aiming to staunch land sales and the resultant bloodshed, which saw tribes place their lands under the mana of a newly created Māori king.[28] Not surprisingly, the colonial state viewed the movement as a challenge to its claim to sovereignty. In 1860, the government pushed through a disputed land purchase in northern Taranaki. Most of the Te Āti Awa tribe, the owners of the land, opposed the sale and the government's intransigence led to a year-long war. Relations between the government and the Kīngitanga became strained when some of the movement's warriors assisted Te Āti Awa in their struggle. The conflict, which ended in stalemate, was followed by several years of cold war between the government and the Kīngitanga. After Tūhaere left for Rarotonga in 1863, Governor Grey provoked Taranaki forces into attacking a group of soldiers in Taranaki. With its casus belli established, the government prepared to roll out its plan to invade the Waikato to crush the Kīngitanga.[29] 'Friendly' and 'loyal' chiefs, such as Pāora Tūhaere, became even more valuable to the government cause.

Te Karere Maori, the government's mouthpiece to Māori, published laudatory articles, including obituaries, on chiefs who were friendly to Pākehā or had improved themselves materially or spiritually in some way. It commended Tūhaere for his 'enterprising spirit' in journeying to Rarotonga and the £330 profit accrued. His voyage was portrayed as

---

25 For example, 'Orakei Maoris', *New Zealand Herald*, 21 August 1940: 12.
26 Kawharu, 1975: 7–10.
27 Edmonds 2010: 2.
28 Te Hurinui 2010: 211–16.
29 Paterson 2006: 167–96.

a good-news story about a loyal chief who was pursuing Pākehā customs. The story linked his achievement with his tribe's location, and with their embrace of the Pākehā settlers:

> The Ngatiwhatua were the original owners of the soil upon which Auckland stands, and were the first to invite the Pakeha to the shores of the Waitemata; and we now find they are the first of the Maori tribes to open up trade with their brethren at Rarotonga, Mangaia, Atiu, Mauka, Waitutaki, and other islands of the South Seas.[30]

This discourse can also be seen in the Napier-based niupepa (Māori-language newspaper), *Te Waka Maori o Ahuriri*, a quasi-official publication that reproduced *Te Karere's* story. The niupepa's paratext began by discussing the prevailing racial anxieties, then stated:

> Let us turn ... to look at things that are pleasing to the heart, peaceful pursuits by which man prospers ... Pāora Tūhaere's journey there [Rarotonga] is a Pākehā custom, that is, commerce.[31]

Not all Māori could do as this chief had done; however, it was stated that 'all people are able to follow this wealth-generating example that Pāora has just shown us'.[32] According to this portrayal by the niupepa, by consciously engaging in European customs and behaving like a Pākehā trader, Tūhaere stood in contrast to Māori who were resistant to the new order, such as the Kīngitanga, or those fighting at Taranaki.

As these two quotations demonstrate, niupepa framed the journey in terms of engaging with a new colonial order, and the same is true with Rarotongan ariki. The latter were well aware of the island's vulnerability and had asked, unsuccessfully, for British protection as early as 1844.[33] In 1862, one of the ariki, Kainuku Tamako, visited Auckland, perhaps as part of a diplomatic mission. Like Māori chiefs visiting this southern outpost of colonial power, he met Pāora Tūhaere, and may have stayed at

30 *Te Karere Maori*, 15 May 1863: 2–3. 'Ko Ngatiwhatua te tuturu ake o te oneone e tu nei Akarana; ko ia te tuatahi ki te kukume mai i te Pakeha ki uta ki Waitemata; a kua waiho ratou hei tuatahi o roto o nga iwi Maori hei takitaki ai i te ara ki Rarotonga, kia Mangaia, ki Atiu, ki Mauka, ki Waitutaki, me era atu motu o tau moana ki te tonga, ki te kukume mai i o ratou tuakana' (trans. from source).
31 *Te Waka Maori o Ahuriri*, 27 June 1863: 1. 'me tahuri tatou ... ki te titiro ki etahi mea manawarekatanga mo te ngakau—nga ritenga waimarie e pai ai te tangata ... Ko te haere a Paora Tuhaere i haere ai ki kona, he tikanga Pakeha—ara, he hokohoko' (trans. author).
32 *Te Waka Maori o Ahuriri*, 27 June 1863: 1. 'e taea ano nga tangata katoa te whai i te tauira whakawhairawa kua oti te whakatakoto nei e Paora' (trans. author).
33 Kloosterman 1976: 59.

Ōrākei.[34] Later, recalling his visit to the Cook Islands, Tūhaere stated that 'Kainuku fetched me',[35] indicating that the pair had planned his visit to the islands when Kainuku had visited Auckland the previous year.[36] The commercial aims of the venture depended on European technology and skills. As Eastern Polynesians no longer sailed great distances in waka, Tūhaere purchased a schooner for £1,400. Although he had a party of about 20 men (who no doubt helped man the ship), a Captain Young was master, and the shipping company Combes and Daldy were his Auckland agents.[37] It appears that Tūhaere became less directly involved as time went on. In 1867, the *Southern Cross* reported that 'Captain Irvine had an interest in the 'Victoria' schooner. Paul [Tūhaere] got a share of the profits'.[38]

Dick Scott, in *Years of the Pooh-bah*, stated that 'since Auckland merchants were "plotting" at the time to sponsor annexation by New Zealand, according to the [London Missionary Society (LMS)] mission, no doubt it was their backing that lay behind the journey'.[39] Scott's work is unfootnoted; however, he attributed his assertion to Angus Ross and Richard Gilson in a bibliographic note. Gilson noted that Reverend E.R. Krause, a German working for the LMS, made this claim, but that he was at odds with the traders and planters on the island.[40] Undoubtedly, the Auckland Provincial Council wanted their city to become the principal trading point for the Pacific Islands.[41] Ross conceded that Pākehā, at times, floated the idea of future Pacific expansion in the mid-nineteenth century, but had sufficient distractions in New Zealand to be concerned with.[42] In contrast, Damon Salesa suggested that any Pacific dreams New Zealand's politicians may have possessed were held in check by London.[43] However, notwithstanding Pākehā imperial aspirations, no real evidence of a 'plot', let alone Tūhaere's involvement in one, is apparent in Scott's sources. Nor is there any indication that Pākehā merchants bankrolled his venture, as

---

34   *Te Karere Maori*, 15 May 1863: 2.
35   *Geelong Advertiser*, 16 January 1865: 3.
36   *New Zealander*, 30 May 1863: 9; 6 June 1863: 4.
37   *Te Karere Maori*, 15 May 1863: 2.
38   *Daily Southern Cross*, 29 January 1867: 4.
39   Scott 1991: 19.
40   Gilson 1980: 43.
41   Ross 1964: 53, 59.
42   Ross 1964: 53.
43   Salesa 2009: 154. See also Salesa 2012: 97–121.

the chief sold land to purchase his vessel.[44] Scott's work on Rarotonga, although anti-colonial in tone, effectively limited Indigenous agency by suggesting that Auckland capitalists orchestrated Tūhaere's voyage.

Certainly, Tūhaere was loyal to the government; his proximity to the Pākehā centre of power would have made any other position untenable. At the 1860 Kohimarama Conference, he declared, 'I am a child of the Queen'.[45] Tūhaere spoke for peace and the rule of law, commerce and progress, and Māori inclusion in the workings of the state, but this did not preclude him from criticising Crown actions.[46] When hostilities resumed in Taranaki during his absence, he seemed genuinely shocked, writing: 'I have heard from the newspapers which have come to this place from Auckland, that there is war in New Zealand—that the Pakeha were attacked'.[47]

Tūhaere was not the only Māori wanting to head to Rarotonga. According to the *Daily Southern Cross*, he took a Waikato man to the island who was intending to purchase powder and ammunition for the future warfare:

> Paul, on discovering his intention, refused to bring him back, saying that the Governor and white men were his friends. He was consequently left behind to return the best way he could.[48]

It is likely that this individual was Henry Nicholas, the son of a Pākehā trader and a woman of Ngāti Hauā, a tribe aligned to the Kīngitanga. Nicholas travelled in the *Victoria* and he remained in Rarotonga, where he married a local woman and was active in the cotton industry, fruit production and printing.[49] In the 1870s, Nicholas had shares in a cutter that traded between Rarotonga and New Zealand, but it appears that his interest was mainly financial.[50]

Rarotonga, with its warmth and supposed ease of living, appealed to the imagination of some Māori. While Tūhaere was still on the island, Waikato Māori came to Ōrākei for an uhunga (ritual tapu removal of

---

44   *New Zealand Herald*, 5 December 1866: 6.
45   *Te Karere Maori*, 14 July 1860: 41. 'he tamaiti au no te Kuini' (trans. from source).
46   *Te Karere Maori*, 14 July 1860: 14–15, 41–42; 31 July 1860: 10; 3 August 1860 (supplement): 66, 70–71; 30 November 1860: 23–25; 16 December 1861: 19–20.
47   *Te Karere Maori*, 18 July 1863: 5. 'Kua rongo au ki nga nupepa o Akarana i tae mai ki konei, kei te whawhai Niu Tireni ki te Pakeha' (trans. from source).
48   *Daily Southern Cross*, 24 April 1863: 2.
49   *New Zealand Herald*, 1 July 1901: 6; Waugh 1971; Davis 1933.
50   *Auckland Star*, 11 February 1876: 2.

bones of recently deceased) and to persuade Ngāti Whātua to align with the Kīngitanga 'in the event of hostilities taking place'. The senior Ōrākei chief, Āpihai Te Kawau, informed them that:

> His nephew Paul had gone to Rarotonga, where the King of that Island had kindly received him, and had also given him the 'mana' of the Island to him and to his people—he (Apihai) had also heard, that it was a quiet and fruitful place—a proper place for old men and orphans—he had therefore made up his mind to go to that Island, and leave this land of confusion forever.[51]

Te Kawau likely used the term 'pani' to define orphan, a word imbued with a sense of ongoing bereavement. He may have used the term to suggest vulnerability or dislocation, with the metaphor implying that Rarotonga was an easier, less-stressful place to live than New Zealand. In doing so, it is likely that he was attempting to divert the attention of his listeners, as he did not leave New Zealand himself. However, others did. In 1864, Tūhaere wrote to the Rarotonga ariki in response to a letter about a man named Maihi, a recent combatant against the New Zealand Government, who had visited the island 'to look for land for his people'. Tūhaere was 'enraged' at this prospect. With the backing of Governor Grey, he talked of arming his men to deter the interlopers who, he believed, had hostile intent, and could easily defeat the Rarotongans 'who know nothing of fighting'. On Tūhaere meeting Maihi, it was reported that:

> [Maihi] said, 'Let us both go [to Rarotonga] and hear what you have to say to them, because when they assembled to ask me to stay at Rarotonga, I said, "It will not be right because Paul is the man who has come to this island. I arrived after him."' I answered, 'That is right.' I continued—'If it had been only yourself and your child, I would have consented.' He said, 'I will go and get my child.' I replied 'The thought is with you, because I will not consent.'[52]

According to the *Hawke's Bay Herald*, Ngāiterangi, after their defeat at Te Ranga in 1864, petitioned the government to relocate them to Rarotonga. They were aware of Tūhaere's voyages, and his 'native space' became a conceptual locality within their own imaginations. The paper noted:

---

51   Fulloon 1863.
52   *Geelong Advertiser*, 16 January 1865: 3.

The constant trading in oranges by the schooner of this chief, to and from Auckland, makes the idea of his residence there very familiar in the minds of the Maoris about this part of New Zealand.[53]

According to *Te Karere Maori*, on first arriving in Rarotonga, 'Paora was proclaimed Ariki over a portion of Rarotonga, with the command of 2,000 men', most likely an exaggeration.[54] It was also reported that he was given 'large plantations of bananas, cocoanuts [sic], oranges, limes, bread-fruit, taro, kumara, and other productions'.[55] When the *Victoria* took the first cargo back, Tūhaere remained on the island. He sent a letter describing the land to his people:

> This is a good country: there is little work done here. I have travelled over the whole place, and have seen that it is good. I have cultivated the soil. It is a good place for the orphan, for the labour of the soil is light.[56]

However, Tūhaere was unsure if he wanted to make it his permanent base:

> They are urging me to remain at Rarotonga to be their chief, but I have not yet consented to their request. When Kainuku and I come to Auckland, then we shall be able to decide, after the matter is discussed.[57]

The newspaper translation suggests that Rarotongans wanted him to be *their* chief. However, it seems unlikely that the ariki there would have been prepared to accept a foreigner as their overlord. Tūhaere's actual words 'hei rangatira mo ratou' could also be translated as 'as *a* chief for them'. Similarly, the tuku (releasing) of the land and men would have been understood, in Polynesian terms, as an exercise of manaakitanga, seeking 'to incorporate those who they chose to have living among them into their hapū structures', with land returning to its original owners when

---

53 *Hawke's Bay Herald*, 25 August 1864: 2.

54 While the population of Rarotonga in 1863 is unknown, Marjorie Crocombe estimates that it was about 7,000 in 1802; however, successive epidemics from introduced diseases had reduced it to 1,936 by 1871. Crocombe 1983: 21.

55 *Te Karere Maori*, 15 May 1863: 2. 'Whakaarikitia iho a Paora e taua iwi; tukua iho nga whenua me nga tangata hei hoa noho mona e 2,000.'; 'he mahinga panana, kokonata, orani, raima, taro, kumara, me era atu kai o taua whenua' (trans. from source).

56 *Te Karere Maori*, 18 July 1863: 5. 'He whenua pai tenei whenua, he iti te mahi o tenei whenua; kua haere au i nga wahi katoa, kua kite au i te pai, kua mahi au i te whenua, he mahi pai to te whenua nei mo te pani, he iti noa iho' (trans. from source).

57 *Te Karere Maori*, 18 July 1863: 5. 'Ko ta ratou tohe kia noho ahau i Rarotonga, hei rangatira mo ratou, heoi, kahore ano au i whakaae noa ki ta ratou korero, erangi kia tae atu maua ko Kainuku, hei reira tatou matau ai ki nga korero' (trans. from source).

no longer used.[58] Unlike early Pākehā who settled in Polynesian societies, Tūhaere would have understood that his new 'possessions' were still the natives' space. Both parties shared a mutual comprehension of what a gift of land meant—it was a means of benefiting the tāngata whenua or 'a reward for services rendered' and was unlikely to be in perpetuity.[59] For the Rarotongan ariki, one of Tūhaere's attractions was his European connections: he had close associations with the New Zealand governor who, in turn, was directly connected to London. The chiefs of Rarotonga and nearby islands feared France as a colonial power; their sympathies lay with the British, largely due to the presence of English Protestant missionaries.

More pressing were the Peruvian slave ships that were stripping vulnerable island communities of their populations for forced labour in South America. Tūhaere raised the issue of slavers with Governor Grey;[60] the *Victoria* carried a letter to Grey from Nūmangātini, the ariki of Mangaia, whose son had been abducted, seeking his assistance.[61] Doubtless too, the Rarotongan ariki would have sought advice from Tūhaere before writing to Grey seeking formal British protection in 1864.[62] In the end, Tūhaere did not settle permanently in Rarotonga; instead, he returned to New Zealand and became active in the Māori politics that foreshadowed the Kotahitanga (unity or solidarity) movement.

While Tūhaere created his own temporary 'native space' in Rarotonga, the relationships, including marriages, that were forged between the two peoples, meant that his own marae at Ōrākei became a 'native space' for Rarotongans visiting or living in Auckland. As early as 1865, Tio, 'a native of Rarotonga', gave evidence in court on a stabbing case at Ōrākei, as

---

58 Mutu 2012: 95, 101. A probably more symbolic gifting was that of land to Ana Pōmare, the daughter of Sir Māui Pōmare who had been the government minister of the Cook Island. According to James Cowan, Lady Pōmare and Ana 'were claimed as kinswomen and chieftainesses' by the Rarotongans. Ramsden states that a 'plantation' was gifted to Ana Pōmare, in honour of her father after his death. Cowan 1987: xii; Ramsden 1938: 23.

59 Mutu 2012: 101; Campbell 2002: 232–33.

60 Archives New Zealand has a record of a letter from Tūhaere dated 2 April 1863 that states: 'Natives of South Sea islands have been kidnapped by Spanish Peruvian ships [and that he] fears losing his ship'. Tuhaere 1863. See Letter from Paora Tuhaere to Sir George Grey, 2 April 1863'. Unfortunately Archives New Zealand were unable to locate this letter.

61 Reilly 2008: 4–7; *Otago Daily Times*, 5 May 1863: 4.

62 'Memoranda by Mr. Sterndale on some of the South Sea Islands': 19.

did Pira, 'a Wahoo', possibly from Hawai'i.[63] More importantly, when Rarotongan royalty and other VIPs visited New Zealand, the Ōrākei marae formally welcomed them, with Tūhaere acting as host for these groups. His guests included Kainuku, the 'King of Rarotonga', in 1879;[64] Queen Makea in 1889;[65] the premier of the island, Tepou-o-te-Rangi, in 1889;[66] and entertainers performing at Auckland's 50th jubilee in 1890 who were quartered at the marae.[67] Such encounters were mediated with formal Polynesian gift exchanges. For example, when Queen Makea came to Ōrākei:

> Paul and his people accorded them a hearty welcome, firing off guns and dancing a war dance … Paul's people made many presents to the Embassy, among them a valuable block of greenstone, greenstone ornaments, a whalebone mere, mats, and last, but not least, twelve native girls approached the Queen, each presenting her with a £1 note as a gift.[68]

Likewise, when the chief of Rarotonga (Tepou) visited, he was:

> Presented with two beautiful and valuable mats, and pieces of greenstone and several hats. The presentation was made by Paul's son, the old chief being laid up with a touch of gout.[69]

Such pōwhiri (rituals of encounter) continued after Tūhaere's death in 1892. For example in 1934, the Ōrākei people hosted a group, with the feast prepared 'in Rarotongan fashion'. The speaker for the tāngata whenua, Ngapipi Rewiti, reminded the gathering of the original friendship and alliance formed between Tūhaere and Kainuku.[70] Ramsden, in 1938, described Ōrākei as 'a Rarotongan marae', stating that 'for any roving Rarotongans in New Zealand there was always food at Orakei. Even to-day there are Cook Islanders associated with that village'.[71]

---

63   *New Zealand Herald*, 13 September 1865: 6. 'Wahoo' derives from Oahu, one of the Hawaiian islands. Pira may have been Hawaiian, or the term might have been used more generally to denote a Pacific Islander. Various Pacific Islanders visited, or lived, in New Zealand during the nineteenth century. See Mallon 2012: 77–95.

64   *Waikato Times*, 14 January 1879: 2.

65   *Auckland Star*, 10 October 1885: 2; *New Zealand Herald*, 14 October 1885: 5.

66   *Auckland Star*, 31 December 1889: 8.

67   *New Zealand Herald*, 16 November 1889: 4; 11 January 1890: 5; *Auckland Star*, 31 January 1890: 5.

68   *New Zealand Herald*, 17 October 1885: 4.

69   *New Zealand Herald*, 30 December 1889: 5.

70   *New Zealand Herald*, 10 February 1934: 14.

71   Ramsden 1938: 6, 23.

Intermarriage, begun when several of Tūhaere's men married Rarotongan women in 1863, appears to have continued, although probably infrequently. In 1898, the *Auckland Star* announced that Nia Tare, 'a halfcaste Maori and Rarotongan' and relative of Pāora Tūhaere's, was leaving Ōrākei with his wife and child to live in Rarotonga.[72] Investigations into land grievances at Ōrākei in 1939 indicate that several Ngāti Whātua women were married to Rarotongans and living on the island.[73] In 1945, the Māori chief Nia Hira Pateoro died at Ōrākei, survived by 'his wife, Tauariki Mihi, a Rarotongan chieftainess' and children.[74] However, it is likely, as Antony Hooper suggested, that, over time, 'those who married New Zealand Maoris have been absorbed into such Maori communities as Orakei'. In 1961, Hooper estimated that there were 'some half-dozen Rarotongans' living in the village.[75]

In 1863, when Tūhaere headed to Rarotonga, Pākehā saw him as a loyal and dependable chief. In 1867, the superintendent of the Auckland Province appointed him to his executive, despite his not being able to speak English.[76] Tūhaere's dependability was also useful in other ways. Although Ngāti Whātua had not joined the Kīngitanga, they were related to the Tainui tribes (a confederation of North Island iwi) of Waikato through the ancestors Tūrongo and Mahinaarangi. Tainui had sheltered some of Ngāti Whātua in Waikato during the musket wars, and it was partly due to the protection of Te Wherowhero (the Tainui ariki who became the first Māori king in 1858) that Ngāti Whātua's presence in the Auckland isthmus was assured in the 1830s.[77] The government invaded the Waikato in 1863, pushing the Kīngitanga forces southward in a year-long campaign. The New Zealand parliament passed legislation allowing the governor to confiscate most of Tainui's Waikato land. Tāwhiao, the second Māori king, and his people, retreated south into unconquered Ngāti Maniapoto lands. This territory, effectively an independent state, lay behind the 'aukati' (boundary) that excluded governmental authority and any unwanted Pākehā. Although fighting had ceased, the government's relations with the Kīngitanga were often tense. Loyal chiefs with genealogical links to Tainui were useful go-betweens, especially up

72 *Auckland Star*, 2 August 1898: 4.
73 'Orakei Lands' 1939: 14, 19.
74 *Auckland Star*, 1 September 1945: 7.
75 Hooper 1961: 16.
76 *South Australian Advertiser*, 5 July 1867: 2; *Daily Southern Cross*, 29 January 1867: 4.
77 Kawharu 1975: 5, 6, 57–58; *New Zealand Herald*, 5 December 1866: 6.

to 1881 (when King Tāwhiao finally reconciled with the Crown). During this period of estrangement, Tūhaere met with Kīngitanga chiefs on behalf of the government, which asked him to mediate in cases where trespassing Pākehā had been murdered by Kīngitanga supporters.[78]

Over time, Tūhaere became more sympathetic to the Kīngitanga's aims. He still acted as an envoy for the government during the 1870s and accompanied official parties; however, he maintained a relationship with the Kīngitanga on his own terms. For example, in 1878, the *Waikato Times* indicated that Tūhaere was hosting Tāwhiao's son and other Kīngitanga chiefs.[79] When he hosted a large Māori parliament at Ōrākei in the following year to discuss how Māori had fared in the colonial state, the Kīngitanga sent three delegates.[80] Tūhaere was still 'loyal' to his people, but the Ngāti Whātua tribal holdings in Auckland had diminished over time and their economic participation in the city had become marginal, allowing a closer affinity with other tribes who had experienced land loss:

> Their principal chief, Paul Tuhaere, who had formerly gone tophatted to Government House parties, began to prefer the company of his compatriots … He became a regular attender at meetings of the King party. Here he exhorted the King party to retain their land, bitterly recollecting his own experience as a landseller; 'Look at me, a man who knows how to suffer.' He urged them not to admit the Native Land Court, to keep out the European surveyors and purchase agents.[81]

Tūhaere's alignment with the Kīngitanga meant that the itineraries of Rarotongan royal visitors generally included visits to the Māori king, or important Kīngitanga chiefs. Tūhaere took Kainuku to meet a number of chiefs behind the aukati at Te Kōpua in 1879.[82] It was Tūhaere who facilitated Queen Makea's visit to King Tāwhiao at Whatiwhatihoe in 1885.[83] These links extended into the twentieth century. The Rarotongan party who were entertained at Ōrākei in 1934 left soon after for Ngāruawāhia to see King Koroki.[84] Later that year, at the Kīngitanga's

---

78 For example, *New Zealand Herald*, 15 June 1869: 6; 10 May 1878: 3; 31 January 1879: 3; *Bruce Herald*, 28 February 1873: 3; *Evening Post*, 5 June 1873: 2; *Auckland Star*, 28 January 1875: 3. Letter from Paora Tuhaere to Sir George Grey, 2 April 1863; *Auckland Star*, 27 May 1873: 3; *Waikato Times*, 26 June 1873: 2.
79 *Waikato Times*, 23 April 1878: 2.
80 *Auckland Star*, 25 February 1879: 2.
81 *Te Ao Hou*, No. 27 (June 1959): 13.
82 *Waikato Times*, 14 January 1879: 2.
83 *New Zealand Herald*, 17 October 1885: 4; *Auckland Star*, 7 November 1885: 4.
84 *New Zealand Herald*, 10 February 1934: 14.

annual Koroneihana (coronation) celebration, a Ngāti Whātua group, with 'several Rarotongans who are resident in Auckland', proved popular, performing Rarotongan songs in 'Island costumes'.[85] Of course, the Kīngitanga also forged its own connections with Rarotonga, with Piupiu Te Wherowhero, the granddaughter of King Tāwhiao, marrying the Rarotongan ariki, Kainuku Vaikai.[86]

The dynamic between Ngāti Whātua and Rarotonga developed over time. With New Zealand's annexation of the Cook Islands in 1900, the Rarotongan chiefly elite gained official channels to work through, not just administrators situated on the island, but Wellington-based politicians. As Rosemary Anderson has observed, before WWII, the responsibility for the Cook Islands fell largely to Māori politicians: Sir James Carroll, Sir Māui Pōmare and Sir Āpirana Ngata. The latter two visited Rarotonga and formed close bonds with the Indigenous elite.[87] Ngata fostered close ties between the island and his iwi, Ngāti Porou, who erected the large Te Hono-ki-Rarotonga meeting house at Tokomaru Bay, opened by the Rarotongan ariki Makea Tinirau in 1934.[88]

Relationships between Rarotonga and Ngāti Whātua continued to change after WWII. The 1936 census recorded only 33 Cook Islanders in the Auckland area,[89] and it is probable that many had connections with Ōrākei. However, as New Zealand's post-war economy boomed, Māori were drawn into the cities to work. Large numbers of Pacific Islanders immigrated to New Zealand at the same time. Although the government had recruited some Cook Islands' women during the war to fill a shortage in domestic labour,[90] the number of Cook Islanders living in New Zealand cities increased markedly from the 1950s (as did other Pacific populations).[91] By 1966, there were 4,391 Cook Islanders in Auckland.[92] This influx of both Māori and Pacific peoples into Auckland meant that Rarotongans were less likely to meet Ngāti Whātua of Ōrākei or have any connection to the village. Moreover, the capability of Ngāti Whātua to host Rarotongan guests in Auckland effectively ceased in 1950 when the

---

85 *New Zealand Herald*, 9 October 1934: 11.
86 Ballara 2012.
87 Anderson 2014: 29–44.
88 Schwimmer 1959: 34; Te Runanganui o Ngati Porou 2014.
89 Curson 1970a: 421.
90 Anderson 2013: 267–85.
91 Anderson 2014: 15–16.
92 Curson 1970a: 421.

government seized the last of the tribe's land at Ōrākei: no cultivations were possible for food and there were no marae where appropriate speeches could be made. Nor were incoming Rarotongans likely to live near the village; instead, they re-created their own 'cultural islands' within other inner-city suburbs, and then in South Auckland. Apart from an area of state rental houses provided for Ngāti Whātua families and a section of public reserve, the land around Ōrākei was given over to up-market housing occupied by Pākehā.[93]

In 1970, P.H. Curson noted a degree of antipathy and 'social distance' between Māori and other Polynesians in Auckland, with some Rarotongans refusing to acknowledge that they might understand Māori language.[94] By the time of the 2013 census, 37,000 people living in the Auckland region claimed Cook Islands descent: of the 142,770 Auckland Māori, just 7,353 identified as being of Ngāti Whātua descent.[95] As Anderson pointed out, it had been the elites that had benefited from the relationships established by Tūhaere, and it was 'unlikely … that the daily lives of ordinary islanders were enhanced by these interactions'.[96] The large numbers of Cook Islanders who settled in Auckland in the later twentieth century effectively swamped what was left of the connection between Ōrākei and visiting Rarotongan dignitaries.

***

By 1863, when Pāora Tūhaere set off to Rarotonga, Western culture and modernity—through commerce, religion and colonial force—had already touched practically all parts of the Pacific. New Zealand was nominally a British colony, despite much of its land remaining in Māori hands, and Rarotonga, although still under independent chiefly rule, could see the benefits of British protection from French assertiveness or South American slavers. The advent of European maritime technology into the Pacific meant that many Pacific Islanders could travel to other places. Most often this movement was along pathways already established by Europeans to colonial outposts of power such as Sydney or to its source in London. In venturing to the Cook Islands, Tūhaere joined an already well-established trading network. What was different was that his encounters

---

93   Curson 1970a: 428, 430; Curson 1970b: 167.
94   Curson 1970b: 172.
95   Statistics New Zealand: Tatauranga Aotearoa 2013. A small number of people identified as 'Rarotongan'. These have been included in the figure for 'Cook Islanders'.
96   Anderson 2014: 47.

with Rarotongans operated on an Indigenous–Indigenous level, mediated by shared Polynesian understandings, through hospitality, marriage and the (temporary) gifting of land. Ongoing relationships, which were diplomatic as much as commercial, were as important as any profit either party might realise. The Rarotongan ariki willingly gifted Tūhaere land and labour because they believed that he was a conduit to the source of British colonial power. Ultimately, he appears to have maintained his diplomatic role far longer than his commercial one, continuing to provide manaakitanga to important Rarotongan visitors. As Ngāti Whātua's land and influence diminished alongside Auckland's growth as a city, Tūhaere's sympathies began to align more with the Kīngitanga, leading him to act as a conduit between kāhui ariki of both the Kīngitanga and Rarotonga. These relationships were imagined and constructed in terms of place, both at Rarotonga and Ōrākei. Like Tūhaere's trading ventures, these may have been temporary phenomena—only possible within the new colonial environment—but they were spaces nevertheless created by Indigenous people for themselves.

References

Anderson, Rosemary 2013, 'Distant daughters: Cook Islands domestics in wartime New Zealand, 1941–1946', *Journal of Pacific History* 48(3): 267–85. doi.org/10.1080/00223344.2013.823008

Anderson, Rosemary 2014, 'The origins of Cook Islands migration to New Zealand, 1920–1950', MA thesis, University of Otago, New Zealand.

Ballantyne, Tony and Antoinette Burton 2009, 'Introduction: The politics of intimacy in an age of empire', in *Moving Subjects: Gender, Mobility and Intimacy in an Age of Global Empire*, Tony Ballantyne and Antoinette Burton (eds), University of Illinois Press, Urbana: 1–28.

Ballara, Angela 2012, 'Te Wherowhero, Piupiu', *Dictionary of New Zealand Biography: Te Ara—the Encyclopedia of New Zealand*, www.teara.govt.nz/en/biographies/3t26/te-wherowhero-piupiu, accessed 30 March 2017.

Campbell, Matthew 2002, 'History in prehistory: The oral traditions of the Rarotongan land court records', *Journal of Pacific History* 37(2): 221–38. doi.org/10.1080/0022334022000006619

Carey, Jane, and Jane Lydon 2014, 'Introduction: Indigenous networks: Historical trajectories and contemporary connections', in *Indigenous Networks: Mobility, Connections and Exchange*, Jane Carey and Jane Lydon (eds), Routledge, New York: 1–26.

Chappell, David A. 1997, *Double Ghosts: Oceanian Voyagers on Euroamerican Ships*, M.E. Sharpe, Armonk.

Cowan, James 1987, 'Preface', Maui Pomare, *Legends of the Maori*, volume 2, Southern Reprints, Papakura: ix–xvi.

Crocombe, Marjorie Tuainekore 1983, 'Maretu's life, work and context', in *Maretu, Cannibals and Converts: Radical Change in the Cook Islands*, Marjorie Tuainekore Crocombe (trans. and ed.), Institute of Pacific Studies, Suva: 1–30.

Curson, P.H. 1970a, 'Polynesians and residential concentration in Auckland', *Journal of the Polynesian Society* 79(4): 421–32.

Curson, P.H. 1970b, 'Polynesians and residence in Auckland', *New Zealand Geographer* 26(2): 162–73. doi.org/10.1111/j.1745-7939.1970.tb00629.x

Davis, G.M. (ed.) 1933, 'Narrative of Mr Charles James Ward of Rarotonga, Cook Islands', New Zealand Electronic Text Centre, nzetc.victoria.ac.nz/tm/scholarly/tei-WarNarr-t1-body-d2.html, accessed 30 March 2017.

Edmonds, Penelope 2010, *Urbanizing Frontiers: Indigenous Peoples and Settlers in 19th-century Pacific Rim Cities*, UBC Press, Vancouver.

Fulloon, James 1863 (26 May), Memorandum, Raupatu Document Bank, volume 55: 21035–37. Archives New Zealand.

Gilson, Richard 1980, *The Cook Islands 1820–1950*, Ron Crocombe (ed.), Victoria University Press, Wellington.

Harris, Cole 2002, *Making Native Spaces: Colonialism, Resistance, and Reserves in British Columbia*, UBC Press, Vancouver.

Henry, Howard 2002, *'The Coming of Tomorrow': European Exploration and 'Discovery' of the Cook Islands,* Sovereign Pacific Publishing Company, Auckland.

Hogan, Helen 1994, 'Stories of travel: He Kōrero Ēnei Mō te Haerenga', volume 2, PhD thesis, University of Canterbury, New Zealand.

Holler, Jacqueline 2007, 'Conquered spaces, colonial skirmishes: Spatial contestation in sixteenth-century Mexico City', *Radical History Review* 99: 107–20. doi.org/10.1215/01636545-2007-005

Hooper, Antony 1961, 'The migration of Cook Islanders in New Zealand', *Journal of the Polynesian Society* 70(1): 11–17.

Kawharu I.H. 1975, *Orakei: A Ngati Whatua Community,* NZCER, Wellington.

King, Michael 2000, *Moriori: A People Rediscovered*, revised edition, Penguin Books, Auckland.

Kloosterman, Alphons M.J. 1976, *Discoverers of the Cook Islands and the Names They Gave*, Cook Islands Library and Museum, Rarotonga.

Lester, Alan 2013, 'Spatial concepts and the historical geographies of British colonialism', in *Writing Imperial Histories*, Andrew S. Thompson (ed.), Manchester University Press, Manchester: 118–42.

Mallon, Sean 2012, 'Little-known lives: Pacific Islanders in nineteenth-century New Zealand', in *Tangata o le Moana: New Zealand and the People of the Pacific*, Sean Mallon, Kolokesa Māhina-Tuai and Damon Salesa (eds), Te Papa Press, Wellington: 77–95.

Maretu 1983, *Cannibals and Converts: Radical Change in the Cook Islands*, Marjorie Tuainekore Crocombe (trans. and ed.), Institute of Pacific Studies, Suva.

Maude, H.E. and Marjorie Tuainekore Crocombe 1962, 'Rarotongan sandalwood: The visit of Goodenough to Rarotonga in 1814', *Journal of the Polynesian Society* 71(1): 32–56.

McClintock, Anne 1995, *Imperial Leather: Race, Gender, and Sexuality in the Colonial Contest*, Routledge, New York.

McIntyre, W. David 1992, 'Imperialism and nationalism', in *The Oxford History of New Zealand,* second edition, Geoffrey W. Rice (ed.), Oxford University Press, Auckland: 337–47.

'Memoranda by Mr. Sterndale on some of the South Sea Islands', AJHR, 1874 Session I, A-03b. Appendices to the Journals of the House of Representatives.

Ministry of Culture and Heritage 2006, *Māori Peoples of New Zealand: Ngā Iwi o Aotearoa*, David Bateman and Ministry of Culture and Heritage, Auckland.

Mutu, Margaret 2012, 'Custom law and the advent of new pākehā settlers: Tuku Whenua—allocation of resource use rights', in *Huia Histories of Māori: Ngā Tāhuhu Kōrero*, D. Keenan (ed.), Huia Publishers, Wellington: 93–108.

Oliver, Steven 2012, 'Tuhaere, Paora', *Dictionary of New Zealand Biography: Te Ara—the Encyclopedia of New Zealand*, www.teara.govt. nz/en/biographies/1t109/tuhaere-paora, accessed 30 March, 2017.

'Orakei Lands: Report of Royal Commission Appointed to Inquire into and Report as to Grievances Alleged by Maoris with regard to Certain Lands at Orakei, in the City of Auckland', AJHR, 1939 Session I, G-06. Appendices to the Journals of the House of Representatives.

Paterson, Lachy 2006, *Colonial Discourses: Niupepa Māori 1855–1863*, Otago University Press, Dunedin.

Paterson, Lachy 2013, '"The similarity of hue constituted no special bond of intimacy between them": Close encounters of the Indigenous kind', *Journal of New Zealand Studies* NS14: 19–40.

Petrie, Hazel 2006, *Chiefs of Industry: Maori Tribal Enterprise in Early Colonial New Zealand*, Auckland University Press, Auckland.

Ramsden, Eric 1938, 'A Rarotongan marae in New Zealand', *The World's News*, 24 December.

Ramsden, Eric 1944, *Strange Stories from the South Seas,* A.H. and A.W. Reed, Wellington.

Reilly, Michael 2008, 'Mangaia in the colonial world, 1863–1899', *Pacific Studies* 31(1): 1–30.

Ross, Angus 1964, *New Zealand Aspirations in the Pacific in the Nineteenth Century*, Oxford University Press, London.

Salesa, Damon 2009, 'New Zealand's Pacific', in *The New Oxford History of New Zealand*, Giselle Byrnes (ed.), Oxford University Press, South Melbourne: 149–72.

Salesa, Damon 2012, 'A Pacific destiny: New Zealand's overseas destiny, 1840-1945', in *Tangata o le Moana: New Zealand and the People of the Pacific*, Sean Mallon, Kolokesa Māhina-Tuai and Damon Salesa (eds), Te Papa Press, Wellington: 97–122.

Schwimmer, E.G. 1959 (September), 'Building art in the Maori tradition: John Taiapa and the carved meeting house of to-day', *Te Ao Hou: The New World* 28: 31–35.

Scott, Dick 1991, *Years of the Pooh-bah: A Cook Islands History*, CITC, Rarotonga.

Statistics New Zealand: Tatauranga Aotearoa 2013, '2013 Census', www.stats.govt.nz/Census/2013-census.aspx, accessed 30 March 2017.

Te Hurinui, Pei 2010, *King Pōtatau: An Account of the Life of Pōtatau Te Wherowhero the First Maori King*, Huia Publishers and Polynesian Society, Wellington.

Te Runanganui o Ngati Porou 2014, *Pakirikiri Marae: Te Korero na Papa Tate Pewhairangi*, www.ngatiporou.com/article/pakirikiri-marae-te-korero-na-papa-tate-pewhairangi, accessed 30 March 2017.

Tuhaere, Paora 1863 (2 April), Letter to Sir George Grey, Item R22399768, ACHK/16569/G13/2/10, Archives New Zealand.

Waitangi Tribunal 1987, *Report of the Waitangi Tribunal on the Orakei Claim (Wai-9)*, Brooker and Friend, Wellington.

Waugh, Richard L.H. 1971, 'Albert John Nicholas of Hikutaia', *Ohinemuri Regional History Journal* 15(June), www.ohinemuri.org.nz/journals/41-journal-15-june-1971/727-albert-john-nicholas-of-hikutaia, accessed 30 March 2017.

11

Reconnecting with South-East Asia

Regina Ganter

The Yolngu people of eastern Arnhem Land and trepang fishers operating out of the Sulawesi port of Macassar share a transnational heritage through the trade in trepang (sea cucumber) that has lasted for generations and created family, community and cultural links between peoples. Their history of mobility interrupts the assumptions of indigenous people as fixed and local that have been so central to colonial discourses of indigeneity. This chapter, like that of Lachy Paterson's in this volume, explores an example of indigenous and non-European encounter through travel, thereby undermining assumptions that Europeans were necessarily central to indigenous travel.[1]

George Windsor Earl, coiner of the term 'Indonesia' and author of *Sailing Directions for the Arafura Sea* (1839), often observed the Macassans[2] working with Aboriginal people in scenes not dissimilar to those drawn

---

1   The research on Asian–Aboriginal contact in northern Australia underpinning this chapter was generously supported by an ARC Discovery grant 1997–2000 and an ARC Future Fellowship 2011–15.
2   'Macassan' is an English-language expression used in historical documents to refer to a mixture of ethnic and religious groups participating in the trepang industry, mostly out of the port of Makassar (Macassar). The language of Makassar (Macassar), capital of Sulawesi (formerly Ujung Pandang) is called Makasar (Macasar). The language adopted through this trade by Yolngu and other north Australian peoples was a trade kriol with roots in several languages from the Malay achipelago. For consistency with other chapters in this volume, the English-language spelling is used: Macassan, Macassar, Masasar.

by Emile Lasalle aboard the *Astrolabe* in 1839. Investing hope in the trepang industry, Earl threw his energies into establishing a trading port at Cobourg Peninsula in 1838, which was to be 'a second Singapore' where business could continue and expand.[3] Contact was also observed by other visitors to the area including Matthew Flinders in February 1803 on the Arnhem Land coast.[4] It was surely more than lucky coincidence that his ship, the *Investigator*, carried a Malay cook who was able to interpret the language and establish a channel for communication.[5] The trepang fishery in Australia was reaching its zenith in the first half of the nineteenth century and several stories tell of Yolngu people travelling to and living in Macassar. However, this transnational mobility would be curtailed by government intervention on account of entrepreneurial, racial and possibly religious competition. The Macassan trepang fishery was prohibited in northern Australia in 1906, rupturing not only family connections and trade, but also deep cultural affinities. As customs officer Alfred Searcy observed, this 'must have been a great blow to the indigenous people'.[6] The colonial administration forced the Yolngu into isolation by confining them to designated parcels of land without access to passports or international travel. Ideological, diplomatic and economic considerations forged this history, and also forged the telling of this history from an Indigenous perspective. The full history has yet to be told.

The historical reflections sparked by the Australian bicentennial celebrations in 1988 reinvigorated interest in this period of contact with the Malay Archipelago, leading to a revival of contact and greater public access to its ritual allusions. As Howard Morphy has observed, the public dances now performed at Yirrkala funerals involve flags, samurai swords, long-barrelled pipes, prayer calls to Allah and references to South-East Asian ports like Djakapura (Singapore), Djumaynga (Macassar) and Banda.[7] After nearly eight decades without contact, the connection has been resumed in a way that both asserts and reclaims new forms of Aboriginality that are no longer premised on social isolation and racial

---

3   Emile Lasalle's image of the Macassan trepang camp at Raffles Bay, visited in 1839 on Dumont d'Urville's *Astrolabe* (NLA reference 20806695) is often displayed and is available online.
4   Matthew Flinders certainly misunderstood the name of the Macassan captain he renders as Pobassoo. Macknight (1969: 67) suggested Pu Basso; Thomas (2013) refers to Puang Basso.
5   There are several indications that Flinders knew what he was looking for. He spent more than five of his 10-month circumnavigation in the Macassan contact zone, and Joseph Banks had given Flinders some information from Alexander Dalrymple about the trading potentials in the archipelago.
6   Searcy 1907: 97.
7   McIntosh 2013: 95–106.

purity. The discovery and commemoration of this history is still in progress; a range of approaches continue to peel back outmoded views of Aboriginality, in the process offering new sources of cultural pride. Within the short span of a century, the contact between Malay and Yolngu people has passed from history to the brink of myth, and from myth to history.

They Have Left Their Spirit With Us

Yolngu people have begun to publicly celebrate their historical and kin connections to Sulawesi in a number of ways, including through song. The Sunrize Band's 1993 track 'Lembana Mani Mani' (the Macassan name for Maningrida) asserts that 'we commemorate and celebrate for those visitors from Macassar', and Yothu Yindi's 'Macassan Crew', released in 2000, makes reference to Dayngatjing who 'came in peace through the Ashmore Reef' and navigated by the morning star, bringing tamarind seeds with him. Dayngatjing, known as Captain Daeng[8] Gassing in Australian customs records, was one of the last Macassans to visit Australian shores.

Another musical expression comes from Milingimbi's Wirrngya Band whose song 'My Sweet Takirrina' refers to the Macassan appellation for Milingimbi that translates to 'abrus seed bay'. Like tamarind, banyan and water buffalo, 'takirrina' was a culturally important biological import from the Malay Archipelago to northern Australia. The song begins with the line 'for many years these stories were told', which alludes to the highly mythologised way in which younger generations have learned about Macassans as if they were mythical beings. The sacred wuramu figures represented them with songkok caps (a style of Muslim fez) and their apparently mythical praus[9] were shown on rock paintings already layered with more recent inscriptions. 'My Sweet Takirrina' captures the moment during the bicentennial celebrations in 1988 when a perahu padewakang (a traditional Macassan trading vessel) arrived from Macassar. Far from being mythical, the ship was captained by a descendant of two of the best-remembered Macassan captains, Husein Dg Rangka and his brother-

8   *Daeng* derives from a royal title in the former kingdom of Gowa in Sulawesi. It is normally abbreviated as Dg (much like Mr or Dr) and has become integrated into the Macassan naming system as an address of respect. It is reflected in some Yolngu names as the prefix 'Dayn-', as in Dayngatjing mentioned earlier.
9   Prau, also spelled proa or (falsely) prow, derives from the Malay perahu for sailing boat, presumably originating from Micronesian languages.

in-law Suleiman Dg Gassing. The elders of Elcho Island off the coast of Arnhem Land embraced this young Macassan as family while local youths looked on in amazement.

The Sunrize lyrics continue: 'They left back for us only their spirit'. The same could be said about Yolngu ancestors in Macassar. Asianist Marshall Clark was present when bulldozers mowed down the best-known site of Yolngu–Macassan transnational heritage, the home of Unusu Dg Remba. Located on Jalan Maipa in the Kampung Bassi district of Macassar, the home was constructed with northern Australian ironwood more than a century prior. In its heyday, it had fishponds, a prayer house and water pump. It was a substantial two-storey building that, even in its dilapidated state, was reputedly sold for the equivalent of US$1 million amid the luxury hotel developments that engulfed Macassar's Losari Beach. At least two Aboriginal men had lived, worked and died in the house. Nobody came to loot the valuable timber that was left lying around during the demolition, as it was considered keramat (sacred). Moreover, the neighbours whispered that the house had been haunted by a hantu Marege[10]—an Aboriginal ghost. The developers may have been hoping that such ghosts of the past would disappear with the rebuilding, as their public information sign read:

> Mohon Doa Restu:
> Lokasi ini akan dibangun Kenari Tower Hotel Unit 2
>
> [Please offer your prayers of blessing: this location will we be used to build Unit 2 of the Kenari Tower Hotel][11]

A banyan tree in Melville Bay, Arnhem Land, is also said to have a spirit that cries whenever it sees a prau coming into or leaving the bay. Banyan trees are often associated with Macassan burials and Melville Bay was the burial site of Sampara Dg Ruppa.[12] Anthropologists Ronald and Catherine Berndt described Melville Bay as a Bayini place associated with deep history and links reaching beyond the Macassan trepang fishery.[13] The Bayini stories might be best understood as a kind of Yolngu spiritual

---

10   'Marege' is the Macassan word for the Arnhem Land coast.
11   Clark 2013: 159–82.
12   Melville Bay, also known as Lembana Panrea, was a trepang site associated with captain Husein Dg Rangka (already mentioned) and the Aboriginal leader Dayngmangu (mentioned below). Spillett (1987) was told that Sampara Dg Rupa was buried there.
13   For a more modern treatment of the Bayini mythos, see McIntosh 2009.

assimilation of pre-British contact history. Yolngu people often remark on their connection with the Macassans: 'Similar dreamings', Joe Djalalinga Yunupingu of Yirrkala stated, while Terry Yumbulul at Galiwin'ku hinted at 'the Hindu flavour of Yolngu ways'. Pastor Joe Mowandjil Garrawirtja at Milingimbi remarked, 'we feel that we are one in spirit'.[14]

Stepping Out of the Myth

The former owner of the residence on Jalan Maipa, Dg Remba, was recorded by Australian customs along with the other two captains already mentioned. Dg Remba captained the *Lakarinlong* and travelled in the same fleet as Dg Gassing and Dg Rangka up to the trade prohibition in 1906, and all three have traceable family connections to Australia. Dg Rangka's daughter, Ibu Saribanong Nganne (born 1904), was interviewed in Macassar by Peter Spillett in 1985; she remembered two Aboriginal men who, until the 1930s, had lived in Dg Remba's house to guard the empang (fishponds), clean the mushollah (prayer house) and look after the water-pumping installation made from bamboo pipes.[15] She also recalled the names of two (among 10 other) Aboriginal children her father had had with several Arnhem Land women.[16] Ibu Saribanong implored Spillett to find her Aboriginal family for her, which he did; the following year she met Laklak Burarrwanga and her cousins from Arnhem Land.[17]

A group of Arnhem Land students from Batchelor College visited Sulawesi in June 1986 in the lead-up to a bicentennial project that Spillett was organising. Then Director of the Northern Territory Museum, Spillett masterminded a project to re-enact Yolngu–Macassan contact. He orchestrated the reconstruction of a traditional padewakang perahu (sailing boat), the *Hati Marege* (*Heart of Marege*), and accepted the honorific Macassan title of Dg Makulle, a Macassan alias that roughly translates to 'Mister Capability'.[18]

---

14   Ganter 2006: Chapter 2 passim.
15   Spillett 1987.
16   Macknight 1976: 87; Cooke 1987; Ganter 2006: 34.
17   Spillett 1987: 14.
18   Jukes 2005: 278.

The Batchelor students were amazed at what they discovered during their visit: people and places with similar names to those back home, words that echoed ones from their own language and ancient rock paintings at Sumpang Bita adorned with hand silhouettes like their own traditions. They observed real praus and real Macassan captains, and finally realised that the stories they had been told were real histories, not legends. Although they felt awkward acknowledging family, they were the pioneers of a grand movement of reconnection.

Not only Aboriginal males, but some Yolngu women also lived in Macassar and had children there. For example, one captain from Kodingareng Island, Dg Mallewa, was said to have abducted a Yolngu woman.[19] According to oral history in Macassar, all of the Aboriginal people in Macassar repatriated to Arnhem Land on the last boat in 1906 when the trepang trade was prohibited.[20] This contradicts the recollection of Ibu Saribanong Nganne, but, in either case, the prohibition on Macassan fishing fleets in northern Australian waters suspended more than important trade for the Yolngu, it also severed families. Presumably this is why that historical moment features so prominently in Yolngu stories of the Macassans.

The termination of this trade occurred amid ethnic tensions and political shifts in Australia. It was occasioned by entrepreneurial competition between the Macassan trepang fishers and the Australian officers who were placed into positions of policing them and who themselves engaged in the same fishery, competing with the Macassans for Aboriginal labour and maritime resources. This was in the lead-up to the Australian Government assuming responsibility for the Northern Territory in 1911, and in the context of federal insistence (since 1901) on a 'White Australia', even in the poly-ethnic north.[21] In 1906, French missionaries of the Sacred Heart took on the Catholic ministry of the Northern Territory. In the expectation of increasing levels of support from the federal government, they projected their intentions into territories hitherto frequented by

19   Ganter 2006: 36; Cooke 1987: 45.
20   The recollection that the Yolngu people were taken back to Marege stems from Dg Remba's son, Mangngellai Dg Maro, speaking to Spillett. The trade was prohibited in 1906, but Husein Dg Rangka set out on a final journey with a letter from Puddu Dg Tombo and gifts for the customs collector, to ascertain whether the prohibition was really going to be enforced, and perhaps also to repatriate Aboriginal people from Macassar. Dg Tompo's letter reads: 'When my proas were at your port, nothing was known about this new regulation. I cannot believe it is really true, but for prudential reasons, now send only one prow, to see how matters lay and I will feel very much obliged to you for instructing my people how they are to act'. Macknight 1976: 16.
21   Ganter 2006: Chapter 2.

Muslim Macassans and established their first mission on the Tiwi Islands in 1911, after which much of the prior Muslim contact histories became 'turned in', to borrow an eloquent phrase from Ian McIntosh.[22]

I Baptise You in the Name of …

The stories of the last visits of the Macassans emphasise the bestowal of Macassan names on Aboriginal people—a symbolic affirmation of kinship and deep connection. This gesture is not unlike the symbolic conferral of a baptismal name—the first initiation into the Christian church and adoption as a 'son of God', a practice that also derives from a polygamous traditional society, albeit in the Middle East.[23] One such story told by Djäwa, as remembered from his youth at Elcho Island, was that during the Macassans' last visit, Captain Dg Gassing gave him the name of Mangalay. Mangngalai is a recurring name in the genealogies of the three Macassan captains mentioned above. Djäwa described how his uncle witnessed this naming, much like a godparent witnessing a baptism.[24]

A similar story is that of Elcho Islander Ganimbirrgnu, an Aboriginal leader at Melville Bay who died around 1925. In some Yolngu stories, this leader has become a Macassan figure represented with a songkok;[25] however, in Macassan stories he is a Yolngu figure. According to oral history, Captain Husein Dg Rangka gave Ganimbirrgnu the Macassan honorific title of Daeng on his last visit, presumably around 1906–07, after which he was referred to as Dg Mangu or Dayngmangung in the two respective languages.[26] One of the Macassan captains remembered Dg Mangu as the 'rajah' of Lembana Panrea, referring to Melville Bay on Yolngu country with a Macassan name. Dayngmangung gave one of his wives to Dg Rangka as an expression of family relationship between the men. Their final farewell involved a ceremonial exchange of gifts that included a mast and a white calico flag 'as a sign that each had an agreement and

---

22   'Turned in' is an expression used by McIntosh for memories of contact that were suppressed from public knowledge. It derives from the concept of protected 'inside' knowledge in traditional society. For the intentions of the Missionaries of the Sacred Heart in the Northern Territory see Ganter 'Gsell, Francis Xavier, Ep.' in *German Missionaries in Australia*, missionaries.griffith.edu.au.

23   *The Catholic Encyclopedia*, www.newadvent.org/cathen/02258b.htm, accessed 26 July 2013.

24   *The Catholic Encyclopedia*, www.newadvent.org/cathen/02258b.htm, accessed 26 July 2013.

25   Spillett 1987: 14.

26   The language of Macassar is referred to as Macasar (or Makasar), and the various Yolngu dialects are collectively called Yolngumatha.

were friends and would remember each other'.[27] Presumably, Dg Rangka and Dayngmangung had a shared sense of paternity for Dg Rangka's Aboriginal children in Macassar and Arnhem Land.[28]

According to Dayngmangung's son, David Burrumarra, the naming practice became a tradition; it was carried on by his grandson, Terichini, who was named after Turije'ne, the collective name by which the maritime nomads of Sulawesi, also known as Sama Bajo, refer to themselves.[29] There are other hints at connections with the Sama Bajo, who were often recruited for the trepang journeys to northern Australia. For example, Galiwin'ku elder Mattjuwi Burarrwanga named his son Lailai Latung after Lailai Island, the home of many Sama Bajo people. Sama Bajo people also settled at Kodingareng, an island in the Spermonde Archipelago, two hours by boat from the port of Macassar; its name is reflected at Gunyangarra, a sacred site otherwise known as Ski Beach at Yirrkala.[30] A Yolngu myth about the turtle hunter Dhurritjini may be another veiled reference to the Turije'ne.[31] Such hints suggest that alongside the relations the Yolngu established with the Muslim Macassan captains, there were also networks of connections with indigenous people crewing the boats. These connections are commemorated in stories and in placenames, and are honoured with the names given to children. While Yolngu people are forthcoming with information about their Macassan links,[32] Ian McIntosh has traced fine-grained rules about the proximity that various people can claim; more recently, Nigel Lendon has commented on the political force of such disclosures.[33]

David Burrumarra is best known in the literature, but others have also offered disclosures about Macassan contact. For example, Wili Walalipa, the son of a Macassan, stated that when his descendant from Elcho Island visited Kampung Maluku and Lailai Island in the 1990s, he was treated like a long lost family member.[34] Another descendant from this contact, a Yirrkala elder, drew on his Macassan pipe while he told a story peppered

---

27   McIntosh 1994: 18, 22. This description of gifts may be a veiled reference to the morning star poles of Elcho Island.
28   Ganter 2006: 39.
29   Interview with Terry Yumbulul at Galwin'ku, June 1995.
30   Ganter 2006: 38ff.
31   Dhurritjini is briefly mentioned in Cooke 1987: 56–58.
32   Janson 2001; Palmer 2007.
33   McIntosh 1992; Lendon 2014.
34   Interview with Willie Danjati Gunderra, June 1995 at Galiwin'ku. Presumably he was also a descendant of Husein Dg Rangka, because he and Terry Yumbulul identified as cousins.

with Malay words.[35] He told of Djaladjari Matullo (who he referred to as father), who worked on the Macassan boats around Caledon Bay, Milingimbi, Goulburn Island, Croker Island and eventually Macassar, where he settled down and had three sons. Djaladjari returned to Yirrkala (presumably around the turn of the century), formed another family and became a bunggawa (or 'headman') because he spoke both Yolngumatha and Macassar.[36]

Masters and Servants

Djaladjari's story has often been cited for its convincing portrayal of a substantial expatriate Aboriginal community in Macassar.[37] Djaladjari enumerated several Aboriginal men in Macassar who had been brought as boys and had married Macassan women and had 'many children'; he could recall four men by their names and tribal affiliations, and referred to 'many others as well'.[38] Djaladjari's story offers a glimpse into the potentially exploitative relationship that existed between the trepang captains and the young boys they recruited along the journey. This aspect of contact has been 'turned in'—perhaps almost forgotten—in some recollections. Djaladjari's name is sometimes rendered as Charley-Charley Sitdown after a lame leg, which he said resulted from physical punishment received on the prau. He was only a boy when he and some companions signed on with the praus and eventually arrived in Macassar. When they finally returned, they became so 'wild with joy' at their first sight of the northern Australian coastline that their captain's cap was lost overboard; the beating that Djaladjari subsequently received permanently crippled his leg.

Djaladjari also mentioned that he did not go to Macassar of his own choosing. At the end of the trepang season, his captain, 'Jadjung', planned to leave him stranded at Port Essington. This sparked an argument with another captain in the same fleet that ended with the two threatening each other with knives. After paying-off Djaladjari (in kind), Jadjung handed him over to the other captain, skipper of the *Patti Jawaya*.[39] It is

---

35 Interview with Bawurr Munyarrun, July 1995, at Yirrkala. He referred, for example, to travelling 'selatang' (south-east), which is similar to 'selatan' for south in Indonesian.
36 Interview Bawurr Munyarrun, July 1995, at Yirrkala.
37 Djaladari's story as rendered by Berndt and Berndt (1954) has been variously cited by Langton (2011) and Stephenson (2007).
38 Berndt and Berndt 1954: 56.
39 Berndt and Berndt 1954: 56.

possible that 'Jadjung' was in fact Husein Dg Ranka, captain of the Patti Jawaya, also known as Jago or Ayam Jantan, a popular nickname meaning 'fighting cock'.[40]

The three captains, Dg Gassing, Dg Rangka and Dg Remba, all worked for Abdulrazak Puddu Dg Tombo, a bunggawa who also financed their journeys in the inner-city district of Kampung Maloku in Macassar.[41] Dg Tombo owned much of the real estate around the main mosque (Mesjid Ansar) at the southern end of present-day Chinatown and presumably he helped to finance the mosque, as this is where his remains are kept.[42] Evidently, he was a man of some social and economic magnitude. This Muslim merchant also appears in Djaladjari's story as the bunggawa who took charge of both the cargo and the Aboriginal boys.[43]

Ibu Saribanong's recollection of the two Aboriginal men serving in Dg Remba's house and Djaladjari's insistence that the Aboriginal men at Macassar were just 'boys' when they first arrived, suggest that ethnic class stratifications operated in a similar manner to those adopted in the poly-ethnic townships of northern Australia. Macassar had 'Kampung Cina' for the Chinese, 'Kampung Malaya' for the Malays, 'Kampung Dadi' for the Japanese and Timorese—as well as various other districts, like the aforementioned Kampung Maluku.[44] These socio-spatial denominations mirror the conventions that underwrote distinctions of social hierarchy circumscribed by class and ethnicity in the northern Australian townships that had 'Chinatowns' and 'Japtowns'.

Mau Ke Mana? (Where Are You Going?)

In view of the extended contact between Aboriginal people and Macassans, it is little wonder that Aboriginal men addressed the European explorers who came to the northern coast in the nineteenth century in a form of Malay. Alfred Searcy, who became sub-collector of customs at Port Darwin in 1882, made many references to this peculiar display of bilingualism.[45]

---

40   Macknight 1976.
41   Macknight 1976.
42   Thomas 2013: 69–94.
43   Berndt and Berndt 1954: 56.
44   Macknight 1976: passim.
45   Searcy 1907: 46.

Yolngu languages are also deeply infused with words and expressions of South-East Asian origin.[46] The typical greeting used by children who ask 'where are you going?' ('mau ke mana?') has been observed in Indonesia and northern Australia.[47]

According to some linguists, Macassan pidgin extended over the northern coast of Australia from the 1750s to the 1940s.[48] When Father Angelo Confalonieri was at Port Essington (1846–49), much of the vocabulary he collected had Malay roots. Linguist Nicholas Evans used this and other sources to examine Macassan loan words at Cobourg Peninsula and found that the Iwaidja language was the 'linguistic equivalent of a well-stratified archaeological language site'.[49] Evans identified four distinct layers of linguistic adaptation; however, because they could not be dated from linguistic analysis alone, he called them early and late adaptations of Malay loan words. Confalonieri's records clearly indicated that such linguistic mutations had occurred by the 1840s, and Evans concluded that the older layer of adaptations must have occurred before the split between Mawng and Iwaidja languages, over a millenium ago. This conclusion explodes the historic framework of contact provided by historical records and rock art analysis, which dates first contact at around the 1750s.[50]

Equally surprising is Edward Robinson's account of meeting an Aboriginal man in 1875 at Blue Mud Bay who had been to Singapore and spoke 'passable English'.[51] Robinson had been to Macassar to recruit divers for a pearling venture and was quite familiar with its traffic; however, Aboriginal visitors to Singapore were still unexpected, even to him. There are many indications of contact yet to be discovered. The butcher paper drawings produced in 1947 by Mawulan Marika for Ronald and Catherine Berndt are one example; guarded by cultural protocols in the Berndt Museum of Anthropology in Perth, they are practically inaccessible for research.[52] Mawulan rendered 43 specialised expressions in relation to work on the Macassan boats, including 15 terms for parts of the ship, 14 terms relating to food and cooking, and six relating to firearms.

---

46 Bilous 2013.
47 Zorc 1986; Walker and Zork 1981; Evans 1992.
48 Wurm, Mühlhäusler and Tryon 1996.
49 Evans 1997.
50 Both Macknight (2013) and Taçon (2013) hold to this timeline.
51 Cited in Macknight 1981.
52 I have attempted to access some of the drawings authored by 'Mawulan' in the Berndt Museum both in person and by written application and am still waiting for access four years later.

One of them is transcribed as 'gwula' (syrup), which clearly relates to the Indonesian 'gula' (sugar). Presumably, Mawulan was demonstrating his transcultural competency by supplying the specialised terms they used in the trade language.[53]

While Yolngu have been forthcoming with stories about their Macassan contact, elsewhere the memory of that contact has been 'turned in'.[54] This 'turning in' of prior Muslim contact may owe something to the arrival of Christian missionaries soon after the prohibition of the Macassan trepang fishery in northern Australia.

Tiwi and Macassans

The first port of call when drifting below the trade winds from Timor towards Marege (the 'wild country' at the top end of Australia) would have been the Tiwi Islands. The white buffalo shooter Joe Cooper, and his Iwaidja wife, lived at Melville Island for about 20 years at the turn of

---

53   The terms given by Mawulan are annotated by Ronald Berndt:

1. Macassan boat. 2. Anchor, balanga. 3. Anchor rope, mundju. 4. The front prow. that is number one bag. 18. Number two rice, second grade rice, garung, which simply means a bag. 19. Baladji, the lilly-grass bag. The rice is kept in that. It is made out of the fibre and the leaves of the lilly grass. 20. Rice in the bamboo, wadji, the sweet liquid rice, a sort of honeyed rice. 21. Coconuts. 22. Banyalanda, a rope attaching a string of coconuts. 23. The pots, budjung, for drinking. 24. Two bottles, budalu, `beer'. It is just a derivation of `bottle'. 25. A window, djrindnga. 26. Two compasses, baduman. 27. The wall between. 28. The rudder, the gwuli. 29. The end of the boat, bugu. 30. The wheel for steering, gindjarang. 31. For rolling sail, bamyulu. 32. Gawa, pot. 33. A jug, sharing Wondjug's mother's name. They could not call it because his mother died a couple of months before and it was too early to call it, so I will have to look up her name, earlier on, as I have not got it noted here. 34. Bodalu, or garumbal, a jar made out of sand and ant-bed termite mound. 35. Badali, rifle. Note the rope joined to the trigger. (a) is the trigger, and up to (b) the hammer and the banda (c). The flintlock with tinder of coconut fibre is (d), and (e) is the powder. 36. A rifle, wangaru. That is the same kind of rifle but wangaru is its inside name, it is a special singing name, and rumbringu which is also a singing name, as well as djinabang. (a) is the rope for the trigger, (b) is the connection to the hammer, (c) is the pan with a stone and tinder, as above. 37. Yimbari, an iron bucket. There is hard syrup in it, gwula. 38. Budjung, water. 39. A pot on stilts containing a wari pot. It is made out of ant-bed termite mound. 40. A double-barrelled badali, rifle, shoot you, same principles as the other. 41. Coloured plates, bani, with lambang design. 42. Boxes, badi, with gunpowder inside. 43. Trepang pots, malara, for trepang and rice cooking. 44. Boxes made out of wood for tobacco, badi, with darabu marks. These are cloud marks (there are other marks too, that look as if they are pretend writing letters). Darabu is the local name for the different kinds of markings, they are really clouds in the normal Aboriginal point of view. 45. Gawa, pot for rice cooking. 46. Garandji, made out of armband tree. It is a cane tray woven from this armband tree. 47. A glass bottle, with firewater in it, that is wine or spirits.

Mawulan's drawing on butcher paper, June 1947, Berndt collection Nr. 7246, University of Western Australia, Berndt Museum of Anthropology.

54   McIntosh 2011: Chapter 17.

the twentieth century (c. 1894–1916). As a local Protector of Aborigines, Cooper had frequent contact with the Macassans who called him 'Djon' (Joe) and his wife 'Daeng Te'ne', a Macassan alias meaning 'the lovely one'. Despite these indications of familiarity, the predominant contact narrative between Tiwi and the Macassans in the late nineteenth century is one of conflict on both sides: stealing canoes, attacking and kidnapping.[55] Only five years after the Macassan traffic was stopped, a Catholic mission opened at Bathurst Island. This probably helped to silence allusions to earlier Muslim contact, for Tiwi people have not been as forthcoming as Elcho Islanders with stories of contact.

Early anthropological accounts assumed that Tiwi had been an isolated people, and Tiwi oral history makes little reference to culture contact, though one Tiwi story recalls the prayer that Macassan shipwreck survivors sent to heaven when at the mercy of Turupla people on the Tiwi Islands—'oh el-la, oh el-la sama ratana oh el-la, oh el-la'—which sounded like an appeal to Allah.[56] According to John Morris, the visiting Macassans learned some basic Tiwi words such as 'pongki', used as a greeting of peace.[57] Some of the same cultural markers observed at Elcho Island are also present on the Tiwi Islands. In the 1920s, anthropologist Charles Hart observed that the Tiwi had a ceremonial language that was not used in everyday interactions; Elcho Islanders say that their ceremonial language is a form of Malay.[58] The Tiwi shifted from bark canoes to dug-out canoes, something which the Elcho Islanders say they adopted from the Macassans (and call 'lipa-lipa'). The distinctive morning star poles at Elcho Island, used in important ceremonies for death and mourning, have been described as reminiscent of lugger masts—an allusion to the departing Macassan fleet at the end of the season.[59] No such esoteric explanation has been given for the equally distinctive Pukumani grave poles on the Tiwi Islands.

There is also evidence to suggest that family connections may have existed between the Tiwi people and the Macassans. Spillett recorded a story about a woman who went to live in Macassar, and Morris recorded a story about the son of a Tiwi woman who was born there and returned

55 Crawford 1969: 208.
56 Spillett 1989: 10.
57 Morris [c. 1960].
58 Interview with Terry Yumbulul, Galiwin'ku, June 1995; see also Hart 1930.
59 Interview with Terry Yumbulul, Galiwin'ku, June 1995; see also McIntosh 1994.

to settle at Cobourg Peninsula.[60] Neither story insists that there are Tiwi people with Macassan ancestry; however, they do suggest the bearings of familial connection. Hart visited the Tiwi Islands in the 1920s and thought its residents had long been 'extremely isolated', so much so that distinctive cultural and genetic characteristics could be observed; the Tiwi were 'taller, sturdier, and better proportioned' than people on the mainland. Hart also found them highly assimilated, 'more adaptable to white conditions' and, therefore, much sought after as 'houseboys' in Darwin. He noted that the islands had a high population density, that landowning was remarkably fluid and that the Tiwi had not suffered decimation as a result of introduced diseases.[61] However, contrary to Hart's opinion, rather than a long period of isolation, each of these factors suggests that Tiwi people experienced intensive contact with Malays. Mixed marriages tend to increase disease resistance and further stretch the rules of land ownership to make room for new relationships; moreover, as the Europeans had a greater predilection for the cultural and physical markers of Malay populations, they would have found mixed descendants 'better proportioned' and 'more adaptable'.

Distinctive cultural markers are generally an indication of extraneous cultural influences rather than of isolation.[62] The material traces of Portuguese or Timorese foreigners on the Kimberley coast[63] sit well with scattered, early European observations about Tiwi. While in Timor in 1840, George Windsor Earl commented that the Tiwi Islands had been 'a major reservoir of slaves for Portuguese slave traders'. Alfred Searcy mentioned in the 1880s that the Macassans referred to the Tiwi as 'amba', or slaves, and Phillip Parker King in 1818 heard a Tiwi woman call out 'ven aca, ven aca', Portuguese for 'come here'. However, any such pre-colonial links that the Tiwi may have had with foreigners from the Malay Archipelago cannot really emerge unless (and until) the Tiwi people themselves and their anthropologists embrace the possibility of such histories.

---

60   Morris [c. 1960]; Spillett 1989: 10.
61   Hart 1930.
62   McNeill 1986.
63   Crawford 1969: 277.

Kayu Jawa: The North-East Coast of Australia

In the Kimberley there is even less tangible evidence of contact, although the Kimberley coast clearly once belonged to the trade routes of the Macassans who called it 'Kayu Jawa'. In stark contrast to Yolngu remembrances of the Macassan contact history, in the Kimberley, as on the Tiwi Islands, conflict dominates most recollections of relations. In April 1803, Flinders' competitor Nicholas Baudin on *Le Geographe* encountered Macassan fishers at Cassini Island ready to head home; they warned him that the local Aboriginal people could be aggressive.[64] Phillip Parker King in 1818 also encountered Macassans on the Kimberley Coast and was similarly warned of Aboriginal people's hostility.[65] J.J. Vosmaer observed in 1839 that the Macassan trepang camps in Kayu Jawa were fortified with earthworks, while Robert Sholl, who visited Camden Harbour (between King Sound and Admiralty Gulf) in 1865, found that the Macassans were afraid of Aboriginal people after being attacked the previous year.[66]

Tamarind trees are normally an environmental indicator of former trepang camps in northern Australia, but the investigation of such sites along the north-west coast has not yielded any substantiation of cultural contact.[67] Searcy found old tamarind trees between the Daly River and Port Keats in the 1880s, but uncovered no other evidence of contact. Further south-west along the coast, the Benedictine monks found strands of tamarind trees in Napier Broome Bay when they were setting up the Drysdale River Mission in 1908. The Balanggarra people of that area were reputed to be fierce, even among the Bardi and Yawuru people, so that Father Nicholas Emo had trouble recruiting guides from Sunday Island to steer through the treacherous waters of Napier Broome Bay, which had long been avoided by the pearlers.[68] The tamarind trees on the Kimberley coast had vanished when Ian Crawford conducted archaeological work at the site dubbed Tamarinda in the 1960s. Crawford, who found no substantiation

---

64   Ganter 2006: 48.
65   Phillip Parker King carried letters of safe conduct in Malay and Javanese supplied by Sir Thomas Raffles, but the Macassans, who used Bugis or Lontara script, could not read either of those scripts. Thomas 2013; Ganter 2006: 48.
66   J.J. Vosmaer 1839, 'Korte beschrijving van het Z.O. Shiereiland van Celebes' and R.J. Sholl, 1865, Journal, cited in Crawford 1969: 103ff.
67   Searcy 1907: 189.
68   Ganter, 'Fr. Nicholas Emo', in *German Missionaries in Queensland*, missionaries.griffith.edu.au.

of contact in local mythologies, concluded that the Macassans stayed on the Kimberley for short periods, often shifted their camps and focused mainly on the offshore reefs. He believed the Macassans abandoned the Kayu Jawa coast between the 1880s and 1900,[69] as this was the period when Australian and British skippers began to fish for trepang, travelling along the same routes and using the same crews as the Macassans operating out of Timor had done.[70]

The possibility of contact between Indigenous people from the Kimberley region and Macassan traders has been subject to debate and conjecture shaped by different theoretical and academic perspectives. Preconceived theories about Indigenous people produced particular interpretations of the linguistic and artistic signposts. To identify traces of South-East Asian influence in the Kimberley languages would require a methodology similar to that applied by Nicholas Evans to the work of Father Angelo Confalonieri at Port Essington.

The earliest sustained language work in the Kimberley was conducted by Spanish and French Trappist missionaries. Their research was continued by German Pallottine fathers, including the eminent Bantu linguist Dr Hermann Nekes and his disciple Father Ernst Worms. Worms was committed to the Kulturkreis (cultural circles) theory promoted by the journal *Anthropos*. Its editor, Pater Wilhelm Schmidt, a Steyler missionary from the Austrian Society of the Divine Word, had produced a structure of the language families of the world, with particular emphasis on Australian languages.[71] Owing to his intellectual allegiance to Schmidt, Worms consistently discounted a South-East Asian influence in the cultural repertoires of the Kimberley that had been suggested by Charles Mountford, Daniel Davidson and Ronald Berndt.[72]

Worms looked for linguistic and cultural influences from outside the Kimberley, but only within the parameters of the Australian continental migrations compatible with Schmidt's work. He used superficial similarities between words from different Australian languages to construct

---

69   Crawford 1969: 287, 290, 107.
70   Ganter 2006: 48.
71   Schmidt 1919.
72   Berndt (1951) was writing about Arnhem Land and did not comment on extraneous influences in the Kimberley, but Worms (1952) identified the terms associated with the Kunapipi cultural complex as also existing in the Kimberley, and found them so deeply rooted in Aboriginal words that they 'must be endogenous'. See also Mountford 1937; Davidson 1947; Worms 1953.

historical connections. Had he been familiar with Sanskrit and Malay, he would surely have noticed the remarkable similarity of some of the terms he discussed, such as between the mythical eagle 'garidja' that brought the fire to the Bardi, 'garuda', the mythical humanoid bird in Buddhist and Hindu mythology, and the word for 'eagle' in Indonesian.[73] Worms also observed that male initiation involved the teaching of a ceremonial language composed of 'obsolete or foreign words for everyday objects'.[74] Among its stages he listed the grades of 'orong ganyano' and 'bungana',[75] words that strongly resemble 'bunggawa', the title of a respected leader in Macassar, and 'orang', the Indonesian word for 'man'. Such terms are hints of grander connections that remain unexplored under the weight of the idea that Australia was an 'isolated continent' prior to British colonisation.

The Kimberley–Pilbara region has two widely divergent but characteristic styles of rock art, the wandjina and gwion gwion (Bradshaw figures). Both have, at times, been ascribed to Malay influence. In 1939, Arthur Capell suggested that the wandjina had come 'from the direction of Timor' and Charles Mountford believed that the gwion gwion style had been learned from Malay pearl and trepang fishers.[76] Worms reported that the 'Gwini' people who lived nearest to the drawings had little interest in them, failed to maintain their appearance, vandalised many of them by painting over them and ascribed them to a different kind of people they called 'giro-giro'.[77] However, as noted, Worms discounted any suggestion of a South-East Asian influence. At that time, a similar debate was emerging over cultural disconnection from ancient art and the possibility of waves of migration on Easter Island (Rapa Nui). This was due to the much publicised work of Norwegian ethnographer, Thor Heyerdahl, who

---

73   Worms 1950b.

74   Worms 1950a.

75   These words were supplied by a Karajarri man from Cape Bossut whose name is given as Made in 1938. Later Worms refered to Gonbal Molade and Gundal Muladi as a main informant who told 25 legends to Nekes and died at about age 70 just before the 1949 publication. Worms 1938, 1940, 1949.

76   Worms 1942; Capell 1939: 391, 389, 403, 390, 403. In 1909, the Trappist Father Nicholas Emo recorded the striking giro-giro (Bradshaw figures, or gwion gwion) at Drysdale River. Emo produced an album of 40 colour drawings taken from 24 caves, most of which were only high enough to lie in. He feared that ornithologist Gerald Hill, who was visiting the mission at the time (since 14 November 1909), would take credit for the drawings. According to Nailon, Emo's album was deposited in the New Norcia archives. Nailon 2005: 135. Presumably this is the same album as that held by the South Australian Museum in the name of Hill.

77   Following the arrival of Europeans, these sites were used to hide tjuringa imported from the Northern Territory and the Great Sandy Desert. Worms (1955) picked up an unfinished stone axe and working chips from this site.

received an Oscar for his 1951 *Kon Tiki* documentary detailing a Pacific voyage by traditional raft.[78] In that debate, too, the effect of missionaries on Easter Island since 1864 was left out of possible explanations.

Reconnecting

Much remains to be discovered about pre-colonial contact between northern Australia and South-East Asia. The mutual visits that have resumed in the last three decades may help to rediscover connections. Perhaps they will also lead to the discovery of more adoptions of Aboriginal customs in the Malay Archipelago, a much neglected question. For example, the Macassan fire dance looked to the Yolngu visitors like a scene from their own initiation ceremony, a similarity also noticed when theatre director Andrish Saint-Clare screened footage of Yolngu dances in Macassar in 1994.[79] Evans, while looking for Malay loan words in Iwaidja, also found Iwaidja loan words in Macassar.[80] On the Indonesian side, there has been renewed interest in rediscovering and celebrating connections. Australian research on pre-British Muslim connections has been frequently mentioned in the Indonesian press and on social media.[81] In 1997, Hari Jadi Gowa (Macassar Foundation Day) included a trepang opera with actors from Arnhem Land and Sulawesi. In 2011, a multidisciplinary group of students from Hasanuddin University in South Sulawesi undertook a 41-day sailing journey from Macassar to Australia, visiting the traditional recruiting areas on the way.[82]

Aboriginal people have been as surprised as researchers about the cultural affinities discovered in Sulawesi. Laklak Burarrwanga, who was shown 'a wishing stone' where the Macassans once prayed for the north-easterly

---

78   Heyerdahl 1990, 1958, 1961.

79   Interview with Peter Danaja of the Sunrize Band, June 1995, and Andrish Saint-Clare, pers. comm., July 2001, referring to his video screening of Yolngu dances in Macassar in 1994.

80   Evans 1997.

81   'Australia: Orang Indonesia Awali Kedatangan Islam', *Faith Freedom,* 14 January 2008; 'Orang Indonesia Awali Kedatangan Islam di Australia', *Muslim Daily Net,* 22 April 2008; 'Islam di Amerika dan Australia jauh Sebelum kedatangan Eropa', *My Quran,* 19 June 2008; 'Diperlakukan Diskiminatif, Ilmuwan Muslim Tuntut Pemerintah AS', *Dunia Pendidikan Anak Islami,* 29 June 2008; 'Orang Indonesia Awali Kedatangan Islam di Australia' *Berita Islam—Wahana Dakwah Islamiyah,* 23 March 2009; 'Orang Indonesia Awali Kedatangan Islam di Australia dan Afrika Selatan' *Syiahali,* 8 September 2010; 'Orang Indonesia Awali Kedatangan Islam di Australia' (abstract), *Berita Pilihan,* February 2012; 'Orang Indonesia Awali Kedatangan Islam di Australia', *Zilzaal,* 22 February 2012.

82   Guswan Gunawan, 'Ekspedisi Pelayaran Akademis Korpala Unhas x 264' www.youtube.com/watch?v=AViiD82z8V0

wind, found 'all the poles and flags similar to home'.[83] (Flag dances in Arnhem Land are normally a reference to Macassans.) Ethnomusicologist Peter Toner detected traces of classical Arabic religious music in the Manikay song cycle genre of Yolngu songs.[84] While touring Sulawesi with a Maningrida dance troupe to perform an extended ceremony in 1993, Maningrida artist John Bulunbulun acquired an ancient ceramic storage pot that looked exactly the same as the ones he had been taught to paint, sight unseen.[85] This storage pot became one of the first objects housed in the Djomi Museum, one of the earliest local museums dedicated to Macassan contact. Bulunbulun subsequently produced a series of 25 paintings depicting Macassan references in the Yirrtitja song cycle, including one created for the Darwin airport.[86] Bulunbulun revealed that his clan totem, 'lunggurrma' (north wind), is a symbol of the arrival of the Macassans at the beginning of the monsoon season.

The memories that had been 'turned in' are slowly being brought out again. This process is attended on both sides—Australia and Indonesia—by politics. On the Indonesian side, the initial interest in contact history came from a nationalist history written by a former governor of Sulawesi in 1967.[87] More recently, the interest has lain in demonstrating the early spread of Muslim influence and its harmonious accommodation with Indigenous people in Australia. In Arnhem Land in 1957, Burrumarra disclosed the meanings of the flag 'rranga' as a symbol of 'adjustment' in the expected lead-up to a treaty to acknowledge and safeguard Indigenous land rights. On the contrary, in the 1990s, debates over the possible extraneous origins of the gwion gwion art in the Kimberley were effectively silenced over concerns that they may impact on native title.[88] Perhaps the Kimberley and Pilbara are still awaiting the Indigenous diplomats who will 'bring out' the hidden meanings of the past to advance a cause in the present. In any event, Marcia Langton has warned that a racialised conception of Aboriginality is unnecessary, untenable and unhelpful, and will not advance the Aboriginal cause.[89]

---

83   Laklak Burarrwanga 2012 'Memories of my Makassan family', paper presented to Macassan History and Heritage conference, 8–9 February 2012, The Australian National University, cited in Thomas 2013.
84   Toner 2000: 22, 33–34.
85   Garde 1993.
86   Bulunbulun also collaborated with the Chinese painter Zhou Xiaoping to explore cultural affinities. Xiaoping 2006.
87   Patunru 1983 [1967].
88   Australian Archaeological Association 1996: 59.
89   Langton 2012.

Clearly, much of the contact has been forgotten or erased. Rock images of praus have been drawn over by more recent images or have disappeared under the onslaught of development; some, perhaps, have naturally withered away.[90] Father Worms commented in 1954 that the rock art galleries at Port Hedland on the limestone ridges from the town to the tidal creeks had already been partly destroyed by quarry works, buildings and the 'ubiquitous initial carvers', despite protection as a state reserve. Worms sought to achieve 'protection of the sites under UNESCO listing of historical monuments', but the world heritage list was still a new instrument and its cultural heritage at that time focused on buildings. Only since 2003 has Purnululu National Park been inscribed on the world heritage list; the Kimberley rock art achieved national heritage status in 2011. The Macassan sites in North Australia are protected under the *Northern Territory Heritage Act 2012*, but no such protection exists for sites of Australian heritage significance in Sulawesi, such as the buildings constructed with valuable 'keramat' ironwood. Paul Thomas suggested that the old trade route from Macassar to Marege is a site of significant international heritage and should be formally listed alongside other 'cultural routes'.[91]

The contact zone has, at times, spanned across a much larger stretch of the northern coastline than has been recovered from Indigenous sources, including stories, art, language and archaeological evidence. In the early nineteenth century, the Macassan trepang fishery ranged from the Gulf of Carpentaria to the Kimberley, and there are some indications that this particular industrial-scale fishery was preceded by other forms of contact, not focused on trepang. In north Queensland, too, the Torres Strait remains a bridge of communication with Papua, though now closely monitored by customs officers. A rupture of Indigenous international communication was brought about with British sovereignty, the outlawing of the Macassan fishery and the confinement of Aboriginal people on designated parcels of land. Indigenous people have broken out of this enforced isolation by visiting Macassar, participating in the United Nations Permanent Forum on Indigenous Issues (since the 1980s) and many other cultural

---

90 The beeswax image dated by Taçon and May (2013) is superimposed on the image of a prau. Worms (1954) described the destruction of much of the rock art galleries at Port Hedland as a result of the town's expansion; according to Petri (1954) the rock paintings described by Sir George Grey at Prince Regent River in 1838 have never been found.
91 Thomas 2013.

connections.[92] Politics of diplomacy are usually at play in the construction and disclosure of such histories, but what is already known about the Macassan contact history undermines the idea of an isolated continent and the untenable notion of a once pure race of isolated people.

References

Australian Archaeological Association 1996, 'Minutes of the 1995 Annual General Meeting', *Australian Archaeology* 42: 59.

Berndt, Ronald 1951, *Kunapipi: A Study of an Australian Aboriginal Religious Cult*, Cheshire, Melbourne.

Berndt, Ronald and Catherine Berndt 1954, *Arnhem Land—Its History and Its People*, Cheshire, Melbourne.

Bilous, Rebecca 2013, '"All mucked up": Sharing stories of Yolngu–Macassan cultural heritage at Bawaka, north-east Arnhem Land', *International Journal of Heritage Studies*, doi.org/10.1080/13527258.2013.807399

Capell, Arthur 1939, 'Mythology in northern Kimberley, north-west Australia', *Oceania* 9(4): 382–404.

Carey, Jane and Jane Lydon 2014, *Indigenous Networks: Mobility, Connections and Exchange*, Routledge, London.

Clark, Marshall 2013, 'Tangible heritage of the Macassan-Aboriginal encounter in contemporary South Sulawesi', in *Macassan History and Heritage—Journeys, Encounters and Influences*, Marshall Clark and Sally May (eds), ANU E Press, Canberra: 159–82.

Cooke, Michael 1987, 'Makassar and northeast Arnhem Land—missing links and living bridges', Batchelor College Report on a Makassan Field Study, June 1986, Batchelor College MS.

Crawford, Ian 1969, 'Late prehistoric changes in Aboriginal cultures in Kimberley, Western Australia', PhD thesis, University of London.

---

92 Many of these transnational connections are canvassed in Carey and Lydon 2014.

Davidson, D.S. 1947, 'Fire-making in Australia', *American Anthropologist* XLIX: 426–37. doi.org/10.1525/aa.1947.49.3.02a00040

Evans, Nicholas 1992, 'Makassan loanwords in top end languages', *Australian Journal of Linguistics* 12: 45–91.

Evans, Nicholas 1997, 'Macassan loans and linguistic stratification in western Arnhem Land', in *Aboriginal Australia in Global Perspective*, Patrick McConvell and Nicholas Evans (eds), Oxford University Press, Oxford: 237–60. doi.org/10.1080/07268609208599471

Ganter, Regina 2006, *Mixed Relations: Asian-Aboriginal Contact in North Australia*, University of Western Australia Press, Perth.

Garde, Murray 1993, 'The Marayarr Murrkundja ceremony goes to Makassar', Bawinanga Aboriginal Corporation, Mangingrida.

Hart, Charles 1930, 'The Tiwi of Melville and Bathurst Islands', *Oceania* 1(2): 167–80.

Heyerdahl, Thor 1958, *Aku-Aku: The Secret of Easter Island*, Allen & Unwin, Sydney.

Heyerdahl, Thor 1961, 'An introduction to Easter Island', in *Reports of the Norwegian archaeological expedition to Easter Island and the East Pacific*, vol. 1, Norwegian Archaeological Expedition to Easter Island and the East Pacific, Allen & Uniwin, London: 21–90.

Heyerdahl, Thor 1990, *Kon-Tiki: Across the Pacific by Raft*, Simon and Schuster, New York.

Janson, J. 2001, *The Eyes of Marege*, The Australian Script Centre, Hobart.

Jukes, Anthony 2005, 'Maksassar', in *The Austronesian Languages of Asia and Madagaskar*, K. Alexander Adelaar and Nikolaus Himmelmann (eds), Routledge, New York: 647–82.

Langton, Marcia 2011, *Trepang: China and the Story of Macassan–Aboriginal Trade*, Centre for Cultural Materials Conservation, University of Melbourne, Melbourne.

Langton, Marcia 2012, 'Indigenous exceptionalism and the constitutional "race power"', Melbourne Writers Festival, BMW Edge theatre, Federation Square, Melbourne: 26.

Lendon, Nigel 2014, 'Relational Agency—the Elcho Island memorial', in *Double Desire: Transculturation and Indigenous Contemporary Art*, Ian McLean (ed.), Cambridge Scholars Publishing, England: 92–116.

Macknight, C.C. 1969, *The Farthest Coast*, Melbourne University Press, Melbourne.

Macknight, C.C. 1976, *A Voyage to Marege—Macassan Trepangers in Northern Australia*, Melbourne University Press, Melbourne.

Macknight, Campbell 1981, 'Journal of a voyage around Arnhem Land in 1875', *Aboriginal History* (2): 135–45.

Macknight, C.C. 2013, 'Studying trepangers', in *Macassan History and Heritage: Journeys, Encounters and Influences,* Marshall Clark and Sally May (eds), ANU E Press, Canberra: 19–40.

McIntosh, Ian 1992, 'The bricoleur at work: Warang Dingo mythology in the Yirritjia moiety of north-east Arnhem Land', *M. Letters,* University of New England, Armidale.

McIntosh, Ian 1994, *The Whale and the Cross—Conversations with David Burrumarra MBE*, Historical Society of the Northern Territory, Darwin.

McIntosh, Ian 2009, 'Missing the revolution! Negotiating disclosure on the pre-Macassans (Bayini) in north-east Arnhem Land Australia', in *Barks, Birds & Billabongs: Exploring the Legacy of the 1948 American-Australian Scientific Expedition to Arnhem Land*, National Museum of Australia, Canberra.

McIntosh, Ian 2013, 'Unbirri's pre-Macassan legacy, or how the Yolngu became black', in *Macassan History and Heritage: Journeys, Encounters and Influences*, Marshall Clark and Sally May (eds), ANU E Press, Canberra: 95–106.

McNeill, William Hardy 1986, *Polyethnicity and national unity in world history*, University of Toronto Press, Toronto.

Morris, John [c. 1960], 'The coming of the Macassans to the Islands of the Tiwi', Northern Territory Reference Library MS, Darwin.

Mountford, Charles Pearcy 1937, 'Rock Paintings at Windulda, Western Australia', *Oceania* 7 (4): 429–35.

Nailon, Brigida C.S.B. 2005, *Emo and San Salvador,* Brigidine Sisters, Echuca.

Palmer, L. 2007, 'Negotiating the ritual and social order through spectacle: The (re)production of Macassan/Yolngu histories', *Anthropological Forum: A Journal of Social Anthropology and Comparative Sociology* 17(1): 1–20. doi.org/10.1080/00664670601168385

Patunru, Abdulrazak Daeng 1983 [1967], *Sedjarah Goa—Jajasan Kebudajan di Makassar*, Ujung Pandang.

Petri, Helmut 1954, *Sterbende Welt in Nordwest-Australien*, Limbach Verlag, Braunschweig.

Schmidt, Wilhelm S.V.D. 1919, *Die Gliederung der Australischen Sprachen*, Mechitharisten-Buchdruckerei, Vienna.

Searcy, Alfred 1907, *In Australian Tropics,* Hesperian Press, London.

Spillett, Peter (Daeng Makkulle) 1987, 'Gotong Royong: Hubungan Makassar-Marege', paper presented to the 2nd International Convention of the Indonesian Educational and Cultural Institute, Ujung Pandang, MS.

Spillett, Peter 1989, 'Dreamtime stories from Makassar and Marege', Museum and Art Gallery of the Northern Territory, Darwin.

Stephenson, Peta 2007, *The Outsiders Within: Telling Australia's Indigenous-Asian Story,* UNSW Press, Sydney.

Taçon, Paul and Sally May 2013, 'Rock art evidence for Macassan–Aboriginal contact in northwestern Arnhem Land', in *Macassan History and Heritage: Journeys, Encounters and Influences*, Marshall Clark and Sally May (eds), ANU E Press, Canberra: 127–40.

Thomas, Paul 2013, 'Interpreting the Macassans: Language exchange in historical encounters', in Marshall Clark and Sally May (eds) *Macassan History and Heritage: Journeys, Encounters and Influences*, ANU E Press, Canberra: 69–94.

Toner, Peter 2000, 'Ideology, influence and innovation: The impact of Macassan contact on Yolŋu music', *Perfect Beat: The Pacific Journal of Research into Contemporary Music and Popular Culture* 5(1): 22, 33–34.

Walker, Alan and David Zork 1981, 'Austronesian loanwords in Yolngu-Matha in northeast Arnhem Land', *Aboriginal History* 5(2): 17–134.

Worms, E.A. 1938, 'Die Inititiationsfeier in NW-Australien', *Annali Lateranensi* 2: 147–74.

Worms, EA 1940, 'Religiöse Vorstellungen und Kultur einiger Nord-westaustralischer Stämme in fünfzig Legenden', *Annali Lateranensi* 4: 213–82.

Worms, EA 1942, 'Die Goranara Feier im australischen Kimberley', *Annali Lateranensi* 6: 207–35.

Worms, Ernest 1949 (April), 'An Australian migratory myth', *Primitive Man* 2(1/2): 33–38.

Worms, E.A. 1950a, 'Djamar, the creator. A myth of the bad (West Kimberley, Australia)', *Anthropos* 45: 641–58.

Worms, E.A. 1950b, 'Feuer und Feuerzeuge in Sage und Brauch der NW-Australier' *Anthropos* 45: 145–64.

Worms, E.A. 1952, 'Djamar and his relation to other culture heroes', *Anthropos,* 47, 539–60.

Worms, E.A. 1953 (October), 'Mountford Charles P. The Tiwi—their art, myth and ceremony', *Man* 53: 164–65.

Worms, E.A. 1954, 'Prehistoric petroglyphs of the Upper Yule River, north-western Australia', *Anthropos* 49: 1067–88.

Worms, E.A. 1955, 'Contemporary and prehistoric rock paintings in central and northern north Kimberley', *Anthropos* 50: 546–66.

Wurm, Stephen A., Peter Mühlhäusler and Darrell T. Tryon (eds) 1996, *Atlas of Languages of Intercultural Communication in the Pacific, Asia, and the Americas*, Walter de Gruyter, Berlin.

Xiaoping, Zhou 2006, *A Dream of Aboriginal Australia* (publication details in Chinese, not translated).

Zorc, David Paul 1986, 'Yolngu-Matha dictionary', Macassan loanwords project, MS.

www.ingramcontent.com/pod-product-compliance
Lightning Source LLC
Chambersburg PA
CBHW040820280326
41926CB00093B/4611